AF335524

# EDUCATION FOR CITIZENSHIP

# EDUCATION FOR CITIZENSHIP

## *Ideas and Innovations in Political Learning*

Edited by
GRANT REEHER
and
JOSEPH CAMMARANO

*Foreword by Benjamin R. Barber*

ROWMAN & LITTLEFIELD PUBLISHERS, INC.
*Lanham • Boulder • New York • Oxford*

ROWMAN & LITTLEFIELD PUBLISHERS, INC.

Published in the United States of America
by Rowman & Littlefield Publishers, Inc.
4720 Boston Way, Lanham, Maryland 20706

12 Hid's Copse Road
Cummor Hill, Oxford OX2 9JJ, England

Copyright © 1997 by Rowman & Littlefield Publishers, Inc.
Chapter 5 copyright © 1997 by William D. Coplin

*All rights reserved.* No part of this publication may be reproduced,
stored in a retrieval system, or transmitted in any form or by any
means, electronic, mechanical, photocopying, recording, or otherwise,
without the prior permission of the publisher.

British Library Cataloguing in Publication Information Available

**Library of Congress Cataloging-in-Publication Data**

Education for citizenship : ideas and innovations in political
   learning / edited by Grant Reeher and Joseph Cammarano.
       p.   cm.
    Includes bibliographical references and index.
    ISBN 0–8476–8365–6 (cloth : alk. paper).—ISBN 0–8476–8366–4
(pbk. : alk. paper)
    1. Citizenship—Study and teaching (Higher)—United States.
2. Democracy—Study and teaching (Higher)—United States.
I. Reeher, Grant. II. Cammarano, Joseph, 1960- .
LC1091.E387 1997
370.11'5—dc21                                                              97–13580
                                                                                 CIP

ISBN 0–8476–8365–6 (cloth : alk. paper)
ISBN 0–8476–8366–4 (pbk. : alk. paper)

Printed in the United States of America

⊗ ™ The paper used in this publication meets the minimum requirements of
American National Standard for Information Sciences—Permanence of Paper
for Printed Library Materials, ANSI Z39.48-1984.

*For our teachers and mentors,*
*David Mayhew, Barbara Salmore, and the late Charles Tidmarch*

# Contents


Foreword *by Benjamin R. Barber*                                    ix

Acknowledgments                                                     xv

Introduction: Some Themes from Recent Innovations and
Questions for the Future                                             1
    *Grant Reeher and Joseph Cammarano*

1  Teaching American Politics through Service: Reflections on
a Pedagogical Strategy                                              17
    *Craig A. Rimmerman*

2  Service Learning as Civic Learning: Lessons We Can Learn
from Our Students                                                   31
    *Richard M. Battistoni*

3  The Urban Agenda Project                                        51
    *Otto Feinstein and James D. Chesney*

4  Citizenship Courses as Life-Changing Experiences              63
    *William D. Coplin*

5  Public Affairs Internships: Coming of Age                      81
    *Glen A. Halva-Neubauer*

6  Enhancing Citizenship through Active Learning:
Simulations on the Policy Process                                  101
    *Joseph Cammarano and Linda L. Fowler*

7  Doing the Rights Thing: Tales of Citizenship and Free
Speech                                                             119
    *Marc Lendler*

  **8** Teaching the Art of Public Deliberation: National Issues
    Forums on Campus                                      135
    *Daniel W. O'Connell*

  **9** Democratizing the Classroom: The Individual Learning
    Contract                                              153
    *John F. Freie*

 **10** Wading in the Deep: Supporting Emergent Anarchies    171
    *Naeem Inayatullah*

 **11** Teaching Deliberation: Citizenship Education and Cross-
    Disciplinary Team Teaching                            189
    *Mark Rupert*

 **12** Using the Internet to Enhance Classroom and Citizenship
    Information                                           199
    *William Ball*

 **13** The Internet as a Tool for Student Citizenship       214
    *Kimberley P. Canfield*

  Bibliography                                             231

  Index                                                    241

  About the Contributors                                   245

# Foreword

"Men are born free but are everywhere in chains": that is the famous declaration trumpeted by Jean-Jacques Rousseau in the opening paragraph of his *Social Contract*. From that moment of revolutionary epiphany in the middle of the eighteenth century, the claim that women and men are born free has become one of the great justifying fictions of modern democratic societies. With it, not only Rousseau but also Robespierre, Thomas Paine, and Thomas Jefferson were able to assert the illegitimacy of arbitrary authority and provide a justification for revolutionary force that wrested from absolute monarchs their power.

Yet the fiction of natural liberty that has been so useful to peoples struggling to overthrow tyrants (this proud Rousseauist history notwithstanding) today risks spreading complacency among those who have long enjoyed freedom. Among them it may create the impression that, born free, they have to do nothing either to secure or to sustain their liberty; that democracy is self-propelling and requires nothing of them; that representative government is an automaton that moves perpetually and by itself; and that liberty finally is free.

The reality is far more daunting. Liberty may be a food easy to eat, but as Rousseau himself observed, it is difficult to digest. Free societies are sustained only by hard work. The price of liberty is citizenship. And if women and men are born free in some abstract potential sense, citizens are always made, not born—which often takes a very long time. That is why quick-fix democracies in Russia and the Third World have failed to take hold: they offer the superstructure of political democracy built on a nonexistent civil foundation, whose absence cripples liberty and whose coming awaits education for citizenship.

The skills that permit citizens to deliberate prudently, think publicly, and collaborate democratically need to be learned. This kind of learning turns out to be especially hard. There is, Tocqueville warned, nothing so arduous as the apprenticeship of liberty.[1]

What would-be denizens of democracy must grasp is that the struggle for democracy is not merely a struggle for government by, for, and of the people, but a struggle for government by, for, and of citizens; and that the distance from a mere people comprised of selfish individuals to a citizenry comprised of engaged and responsible patriots is precisely the distance from mob rule to true democracy. For democracy will be little better than mob rule—Hamilton's "great beast"— unless the demes are educated in deliberation, prudence, and public judgment; unless they can transform the logic of private interests into a logic of the general will; unless they can distinguish their private wants from the public good and their private wealth from the essential commonwealth.

Thomas Jefferson thus insisted on public education as a concomitant of a democratic Virginia and attached far greater importance to his founding of the University of Virginia than to his two-term presidency or his acquisition of the Louisiana Territory. Only his authorship of the Declaration of Independence and the Virginia Statute for Religious Freedom and his fathering of the University of Virginia found a place in his epitaph. John Adams of Massachusetts likewise argued that "wisdom and knowledge . . . are necessary for the preservation of [the people's] rights and liberties," and he put flesh on the bones of his argument by establishing a public school system for the Commonwealth of Massachusetts that rivaled the schools of England. To the founders, the Bill of Rights was but a piece of paper—"parchment parapets," as James Madison wrote—from which no effective defense against tyranny could be mounted. And so for Jefferson, without public education for all citizens there would be neither a democratic public nor a democratic politics at all. For without citizens there would be no republic, and without education there would be no citizens.

In pairing the Declaration of Independence and the Virginia Statute for Religious Freedom with the founding of the University of Virginia, Jefferson's epitaph disclosed the hidden logic that linked rights with responsibilities, American independence and democratic self-sufficiency with an educated citizenry. If there was to be a common American people capable of pursuing a common American good in the name of their natural rights, there had to be common schools. Although he boasted in the Declaration of Independence that men were "born free," Jefferson knew well enough that liberty is acquired and that citizens are educated to a responsibility that comes to no man or woman naturally. Without citizens, democracy is a hollow shell. Without public schools and universities, citizenship is an empty boast.

This civic strain of thought persisted from America's colonial days through the nineteenth century. The Common School movement informed our nineteenth-century educational practices with a sense of civic mission that left no school or college untouched. Not just the land grant colleges, but nearly every higher educational institution founded in the eighteenth and nineteenth centuries—religious as well as secular, private no less than public—counted among its founding principles a dedication to training competent and responsible citizens. Rights were understood to be tied to responsibilities; the freedom to live well and prosper was seen as a product of civic obligations discharged with vigor; and the security of the private sector was thought to depend on the robustness of the public sector.

Sometime toward the end of the last century, with the professionalization of higher education that came to American shores with the German research university model (after which Johns Hopkins University was patterned) schools began to move away from their civic responsibilities. By the end of World War II, higher education had begun to professionalize, vocationalize, and specialize in a manner that occluded its civic and democratic mission. Rights and responsibilities were decoupled and citizenship relegated to the occasional boring "civics" lecture—usually a harangue monumentalizing a mythical founding by a set of sterotypical heroes, from George Washington to Abraham Lincoln, with whom (at least as they were presented) the increasingly nonwhite population of public schools could have little sense of common cause. So far had rights wandered from responsibility that young people who explicitly professed that they deeply cherished the system of trial by jury nonetheless also argued that no one should be "required" to do jury service. At the same time, the citizen army of conscripts gave way to the "volunteer army" made up, at least in part, of those, black and white, for whom society offered few other opportunities. Today the Department of Defense no longer dares to advertise military service as public service or civic patriotism at all and instead offers workplace credentialing, school-to-work vocational learning, and a good job after military service is over. The "service" in military service has simply vanished, to be replaced by "professionalism" and "alternative employment."

If our nation is to repossess its civic soul, it needs to recapture the central civic responsibilities of public schools, indeed of schooling in general, K through 12 and university, public and private. This means that if American schools are to be defined by the search for literacy, then civic literacy must take its place alongside science, math, English, and cultural literacy. It means that if education is to support school-to-work initiatives that adapt pedagogy to the needs of the workplace, it must also support school-to-citizen initiatives that adapt pedagogy to the needs of the public square—the civic marketplace of civil society. Lawyers and doctors are no more likely to make good citizens than dropouts if their training is limited to the narrow and self-interested world defined by vocational preparation and professional instruction. Youngsters preparing to turn their schooling to the purposes of economic competition with Japan and Germany must also be able to turn their schooling to the purposes of civic cooperation with their fellow Americans in making democracy work. Civic literacy is as important as numeracy and English literacy. Standards have to incorporate civic as well as academic challenges.

To rejoin education and liberal citizenship requires only that we take "liberal" education seriously. Liberal arts education and civic education share a curriculum of critical reflection and autonomous thought. That is how the liberal arts emerged in the modern era in contrast to the feudal servile arts. The latter were job training for the indentured and subordinated learning to an apprenticeship in the vocations. The former were devoted to free thought and to what Tocqueville would many centuries later deem "the apprenticeship of liberty." In feudal times, the liberal arts were intended to serve that small minority lucky enough to be born "freemen." If schooling is to be guided once again by its democratic mission, it needs to be not only supported financially but also reendowed with a sense of civic passion.

This means that public schools must be understood as public not simply because they serve the public, but because they establish us as a public. Too much market ideology has left our private and public worlds all topsy-turvy. We have made Madonna's private parts public at the very moment we are demanding, via vouchers, that our last genuinely public institutions be made private. We need incentives to draw parents back into public schools, not vouchers to lure them out. We need to fix, not abandon, those inner-city schools that are least effective. We need to make education more experiential and make experience more educational, to put community service into the middle of the curriculum, and to test the curriculum on the streets of the community.

To do these things is to insist that:

• The "public" in public schools be understood to signify plurality and diversity. America is not a private club defined by one group's historical hegemony. Consequently, multicultural education is not discretionary; it defines demographic and pedagogical necessity. If we want youngsters from Los Angeles whose families collectively speak more than 160 languages to be Americans, we must first acknowledge their diversity and honor their distinctiveness. English will only thrive as the first language of America when those for whom it is a second language feel safe enough in their own language and culture to venture into and participate in the dominant culture. For what we have in common is not some singular ethnic or religious or racial unity but precisely our respect for our differences: that is the secret to our strength as a nation and the key to democratic education.

• Schools need to be as democratic as the civic ideals they wish to teach, consistent with the authority of sound pedagogy. This suggests cooperative learning where the facile help the less facile to the benefit of both rather than tracking (where the quick advance at the expense of the slow), or large, undermanned detracked classes (where the slow advance at the expense of the quick). The goal is not to level down but to secure an "aristocracy of everyone" in which excellence is the common denominator.[2] This suggests systems of secondary and higher education that leave room for a role for students in governance and administration. To be sure, students are a transient constituency, and there are issues of hiring, curriculum, and peer review where their role should remain extremely limited. But there are other domains where their participation, at the minimum on a consultative basis, is not only feasible but beneficial to the students and to their educational institutions. Simultaneously, such participation models the kind of democratic culture we presumably wish to teach.

• Learning, above all civic learning, needs to be experiential as well as purely cognitive. Serving others is not just a form of do-goodism or feel-goodism, it is a road to social responsibility and citizenship. When linked closely to classroom learning ("education-based community service"), it offers an ideal setting for bridging the gap between the classroom and the street, between the theory of democracy and its much more obstreperous practice. Our schools and colleges are not social agencies but teaching and learning communities. Service is an instrument of civic pedagogy. It is a response to William James's quest for a "moral equivalent of war." In serving community, the young forge commonality; in acknowledging differences, they bridge division; in assuming individual responsibility, they nurture social citizenship.

If it is to serve democratic education, service learning must be a responsibility of everyone, not just a requirement for the criminal or the needy. Teaching the young that white-collar felons or blue-collar loan seekers owe their country civic service while the well-off and wealthy do not is a poor way to inculcate the ideals of civic equality. Service is a universal entailment of what it means to live in and enjoy the rights of a free society. Loans for those who need them ought to be offered as a reciprocal right of good citizens, a consequence rather than a prerequisite of citizenship. This is the justification for the vital link the Corporation for National Service has established between education vouchers and community service.

*   *   *

These revisions of the mission of education, aside from their possible impact on democracy, potentially have a crucial political payoff: they make schools more relevant to the needs of society generally and more pertinent to the concerns of citizens without school-age children. They thus offer burdened taxpayers reasons to support the flow of tax dollars to education. Polls show again and again that citizens object not so much to paying taxes but to the perceived lack of impact of the taxes they pay. They seek not so much lower tax rates as higher payoffs—better results. That our schools are committed not only to educating our children but also to preparing them to take responsibility for preserving and extending our democracy may make education look like a better bargain.

The rights and freedoms of all Americans depend on the survival of democracy. There is only one road to democracy: education. And in a democracy where freedom comes first—educators and politicians alike, take notice—the first priority of education must be the apprenticeship of liberty. Tie every school reform to this principle and not only education but democracy itself will flourish, and the reforms may even pay for themselves. Let schools sink further into poverty and privatization and we will not only put our children at risk but may imperil the very foundation of their liberties and our own. This is why all education must, whatever else it is, also be education for citizenship.

Benjamin R. Barber

## Notes

1. Alexis de Tocqueville, *Democracy in America,* trans. Henry Reeve, vol. 1 (New York: Vintage Books, 1990), p. 247.

2. Benjamin R. Barber, *An Aristocracy of Everyone: The Politics of Education and the Future of America* (New York: Oxford University Press, 1992).

# Acknowledgments

This volume would not exist without the work of the contributors, and so we thank them first. We are also grateful for a Dean's Fund at Syracuse University's Maxwell School of Citizenship and Public Affairs, which provided support for conference participation that led to this volume's creation and later helped to refine its contents. The early enthusiasm on the part of Jennifer Knerr at Rowman & Littlefield was instrumental to the volume's success; as usual, she was extremely helpful throughout the process. Additional helpful editorial assistance was supplied by Brenda Hadenfeldt and Julie Kirsch. Linda Hartley and David Reeher carefully read the manuscript at important stages in the publishing process. We also appreciate the support and comments supplied by our present and former colleagues at Syracuse University, some of whom are included among the contributors. Finally, we thank our students at Syracuse University, who continue to inspire and agitate us in our thinking about education, citizenship, and democracy.

*Introduction*

# Some Themes from Recent Innovations and Questions for the Future

*Grant Reeher and Joseph Cammarano*

This book stands at the crossroads of two perennial social and political concerns that have recently enjoyed renewed interest: education and citizenship.

Over the past thirty years there has been a growing sense that our educational system is in a state of crisis, particularly at the primary and secondary levels. The concern is that students are falling behind those in other peer nations, and more generally that they are increasingly ill-prepared and ill-tempered to succeed in life. Higher education has not been spared from this sense of crisis, but the concerns have taken different forms. Setting aside the critique that college instruction has been overly influenced by a politically liberal and in some renderings even left-wing approach, educational observers have worried that simply imparting information, even at high levels of sophistication, is no longer sufficient. According to their concerns, higher education has become stale, brittle, remote, unimaginative, and generally ill-suited to the world students enter upon graduation. Higher education must thus go beyond imparting information to the active engagement of analytical and communicative skills that will allow any adult to adapt, participate, and succeed in a rapidly changing world.

Concomitant with the sense of crisis in education has been a growing sense of crisis in political citizenship. Perhaps the best-known benchmark for this crisis is the marked decline in voter turnout since the early 1960s, but the problems indicated by lower turnout rates run much deeper than people failing to register and vote. Foremost among these problems, which plague voters and nonvoters alike, are a widely felt and profoundly held sense of political alienation; a distrust of organized political institutions, particularly the government; an anger toward or ambivalence about politics more generally; and a felt absence of constructive avenues for meaningful political engagement.[1] Political observers have located these problems in the erosion of traditional institutions engendering citizenship, most notably political parties (and arguably families), along with the inability of other institutions, such as the media, to provide useful alternative bases for active citizenship. They have thus looked with increasing hope and desperation to other realms, such as populist mutual aid communities (Boyte and Reissman 1986), integrated networks of ongoing public deliberation (Barber 1984), communitarian movements (Etzioni 1993), and alternative or renewed institutional links among individuals and between individuals and the common sphere (Bellah, et al. 1991).

One important institution potentially providing those links is education, and it is the confluence of higher education and citizenship that animates this book. Many of those in and around higher education have looked increasingly to higher education to prepare students to be active citizens as well as scholars, professionals, and entrepreneurs (see Boyer 1994). Indeed, this is not the first attempt to consider the link—or chasm—between higher education and citizenship. But most recent work at the intersection of education and citizenship has concentrated on *what* students should be learning rather than the *ways* in which they should learn.[2] While we will touch on the former, our primary focus is the latter. How must we, as educators concerned with citizenship, adapt to the changing realities of higher education? What kinds of active and innovative teaching techniques within the academy also enhance active citizenship outside of it? To what degree can the experiences offered by higher education supply the "connective tissue" (Greider 1992) between the individual and the public realm that is necessary for efficacious citizenship? To what degree can education for citizenship contribute to the development within our students of essential analytical and temperamental skills? These questions would have sounded quite familiar to ancient Greek and republican political philosophers, and would today be familiar to anyone who has read the *Republic*. Thus the essays gathered here represent new variations on a timeless concern.

These essays take up the challenge of education for citizenship at a specific, concrete level. They relate front-line attempts to place education "at the center of our common life" by placing our common life at the center of our education (Bellah, et al. 1991). In an important respect, they are examples of efforts to create among our students a new set of what Alexis de Tocqueville called *mores* or culturally defining "habits of the heart," which will enhance citizenship, foster a sense of connectedness to a community stretching beyond the university, and ultimately support the practices, basic values, and institutions necessary for the democratic process.

A great part of that democratic process, as both journalist William Greider and political philosopher Benjamin Barber note, begins in conversation. And as Plato demonstrated, conversation also supplies the foundation for genuine education. Thus, perhaps most fundamentally, our colleagues are engaged in an effort to begin the process of conversation among their students, to enlarge its circle of inclusion, and to develop both the honesty and the critical capacity of those engaged in it while at the same time instilling within the participants a deep sense of mutual respect (Greider 1992).

This is a Herculean task, to say the least, but its importance cannot be overemphasized. In teaching our courses both of us have been struck by the degree to which our students seem to be floating adrift in political waters. Even political science majors appear to lack both interest in and knowledge of American political life; many are distinctively repulsed by what they consider to be "the political" (see also Luger and Scheuerman 1993).[3] There is probably nothing new in this; alienation and disconnection always accompany times of rapid political and technological change. And of course the past may not have been that much better. Nonetheless, our task as educators concerned with citizenship is to provide new grounds and new formats for connections that sustain and expand liberty. New technologies and new politics occasion new opportunities for despotism as well as freedom.

## Emergent Themes

One of the more specific themes that unites the essays gathered here, and that underscores the importance of conversation, is the focus on various kinds of active learning, both inside and outside the classroom. There has been an explosion of recent works on active learning at all levels of education. The upshot is that students best learn to do by doing. Within political science, there has been much consideration of democratizing the learning environment as a way of encouraging more active learning. One learns about democracy, and for democracy, by practicing it. Students must be less acted *upon*, and more acted *for*. Education and citizenship thus reinforce each other. Most of the contributors to this volume are concerned with discovering ways to introduce elements of democracy into the learning process and, more generally, with making learning a more active process.

Instituting active learning, increased participation, and activities outside the classroom may also tap into and take advantage of alternative intelligences possessed by students, which have heretofore been underengaged, such as body-kinesthetic, interpersonal, and intrapersonal intelligences (see Gardner 1982; Lawrence 1995; Canfield and Reeher 1996). When teaching engages such alternative intelligences—or, if the reader prefers, alternative forms of intelligence or alternative learning styles—students learn more completely and at a deeper level, and more students are drawn into the process of learning. Once again, education and citizenship reinforce each other.

At the same time, rigor and content must not be compromised. This danger is a deep concern for the contributors. Democratic citizenship is not just action, but action of a certain kind which includes deliberation, judgment, even regret (Barber 1984). Education for citizenship must not only engender activity, but also refine it. It is therefore important that more active learning processes take place within an analytical and critically reflective context.

A second theme that emerges from the essays gathered here is a more psychological one, concerning both teachers and students. It is clear that in order to be successful in engendering citizenship, teachers must be keenly aware of their students. They must know something of their backgrounds, their attitudes toward political life, and their impressions of their fellow students and the world. They must also know campus life and the social and political issues that animate and perhaps divide it. For individual students, teachers must be aware of particular fears of and resistance to speaking in front of others and acting publicly. But at a deeper level, taking education for citizenship seriously involves psychological risks for both students and teachers, in that it requires a different mode of social interaction; it necessarily requires moving beyond the conveyance of information in an authoritative way and into the engagement of *arguments*, where views might indeed change (Lasch 1995, 170). Accepting this risk is part of the education for citizenship.

For the teacher all of this takes effort, and also threatens the traditionally held role of the professional that so many of us cling to. Another aspect of this psychological theme, then, is that teachers need to pay attention to their own experiences and attitudes. As academics, we are trained to be experts in a field of knowledge. There is an obvious tension here, as this role is explicitly antidemocratic. Becoming educators for citizenship threatens our social position; in teaching citizenship, we ourselves become less the professional and more the citizen. We become more subject to the claims of others, and our independent standing is necessarily threatened (see Reeher 1995). Citizens must listen and respond to other citizens. But as our contributors have found, this transition is well worth the cost. The transition might even prompt us to reconsider our roles as researchers, specifically to broaden our notion of scholarship and to become citizen-scholars rather than professional-scholars. In the end, the process of education for citizenship should lead to deeper self-understanding for both students and teachers.

A third emergent theme is more subtle and embedded in the efforts related here. Reflected in the way education for citizenship is approached is a larger view about the political economy of education. As teachers, we view our students first as the future citizens of the nation, not simply as the future workforce. As Daniel Ritchie, chancellor of the University of Denver, succinctly stated, "We don't want to graduate barracudas" (Marriott 1996). To invoke an earlier observer of the educational process, we might consider ourselves engaged in a present-day (and necessarily watered-down) version of what Jean-Jacques Rousseau might have called the "overcoming of the bourgeois" (Bloom 1979, 6). We are trying to develop the better angels of the students' nature, not the "greedy little varmint" inhabiting an overly individualized society (Barber 1984, 23–24). Though many of us are located in ostensibly private institutions, in educating for citizenship we are involved in a distinctively public enterprise.[4]

## Questions for the Future

As with any work of this kind, these essays raise more questions than they answer. The efforts described here, and their limitations, suggest some specific paths for future investigation. First, how do we set about building institutions within the academy in order to make education for citizenship a more general and permanent feature of college education? Many of the attempts related here take the form of specific practices instituted in specific courses, at the discretion of individual instructors. Second, how lasting are the effects of education for citizenship? Do they stir only temporary interest in political life? Third, how must we rethink and expand the very notion of citizenship that informs the present efforts to engender it? Our efforts may be too entrenched in and limited by a notion of citizenship centered around traditional political participation. Fourth, must we rethink and expand our notion of the classroom? Many of the efforts related here struggle with its boundaries. Fifth, must education for citizenship, if taken seriously, include students in the actual governance of the university, beyond the symbolic role they are presently permitted to play? Education for citizenship requires taking students seriously, and taking students seriously might require this change. Sixth, is there a particular ideology that attends citizenship for education? We are encouraging students to become active in the public realm, after all, and presumably the impact of this encouragement is that the public will become more salient in people's lives and livelihoods. Finally, how must we guard against the danger that the new technologies available for education for citizenship, such as the Internet, reinforce existing inequalities and hierarchies? Furthermore, might not the new technologies ultimately instantiate more passive qualities among those students using it (see Stoll 1996)? These are all thorny questions, to which future work should be directed. But let us turn now to a more detailed description of the present efforts to educate for citizenship.

## Education for Citizenship

The essays fall into four broad categories: attempts to instill active citizen involvement among students through service learning and other similar components that recently have been springing up all over the nation; attempts to use the classroom environment itself to stimulate citizenship and democratic conversation; attempts to confront and enlist issues of diversity, pluralism, and interdisciplinary instruction; and attempts to use the technology of the Internet for the purposes of citizenship.[5] But just as the endeavor to instill citizenship may require a broadening of the very conceptions of political activity and involvement, these essays themselves do not fit neatly into a single category; most overlap with others.

Craig Rimmerman of Hobart and William Smith Colleges leads off with an essay that serves particularly well as a starting point, as it first sets forward the fundamental characteristics required of any course devoted to critical education for citizenship, and then describes in more detail the community service component of his own course on American politics. Rimmerman argues that for students to develop an accurate picture of democracy and citizenship, they must practice as well as study such ideals. His course is designed around questions regarding the role of citizens in the American political system and the proper scope of the federal government in the United States. Course readings and assignments address these themes, and they integrate students' community service experiences into the course structure. Rimmerman's goal is to merge the theoretical issues of democracy and citizenship with the realities of public and private life, and to encourage students to think about citizenship as a complex, interrelated activity rather than simply a passive, individualistic exercise.

Rimmerman argues that any course attempting to provide a critical education for citizenship should do at least five things: (1) present a full critique of American democracy as currently practiced; (2) demonstrate to students the importance of participating in public decisions; (3) encourage students to conceive of democracy and participation broadly to include community discussions, community action, workplace action, public service, and protest politics; (4) encourage students to take account of the important relationships among gender, race, and class in the participatory process; and (5) prompt students to confront their prior assumptions regarding power and leadership, and the sources of those assumptions. By including a community service requirement in his course, he offers students the opportunity to learn about politics through experience, and a chance to understand that there is an alternative to passivity and indifference.

Richard Battistoni of the Feinstein Center for Public Service at Providence College is also a strong advocate of service learning programs. He, like Rimmerman, has been actively involved in developing community service requirements for students. In particular, he critically examines the assumptions about the connections between service and engaged citizenship, and describes the specific civic skills that service learning can impart to students. His experience with students leads him to argue that the generally limited connection between service learning and increased citizenship is due not to students' inability to make connections between service and citizenship, but rather to the limited, narrow conception of citizenship held by scholars and researchers. And by focusing on the obvious and more individualistic aspects of citizenship—such as voting in elections—skeptics of service learning fail to discover the full effect of such programs. An effective service learning course teaches both the intellectual and the practical skills of citizenship, and seeks to broaden the concept of citizenship itself to include all forms of community interactions, not simply the most obviously political ones.

In his work at Providence and at Rutgers University, Battistoni has found that the benefits of service learning are fourfold. First, students learn more about the community in which their institution resides. By going into the community and being exposed to the experience of other residents, students get a clearer understanding of the lives of those around them. This encourages them to become better neighbors. Second, students learn that being a good citizen relates to both individual behavior and relationships with others which, in turn, leads to a greater sense of responsibility for their actions and the needs of the community. Third, students are forced to confront questions regarding their place in an increasingly multicultural democracy. Such confrontation is a two-way process. Students who are not accustomed to the diversity offered by metropolitan life learn that their community is not as homogeneous as they thought; by the same token, they must also confront the fact that their own characteristics and lifestyles are different from those in their community, and that people can be hostile to the diversity they introduce. Finally, Battistoni argues that service learning must include classroom meetings in which the environment is democratic, egalitarian, and participatory. When service learning is thoughtfully done, students not only learn the values of citizenship, they also become active in those areas of community life that matter to them.

Service learning usually takes the form of having students volunteer at some program in the local community for the duration of a course. But this is not the only way to incorporate service learning into citizenship education. Otto Feinstein and James Chesney of Wayne State University have ten years of experience with a service learning component in their American government courses, called the Urban Agenda Project. The project attempts to provide students with "civic literacy" based on participation in the following activities: (1) formulating, as a class, an urban agenda through participatory and representative democratic procedures; (2) attempting to place that agenda on the actual working agenda of the local governing bodies in the Detroit area; (3) conducting a voter registration and pledge to vote drive; and (4) researching the issues related to the agenda and producing a local television program based on that research and on interviews with candidates for local offices. Two years ago, the project was expanded from Wayne State to thirty-one surrounding middle and secondary schools.

This approach to service learning is somewhat different from those of Battistoni and Rimmerman. Although they too are concerned with the development of students' personal conceptions of citizenship, Feinstein and Chesney add an additional dynamic into their course: the power of collective action. The overall goal of the project is to raise important issues related to citizenship, and then do something about those issues. By developing an agenda and then actually setting out as a class to accomplish political action, Feinstein and Chesney help students to see the connection between their individual actions and the achievement of real-world results. Students also see firsthand the effectiveness and the rewards of group-based activity.

Another innovative approach to service learning is that used by William Coplin of the Public Affairs Program at Syracuse University's Maxwell School of Citizenship. For more than twenty years Coplin has taught an introductory public policy course that relies on an active, problem-based learning process that takes students into the Syracuse community. Coplin starts with the assertion that higher education is much too concerned with intellectual learning and too little concerned with practical learning. His course is thus designed to give students a chance at gaining knowledge through practice. The course begins with the assumption that the students are in a training program for a company that proposes public policies to solve community problems. Class time is taken up with visits from public officials from the Syracuse area, experiential exercises aimed at getting students to consider questions of power and influence, and discussions of how individual behavior can result in large social problems. Coplin includes several exercises intended to teach students about the process by which public policy is made. These exercises drive home the point that politics is not necessarily a process of achieving equality, and that the unequal distribution of political resources has serious consequences for public policy. Throughout the course, Coplin uses unconventional methods, such as confronting students about their illegal behavior, in order to provoke them to think about themselves as part of a larger community.

Perhaps the most widely used and universally established form of service learning is the internship. The confluence of two recent trends has made internships an important part of political science education. The first trend is the increasing demand on liberal arts education to make courses of study more relevant to career opportunities for students. As part of a response to the increasing professionalization of undergraduate education, internships give students practical experience which in turn enhances their knowledge of politics while increasing their marketability once they graduate. The second trend is the expansion of opportunities for students to work in both public and private organizations. New organizations have emerged in and around government as politics becomes more professionalized, decentralized, and complex. Organizations have also turned to internships to cope with pressures to increase service while controlling costs. Needs of organizations to enlist students merge nicely with the desire of students to gain real-world knowledge and experience.

An example of an innovative program that uses internships as a vehicle for citizenship education is the program run by Glen Halva-Neubauer of Furman University. The Furman internship program rests on the principles of immersion in the political experience, integration of relevant social science literature with the student's experience, and activities that produce reflection on questions of citizenship. Halva-Neubauer finds that the students who participate in the program return to campus with a more sophisticated understanding of public service. Regardless of where students are placed, they end their internship with a keener awareness of the importance of public service for citizenship. This awareness is accompanied by an appreciation for the work of public servants. Once back on campus, students are more active, engaged learners who are informed and passionate about current public affairs. Looking at long-term effects, Halva-Neubauer argues that the internship also has a positive impact on the political behavior of alumni.

The second major path in citizenship education is the use of various active learning strategies within established courses, including class discussions, group projects, debates, and other activities that require interaction. The basic assumption behind these active learning strategies is that learning is not simply related to mastery of course content, but also to the *processes* of politics. There is nothing new about this notion, but there are recent adaptations of active learning strategies that help students to examine their own actions and behavior as examples of citizenship.

A widely used exercise that enhances students' understanding of and motivation toward citizenship is the simulation. Simulations are well suited for courses on politics because they help students understand complexities within political institutions and in political behavior. They also underscore the importance of individuals in political processes. The use of simulations in political science is widespread;

consider, for example, programs like the Model United Nations and Model Congress, as well as the countless moot court simulations used in courses on constitutional law. The pedagogical strength of simulations rests in merging academic knowledge with role-playing exercises such that the academic material is made concrete to students.

An example of the effective use of simulations is seen in the cross-course simulation used by Joseph Cammarano, of Syracuse University, and Linda L. Fowler, of Dartmouth College (formerly of Syracuse University). Together they conducted a budget process simulation with students in two courses, one on Congress and the other on the presidency. They argue that this form of active learning provides an excellent tool for promoting citizenship (without neglecting course content), in large part because the experience demonstrates to students the realities of budgetary politics, in particular the messiness of the process, the necessary bargaining, and the sheer complexity involved. This in turn inclines students toward additional political activities, creates empathy among them toward real-life political figures, and demystifies the political process more generally. Indeed, their students have repeatedly cited this simulation experience as among the best and most important parts of their political science education. In addition, those who have gone on to careers in politics note that the simulations have given them a clearer and more accurate understanding of the demands they face in their public sector jobs.

Simulations are an effective way to bring the world into the political science classroom. However, no matter how well organized and implemented, simulations are still acts of fiction. Through some of his courses, Marc Lendler has made the issue real. Lendler integrated actual on-campus free speech controversies into his courses on speech rights. During one course, a campuswide controversy erupted over the rights of student artists to display work considered offensive by several campus employees who regularly viewed it while they were at work. The conflict did not end with the end of the display, however, and Lendler had an extended opportunity to integrate the issue into his courses. Through this integration, in which the participation of students in these practical debates both strengthened and was strengthened by their study of Supreme Court decisions and works of ethical reasoning concerning free speech, Lendler traces a substantial development in student thinking over time: What began as simple libertarian individualism grew into a more complete understanding of reciprocal rights and the claims of community. He also comments more generally on the ways in which actual community debate and classroom discussion interact.

Lendler finds some broader lessons in his experience with the on-campus controversy. Most importantly, he finds that students can learn a great deal about the concepts of governance through a discussion of on-campus issues. There was no need for students to leave campus to learn about politics because issues of power, liberty, tolerance, and community all occurred in the on-campus free speech controversy. Additionally, he finds that the controversy itself led students to be more interested in developing their own conceptions of power and authority. Finally, Lendler shows why faculty must be ever-aware of contemporary issues that relate to their courses, and how, by focusing on things students care about, teachers can encourage students to apply academic issues to events occurring on campus.

In a similar vein, Daniel O'Connell of Palm Beach Community College, and a board member of the National Issues Forum (NIF), makes use of public deliberation processes in the classroom and on campus. Established by the Kettering and the Public Agenda foundations, NIF produces books on important public policy issues, coordinates the efforts of the nationwide network of instructors who use NIF publications, and solicits and administers grants to promote deliberative democracy. NIF assumes that learning about citizenship includes four elements: public service; deliberation on issues; on-campus participation; and rigorous academic study in the classic academic model. Although there are ample opportunities for internships, campus politics, and, of course, classroom learning, there are fewer chances for public deliberation, and NIF seeks to bolster this form of learning. The flexibility provided by NIF is an important strength of the program. Instructors may use publications as supplements to class materials, or they may structure an entire course around the issue books. The publications are also useful to many different academic courses, not only those on government. In addition, school administrators can use NIF to coordinate campuswide meetings, or meetings across different campuses.

By using current issues and structuring class and campus activities around them, O'Connell finds that students benefit in several ways. First, they gain a clearer understanding of important political questions and controversies. Second, they become more aware of possible answers. Third, they see the connections between their own lives and public policy issues. Again, by using the real world in real time, O'Connell merges politics with political education, resulting in a more interested and engaged student citizen.

John Freie of LeMoyne College describes another way to bring the world into the classroom. Instead of focusing on bringing the outside world into the classroom, Freie changes the classroom to resemble the realities of democratic society, through the very manner in which a course is organized. Observing that the process of organizing and conducting a course is inherently political in that it involves authority, relations of power, and issues of responsibility, Freie has come to the understanding that the autocratic development of course content is not only a bad example for students, but also fails to impart any sense of responsibility or obligation. Borrowing from research that supports the importance of democracy within classrooms, Freie designs his courses *with* students, not *for* them. To achieve this he uses the Individual Learning Contract. Freie argues that the Individual Learning Contract, which involves an interactive process between student and professor, is ideally suited to teach citizenship because it requires both the professor and the student to democratize the learning experience and to work together in that process, while at the same time remaining within the traditional college framework.

Freie's use of a learning contract for democratizing the educational experience suggests the broader use of the classroom environment to provide alternative models of authority, and to serve as a catalyst for developing more diverse, pluralistic experiences for students. Naeem Inayatullah of Ithaca College takes this a step further. Inayatullah has contemplated the relations between the dynamics in the classroom, specifically its hierarchical nature, and the thorny issues of cultural interaction and international citizenship. He describes his own efforts to build meaningful participation and responsible action through a classroom context of "creative anarchy" and decentered power. His approach forces students to be proactive rather than reactive in his classes, and challenges them to think about their courses in a more comprehensive, interrelated way. This approach to teaching challenges students to form their own notions of education and citizenship that are based more upon internally driven motives than externally dictated structures.

Mark Rupert of Syracuse University considers the issue of diversity, education, and citizenship from the perspective of academic discipline rather than culture or race. He describes the development in the Maxwell School of Citizenship of two introductory-level multidisciplinary courses that have attempted to expose students to various ways of constructing social knowledge and their practical implications. These courses have prompted students to rethink the conventional boundaries that separate disciplines as well as those that traditionally delimit economics from politics, public from private, domestic from international, and, most importantly for citizenship, knowledge from practice. He argues that these courses and others like them might foster within students a more critical awareness of the possibilities open to them as knowers and doers in the world.

The final area of innovations concerns the adaptation of technology to teach citizenship. The transforming effects of technology on education cannot be denied; indeed, it seems that there would be ample opportunity for political scientists to use technology to promote a new notion of citizenship among their students. William Ball of the College of New Jersey and Kimberley Canfield of Syracuse University and the State University of New York at Oswego have both made efforts to promote citizenship through the Internet. This is a tool that is only beginning to be investigated in any systematic way, and both authors have extensive experience using it with students.

Ball uses the Internet in his introductory American politics course in two ways. First, he uses the Internet to increase the level of discussion among students. The nature of Internet communication transcends the traditional boundaries of space and time. Students are able to conduct conversations about course materials in ways that are less threatening and more deliberative than regular class discussions. Second, he uses the Internet as a "virtual library," a source of information that is specific to the course. This use of the Internet allows students to analyze the reporting of the same issues by different media outlets and to study how political organizations present themselves through the Internet. Using it in class also enlivens his own lecture materials. Ball believes that the Internet has a positive influence on political education because it helps students to gain more detailed, complex information about politics, and to learn in a more realistic way the intricacies of politics. It also helps students to demystify politics, since learning from real sources shows students that political participation is neither obtuse nor overly difficult.

Canfield has used the Internet in much the same way as Ball and also finds that it helps students to better understand American politics. She contends that the Internet offers a particularly intriguing tool for citizenship as it is both intensely individualistic and community oriented. Power is decentralized on the Internet, and this fact encourages individualism in the actions and behaviors of its users. On the other hand, the Internet provides a chance for the development of interest communities, groups of people who gather together in cyberspace because they have a common interest or concern. The tension between the actions of individuals and the needs of the community that has arisen on the Internet is elegantly parallel to the tension in American politics between individual and community. Therefore, the Internet provides a conceptual advantage in teaching about American politics and citizenship.

## Synthesizing Education and Citizenship

These attempts to imbue a sense of citizenship in our students only scratch the surface of possible efforts. There are many ways in which political science teachers can educate students for citizenship. What emerges from this discussion, however, are some general ideals and principles. First, we must remember that there is no division between education and citizenship. Instead, they are part and parcel of the same thing: the pursuit of informed, critical, and active citizens. Second, the division between academic learning and practical experience is artificial. Classroom learning prepares our students to interact in the world and to understand it; conversely, what occurs in local, national, or global society can inform and enhance traditional academic learning. Third, as educators we need to rethink the purpose, structure, and content of our individual courses and of our discipline, and to be more conscious—and conscientious—not only about the content of our teaching but also about our methods of course design and structure, and the lessons they impart about the role of leadership and citizenship. Finally, we must be willing to experiment with our own ideas about education. All of the contributors have taken risks in their classes, but not all of these risks were successful. This too is a message to our students about citizenship. The willingness to try new things, to develop ideas into concrete teaching strategies or tactics, to challenge students to change their existing attitudes and behaviors, and to fail is well within the tradition of the liberal arts, and firmly entrenched in the pluralistic tradition that is so evident in our polity.

## Notes

1. See for example Bellah, et al. 1985; Harwood 1991; Greider 1992; and Putnam 1995. For an even deeper critique, which locates the problem in our fundamental political, epistemological, and psychological frameworks, see Barber 1984. For arguments and data suggesting that, aside from voter turnout,

Americans have actually become *more* politically involved, see Verba, Schlozman, and Brady 1995; and Morin 1996.

2. For an interesting set of essays that considers the appropriate content of education for citizenship, see "Educating for Citizenship" 1984. This topic has also driven some of the most intriguing recent conservative writing on the topic; see for example the work of Allan Bloom and Thomas Pangle.

3. In this regard, it is both interesting and telling to note that in the eyes of many students, one of the most attractive elements of "service learning" or community activity–based projects is their apparently apolitical nature.

4. Note also that this is not by any means a utopian effort. The kinds of orientations and skills developed by education for citizenship are increasingly in demand by private corporations, in particular those of inclusiveness, teamwork, and participation.

5. For a good general survey of service learning and community service efforts in colleges and universities, see Marriott 1996.

*1*

# Teaching American Politics through Service: Reflections on a Pedagogical Strategy

*Craig A. Rimmerman*

Our educational system must transmit an understanding of what democracy really means to all of our citizens.

—Robert Bellah, et al., *The Good Society*, 144

The successful resuscitation of the idea of service will not proceed far without the refurbishing of the theory and practice of democratic citizenship, which must in turn become any successful service program's guiding spirit.

—Benjamin Barber, *An Aristocracy of Everyone*, 236

This essay explores the connections between course-based service learning and the notion of "critical education for citizenship" within the context of an introductory American political system course, taught at Hobart and William Smith Colleges during the 1996 winter term. The course required all students to participate in a community service project for two hours per week, in the surrounding Geneva, New York, community.

A course rooted in critical education for citizenship should: (1) present the full critique of American democracy to the students; (2) allow students to see the importance of participating in public decisions; (3) ask educators and students to conceive of democracy broadly to include community action, worker self-management, public service, and protest politics; (4) encourage students to take into account the impor-

17

tant relationships among gender, race, and class concerns in the participatory process (that is, "the politics of difference"); and (5) ask students to confront their assumptions regarding power and leadership as well as the sources of such assumptions (Rimmerman, 1997).

This approach is grounded in a participatory democratic conception of citizenship, one that assumes that the purpose of an undergraduate college education is to encourage students to develop the skills needed to participate actively in the public sphere upon graduation. This means that students should have an opportunity to develop a program of study that will enable them to link their work in the classroom with the surrounding community in which they live. In doing so, they will develop the analytical and problem-solving abilities needed to address public problems in meaningful ways. Finally, students should be exposed to various perspectives on ethical and moral reasoning. Ultimately, a participatory conception of citizenship asks citizens to address what constitutes the good society—a normative question that a university education and political science departments are uniquely situated to engage. This central question underlies the critical education for citizenship model.

The purpose here is to examine the various theoretical and pedagogical issues growing out of my attempt to meet the critical education for citizenship criteria within the context of my American political system course. In doing so, I will address the following questions: Why require students to complete a community service project as a part of a college-level course that examines the American political system? What are the advantages and disadvantages of doing so? What is the connection between community service and broader issues of democracy, citizenship, community, justice, and difference? What are various approaches to citizenship education? I conclude that the course was only partially successful in meeting the criteria for critical education for citizenship. This is due to the narrowly constructed conception of citizenship associated with most models of service learning.

## Approaches to Citizenship Education

Ultimately, a college curriculum should enable students to define for themselves what they mean by democracy and then have the opportunity to develop the skills that they need for participation on their campuses, in their communities, and in the larger society. Students must see the connection between their college educational experiences and their participation in the larger society upon graduation. Indeed, education is an important predictor of civic engagement. The Kettering Foundation has addressed these issues in a number of meaningful ways, including a national town meeting program called the National Issues Forums, as well as a variety of written documents. The Kettering pamphlet *Politics for the Twenty-First Century: What Should Be Done on Campus?* (Morse 1992) offers several approaches to citizenship education that are particularly relevant as we explore the full meaning of critical education for citizenship and its connection to challenging civic indifference.

A first approach, rooted in community service, is "learning by doing—the public service component." The argument here is that students must look to the larger community if they are to be properly prepared for their roles as citizens in a democracy. From this vantage point, students should participate in their communities through involvement in service opportunities, organizing for social change, or political campaigns. Regardless of the form that involvement actually takes, students learn that hands-on experience outside their college campuses is a crucial component of their college education (Morse 1992, 5).

A second option, "learning by talking—acquiring deliberative skills," rejects the notion that service should be at the core of an undergraduate education. Instead, this approach argues that service cannot begin to train people for politics, "because politics is actually about what we mean by the 'public good.'" The key here is that all students and citizens must be afforded the opportunity to develop their public deliberation skills, so that they will be better equipped to participate meaningfully in politics at the community level. Proponents of this second approach think that "all citizens need to engage in reasoned political discussion about the sort of world they want to live in, and that a college should itself provide opportunities to practice deliberation and to hone the skills that public talk requires" (Morse 1992, 5–6).

A third perspective might be entitled "learning by practicing—democratizing the campus." Those who support this approach to citizenship education point out that direct participation by students in the creating of their own education and the structuring of their lives within their college or university affords them the best possible training in politics. The goal here is for students to transform the campus itself into an egalitarian, participatory community. As they do so, they will learn that "deliberation is meaningless without power and responsibility." In addition, they will come to reject hierarchy in all of its forms and recognize that "citizenship has to be practiced in order to be learned" (Morse 1992, 6).

Those who believe that "the key to a strong democracy lies in individuals who are well prepared intellectually" constitute a fourth approach. This approach might be called "learning by learning—a classical academic model." Proponents of this perspective believe that the college or university should remain neutral in political affairs and students should not become too politicized. Instead, they should devote their attention to their studies and become trained in various intellectual disciplines, with the hope that they will develop the rigorous training needed to successfully analyze complex issues as we head into the twenty-first century. In this way, they will actually strengthen democracy (Morse 1992, 6).

As the Kettering authors point out, these four approaches to citizenship education are not mutually exclusive. In fact, all four approaches can contribute in valuable ways to the elements of critical education for citizenship identified earlier. In addition, each approach either implicitly or explicitly challenges students to overcome the civic indifference often associated with their age (Rimmerman 1997).

Of the four, the first—"learning by doing"—has received the most recent attention and underlies many of the efforts by college faculty to build community service requirements into their courses.

## The Case for Service

Many studies in recent years have provided considerable evidence to support the conclusion that young people are largely apathetic, uninterested, and indifferent when it comes to politics. Indeed, recent studies of the political lives of today's youth provide more support for this claim (Higher Education Research Institute 1995, 1; and Higher Education Research Institute 1996, 1; People for the American Way 1989, 1213). Why is there this apparent indifference to politics among America's youth today? One possible explanation is that this generation of youth is more preoccupied with career goals and making money than previous generations. In support of this explanation, Harry Boyte and Nancy Kari conclude that "America's youth culture in the 1990's is characterized by pervasive passivity in the form of consumerism and the never-ending search for personal fulfillment" (Boyte and Kari 1996, 173). What Boyte and Kari overlook, however, is that today's students perceive that they face enormous economic pressures, pressures that are heightened by a changing and more unfriendly economy, one that simply does not provide the opportunities available for college graduates in years past. Given this negative economic climate, who can blame students for pursuing careerist kinds of concerns rather than politics? A second possible explanation for civic indifference on the part of America's youth is that college students are so convinced that politics does not solve real problems that they see no real reason to participate. Yet on a more optimistic note, they can imagine a different kind of politics, one that would take their concerns more seriously than the current "politics as usual." Proponents of service justifiably argue that requiring students to participate in community service projects will enable them to begin to imagine that "different kind of politics," one that embraces a more positive relationship with the public sphere. This revised conception of politics requires them to link their individual interests to the larger community in which they live. It is this sense of community that underlies most approaches to community service and that is often embraced by faculty building required service projects into their courses.

For those of us in higher education, it seems that we are uniquely situated to evaluate citizen disaffection and to devise strategies rooted in a curriculum that enables our students to grapple with the meaning of citizenship, democracy, and public participation in compelling ways. Political scientists have much to offer as we tackle these issues in our teaching, our research, and our community work. Indeed, requiring our students to participate in community service projects as a part of regularly taught political science courses is a way to ask them to connect ideas that they confront in the classroom with their service experiences in the surrounding community. The goal, then, is to ask students to bring together the intellectual with the experiential. A central mechanism for doing so is by assigning texts, papers, and journals that will enable students to reflect critically on broader issues of race, class, gender, democracy, and citizenship concerns growing out of their service experiences. Class lectures and discussions should then connect the assigned course readings with student service experiences. The hope on the part of many service proponents is that students who participate in service activities will begin to ask why tragedies such as illiteracy, hunger, and homelessness even exist. In doing so, such students, many of whom are apolitical, will begin to develop a social consciousness through their service experiences and link these experiences with their daily classroom assignments.

Finally, if service learning is to be successful, proponents claim that it must link issues of social justice to social transformation, political empowerment, and the moral development of the individual. The argument here is that democratic citizenship is certainly not a part of the political socialization experience in the United States; instead, it is learned by interacting with others from different class, race, ethnic, gender, and sexuality backgrounds in the community. Service learning, then, enables students to demystify "the other," those who reside outside their immediate social experiences (Guarasci and Rimmerman 1996). In doing so, service affords students the opportunity to link their political and moral development with their service experiences in the surrounding community.

## The Critique of Service

Those opposed to courses that require students to participate in community service often argue that such service simply cannot possibly achieve all that it is supposed to achieve, and that it is far too limited in its scope. For example, Boyte writes that "community service is not a cure for young people's political apathy" because "it teaches little about the arts of participation in public life" (1991, 765). In addition, most courses that require community service fail to afford students the opportunity that they need "to work effectively toward solving society's problems" (Boyte 1991, 766). Critics also suggest that service fails to connect students directly to the daily political process.

Other critics of service-based experiences contend that most student participants fail to tackle larger policy questions and issues as a part of their service experiences. They argue that it is simply not true that students will necessarily connect their service experiences with the broader policy process. Indeed, it is possible and perhaps likely that they will resist doing so. Boyte points out, for example, that the language of community service is infused with the language of "helping" rather than "a vocabulary that draws attention to the public world that extends beyond personal lives and local communities." Service volunteers rarely have the ability to engage the complex intersection of race, class, and power that develop as college-age youths participate in service projects in low-income areas. Community service adopts the worst form of "therapeutic language" in the absence of

> a conceptual framework that distinguishes between personal life and the
> public world. This therapeutic approach, with its focus on the individual,

cannot begin to deal with the inequalities that structure the relationship between the so-called servers and the served. In the end, then, service activity is devoid of politics, and as a result, is an empty way of tackling complex structural issues that arise out of the conditions that prompt service activity in the first place. (Boyte 1991, 766)

To some critics, service is problematic because it fails to address the relationship of the individual to the state in a meaningful manner. Eric Gorham, for example, believes that "community service is an institutional means by which the State uses political discourse and ideology to reproduce a postindustrial capitalist economy in the name of good citizenship" (1992, 1). For Gorham and other critics, community service tacitly accepts the structural inequalities growing out of the limited American welfare state and reinforces the worst form of clientelism. It does so by largely working within the confines of our current system without always affording students the opportunity to critique that system in a meaningful and fundamental way. Therefore, it supports the worst aspects of the American social and economic framework. Furthermore, service assumes that all participants can afford to volunteer for little or no pay. Unfortunately, some students cannot participate in service opportunities because they must work one or two jobs merely to make ends meet while they complete their undergraduate education (Rimmerman 1997).

A final major criticism examines service from the vantage point of those community members "being served." What can they be expected to gain from the relationship? What do they actually gain? Or is the relationship one that is primarily supposed to "benefit" the person who does the serving, by fulfilling a classroom requirement, and contributing to that individual's overall education? What happens to the service relationship once the academic term is over? These questions touch on some of the toughest practical issues that proponents of service must address in response to their critics. Ideally, community members should be brought formally into the course planning, implementation, and evaluation processes. Students and faculty members should receive feedback from community members prior to, during, and after their service experiences. But this often does not happen in practice. Service proponents hope that virtually all students who participate in service learning courses will continue with their community participation long after the formal course concludes. If they fail to do so, then their relationship to community members will possibly be viewed as an exploitive one from the vantage point of the community.

Student continuity and commitment are crucial if service learning is to be successful from the vantage point of community members. From the vantage point of service critics, however, that continuity and commitment are rarely achieved in practice.

The first part of this essay has established the broad theoretical context for evaluating community service, while exploring the case for service learning and its critique. I am now in a position to examine these broader issues within the context of an Introduction to the American Political System course taught at Hobart and William Smith Colleges.

## Service Learning in Practice

Four key questions underlie my American political system course and frame the analysis presented over the course of the academic term. These appear on the course syllabus and are introduced to students on the first day of class: What is the role of the citizenry in the American political system? What should the role of the citizenry be? What is the role of the federal government in the American political system? What should the role of the federal government be? These questions are then addressed from a variety of perspectives throughout the course of the term. Assigned readings and lecture, film, and discussion materials are chosen that will enable students to develop the critical faculties necessary to be thoughtful and engaged citizens in a country that purports to adhere to democratic principles. In this course, students are asked to read several books that touch on themes of democracy, citizenship, service, and social policy—Robert Bellah and his co-authors' *Habits of the Heart*; Jonathan Kozol's *Amazing Grace*; Charles Murray's *Losing Ground*; William Greider's *Who Will Tell the People*; and Steven Waldman's study of Bill Clinton's National Service proposal to Congress, *The Bill*. All three major course writing assignments ask students to reflect upon their service experiences within the context of the reading, lecture, discussion, and film materials. Ultimately, the goal is to integrate into my course the various elements of the critical education for citizenship model outlined earlier in this essay. In doing so, I want students to grapple with the broader connection between the public and private spheres within the context of their own lives.

Faculty members face three key barriers as they attempt to inspire students to connect their own private interests with the larger public sphere and develop a critical approach to citizenship. The first barrier is a political socialization process that encourages us to extend the private aspects of our lives, rather than develop how we can engage the public sphere in meaningful ways. A second barrier is the enormous impact that popular culture (television, in particular) has on a daily basis in encouraging our students to become passive receptacles for someone else's ideas (Ehrenhalt 1995; Putnam 1995), thereby deterring them from participating meaningfully in politics and in their communities. As Robert Wuthnow suggests, "young people are, in fact, more exposed to the influences of contemporary culture than many adults are because they have yet to acquire the resources to resist these pressures" (1995, 12). And finally, as discussed earlier, many of our students are driven by the central goal of careerism as they choose their majors and plan their college careers. This is certainly understandable, given the economic uncertainties faced by today's college graduates. These are all enormous barriers that must be overcome by educators who wish to inspire our students to consider their roles as citizens and to develop a critical approach to citizenship.

To be sure, I face all these barriers on a daily basis as I interact with my students in the classroom. It seemed to me that building a community service requirement of two hours per week into my course would enable me to confront these barriers in a compelling way. It would also afford me the opportunity to explore many of the broader issues growing out of the critical education for citizenship model and the different approaches to citizenship education outlined earlier. In addition, I wanted students to see firsthand the financial struggles of nonprofit agencies that had depended on government subsidies prior to the massive cutbacks in federal, state, and local grants imposed under the guise of fiscal austerity. In this way, I was able to address the role of the state in a liberal capitalist society.

None of this could have been accomplished, however, without the administrative support provided by the coordinator of public service through the Office of Public Service at Hobart and William Smith Colleges. I wanted students to see the importance of the community service requirement from the first day of the course. With that in mind, I invited David Mapstone, a recent graduate of Hobart College and the public service coordinator, to address the class on the very first day. I provided a theoretical overview of how service would supplement the broader course themes of democracy, citizenship, justice, and the role of the state, while Mapstone explained the purpose of the Hobart and William Smith service program and outlined service opportunities available to the thirty students enrolled in the course.

All students were required to participate in an evening training session that asked them to address important ethical and practical matters of what it means to engage in service in the Geneva, New York, and surrounding communities. The two-hour intensive session engaged many of the above concerns raised by the critics of service learning. Upper-division students who had considerable community service experience served as peer facilitators of the service session. Their training program required my students to participate in an array of role-playing exercises designed to force them to consider some of the ethical issues that they might face as they performed their service in the Geneva community. Both Mapstone and I agreed that students could not be sent out into the community without having had at least some minimal training.

Within two weeks, all students were placed in an array of service opportunities, including Geneva Head Start, the Geneva Food Pantry, the Geneva Rape Crisis Service, RISE Day Care, Geneva Community Lunch, and a literacy volunteers program at the Geneva Agribusiness and Chartres Homes. Attempts were made to link student interests with appropriate service opportunities.

How well did the implementation of the community service requirement enable my students and me to meet the articulated course goals? Throughout my course, some students were reluctant to relate the course reading and discussion materials to politics and broader issues of democracy and citizenship. There are two possible explanations for their unwillingness to do so. There can be little doubt that most of our students have been socialized to accept the basic elements of American "democracy" without the questioning or critical self-reflection that my course and the notion of critical education for citizenship requires. As a result, we should not be surprised that students resisted engaging in this important critical process. Second, as Harry Boyte and others have pointed out, it may well be that there is a flaw in the structure and nature of courses that require service to the extent that they fail to connect service appropriately to issues of democracy, politics, and citizenship. Some of my students probably resisted discussing issues of democracy, politics, and citizenship because in their minds their service activities had little relevance or connection to these broader issues. Indeed, some of them were excited about service learning precisely because it did *not* involve politics.

I am also convinced that one course cannot possibly tackle issues of democracy, citizenship, diversity, and difference with the level of depth and attention to detail that such important concerns deserve. For some of my students, they simply could not make appropriate connections among these important issues within the broader context of one ten-week course on the American political system. Participation in service learning affords some of our students an opportunity to confront some of these concerns, but it is in the classroom that the difficult task of making important connections must take place. One ten-week course cannot possibly do justice to the magnitude of the issues raised by service learning and the literature on democracy, citizenship, and service (Guarasci and Rimmerman 1996).

At the same time, however, a number of students in the course believed that their community service participation afforded them invaluable learning experiences. In response to the question of how their service experiences enabled them to understand the American political system better, students offered a number of insightful comments. A student who worked at Head Start said that she now understood the importance of federal and state funding in supporting local Geneva agencies. This was an important comment given the amount of time I devoted in the course to studying various perspectives on the role of the state in the social policy arena. A second student who worked at Project Rise lamented the number of federal and state regulations that she perceived hindered the ability of Project Rise staff to do their jobs well. Other students said that their service experiences made the seriousness of social problems in the United States today more of a reality. In drawing this conclusion, they made direct connections to the problems described in Kozol's *Amazing Grace*. Finally, a number of students said that participation in service opportunities afforded them a sense of hope regarding the American political system. This conclusion, they claimed, was in direct contrast to their attitudes regarding their political system before enrolling in the course.

It was clear from course evaluations and oral comments from my students throughout the term that they viewed the community service requirement as one of the most important parts of the course. All students encouraged me to build such a requirement into the course in future years.

## Broader Implications of My Community Service Experience

Why is it that my students were so enthusiastic about the community service requirement in the course? Is it because this requirement allowed them to make a contribution to society without engaging in politics? On the last day of class, I raised these questions and offered a critique of service in light of the model of critical education for citizenship introduced at the outset of this essay. I told students that I thought service only partially met some of the criteria associated with what it means to be a critical, engaged, and informed citizen. A thoughtful student, one who had a wonderful community service experience, responded to my critique in this way:

> *Service is the first step in getting people to connect with the public sphere. This is especially important for young people, who have lived essentially "private" lives before coming to college.*

From the vantage point of this student, service is the first step in developing public citizens. She and other proponents of service would argue, too, that people cannot participate meaningfully in politics unless they first connect to the public sphere.

Reflecting back on my teaching experience some six months later, I am persuaded by this argument. But I also realize that if service is to begin to develop the public aspects of citizens' lives, it needs to be placed within a broader systemic framework of the kind associated with the critical education for citizenship. Unfortunately, this approach is defined far too narrowly by many faculty members and students who embrace service learning as the most important approach to education. In this way, they limit the opportunities available to students who might otherwise be open to conceptualizing their participation in the public sphere much more actively and broadly.

Indeed, citizenship education programs must have a significant opportunity for participants to engage in public problem solving and political action. One successful program in this vein is Project Public Life, which is associated with the University of Minnesota's Humphrey Institute. The purpose of this program is to reengage citizens in politics by encouraging them to redefine politics in terms of public problem solving rather than a narrow focus on community service. In the words of Harry Boyte and Rebecca Breuer, problem solving cannot be defined narrowly. Instead, "it is the public process by which people engage in the complex, difficult work of creating their larger environments, requiring attentiveness to the relation of problems to the larger whole and to the long term implications of any course of action" (Boyte and Breuer 1992, 1). As argued earlier, the university is well situated to impart to its students the skills necessary to engage in this active conception of citizenship, one rooted in public problem solving.

I am convinced that students need the opportunity to integrate all four approaches to citizenship education—learning by doing, learning by talking, learning by practicing, and learning by learning—during the course of their undergraduate careers. They must also have a chance to ask two key questions that underlie my American political system course: What is the role of the citizenry in the American political system? What should the role of the citizenry be? A course-required community service project may not fulfill the criteria of the critical education for citizenship on its own, but it does enable faculty and our students to interrogate an array of approaches to citizenship education. More importantly, in requiring service, faculty will also hopefully challenge the prevailing student passivity and indifference to politics that is a chief characteristic of our time.

**2**

# Service Learning as Civic Learning: Lessons We Can Learn from Our Students

*Richard M. Battistoni*

Over the past several decades, we have witnessed numerous proclamations about a "crisis" in education, along with a barrage of prescriptions for cures to what ails education. Among the more recent cries of crisis are concerns about the ways in which higher education is leaving students unprepared for a life of democratic citizenship. In 1992, Benjamin Barber called upon American colleges and universities to return to their earliest mission of educating citizens for democracy and liberty. In 1993, an influential group of college educators met and issued the Wingspread Group Report on Higher Education, *An American Imperative: Higher Expectations for Higher Education*, challenging higher education to reclaim its role of preparing ethical citizens who responsibly lead the larger society: "We challenge you to assure that the next year's entering students will graduate as individuals of character more sensitive to the needs of community, more competent to contribute to society, and more civil in habits of thought, speech, and action" (Wingspread Group 1993).

Over the past decade, a common strategy for meeting this challenge has been to adopt programs that will place students in community-based service activities. Colleges and universities, especially their presidents, have assumed that there is a clear relationship between service and citizenship. They have proceeded on this assumption, often ignoring the cautions of experiential educators like John Dewey, by sending

31

students out into communities with little opportunity for preparation or reflection, thinking that service alone will engage students as active citizens.

This assumption begs the question, "Are service and citizenship necessarily connected?" There is a growing body of evidence to suggest a negative answer to this question. Our students often equate citizenship with politics, which they reject as corrupt and "dirty." In fact, many students actively involved in community service say that they have chosen service as an antidote to politics. The Kettering Foundation's Harwood Group report, *College Students Talk Politics* (1993), as well as Alexander Astin's most recent Freshman Survey data (Higher Education Research Institute 1996) provide further evidence that students are rejecting politics and citizenship. Harry Boyte (1993) challenges the connection between service and citizenship, and goes so far as to question the former if one wants to achieve the latter.

On the other hand, there is evidence that when accompanied by proper preparation and adequate academic reflection, service learning can be a potent civic educator. Craig Rimmerman's chapter in this volume clearly makes this claim. Preliminary studies of data collected by Rutgers University's Walt Whitman Center for the Culture and Politics of Democracy as part of its Measuring Citizenship Project indicate that students enrolled in citizenship-based service learning courses at Rutgers had a stronger sense of civic capacity and membership than students enrolled in two different comparison courses. On a "civic leadership" scale of the Measuring Citizenship survey, a scale consisting of twenty-three items that ask respondents to compare themselves with others with regard to a variety of civic leadership skills and capacities, Rutgers service learners scored significantly higher from pre- to post-test than those in nonservice learning political science and journalism classes (Walt Whitman Center 1996). In a similar study conducted by Gregory Markus and colleagues at the University of Michigan, students in service learning sections of an introductory political science course were compared with students in more traditional sections of the same course. The study concluded that in addition to the enhancement of their academic learning in political science, students' personal values and orientation to the community were affected by participation in course-relevant community service (Markus, et al. 1993).

Teaching service learning classes and directing campuswide programs at three different urban campuses, I have found that citizenship education can be a powerful foundation and outcome for service learning. Students' essays and journals indicate that a civic education model of service learning can achieve the goal of educating our students about their responsibilities in a democratic society, allowing them to think about what it means to be a part of the multiple communities in which they find themselves. Listen to these themes found in samples from student journals:

> *Why do I serve? I serve because . . . service is part of my civic responsibility. Providing a service to others . . . is my duty as a citizen. The readings and discussions in this class helped me to formulate this idea. If I am to enjoy the rights and privileges of American life, then I must provide something in return. . . . I fear that the supply of rights will run out if Americans do not constantly restock the shelves. . . . My individual work at [my service site] makes some impact here.*

> *Over the course of this semester I have become a citizen of New Brunswick. It could be argued that I was a citizen here well before registering for the course, but I did not feel as if I were one. Having taken the course, I now know why I felt as I did. A citizen must play an active role in his or her community. A citizen must work for change, and never accept the status quo—things can always be better. I am now aware of what is happening around me. New Brunswick extends beyond the E bus route. It is filled with people who need aid, people who give aid, people who cannot be bothered to give aid, and people who, like me, don't realize they are citizens at all. . . . I now see the city differently. I'm no longer scared walking to [my service site]—far from it. I feel like I know that small portion of the city now. Now when I pass people on the street, some say hello to me, and call me by name. Through my work I've gotten to know individual people, and they've gotten to know me. I enjoy my community service. It has opened my eyes as to the role I play as a citizen in my community.*

> *Ten years from now I might not remember what molecule is responsible for fast-anterograde axonal transport in a ganglion cell of the central nervous system, or what the symbolic significance of the moon was in William Wordsworth's "Goody Blake and Harry Gill," but I will recall what it means to be a responsible member of society.*

So where is the disconnect between my and my students' experiences of engaged citizenship resulting from participation in a service learning program and the findings of others that students have lost a concept of themselves as citizens, and that service, a personal act of caring, has replaced citizenship, a public expression of values? I would contend that much of the problem lies in our monolithic assumptions about the meaning and language of citizenship. If we define citizenship as a national identity, either as patriotic flag-waving or connection to a single "commonwealth," we are more likely to conclude that students engaged in service are not developing adequate notions of engaged citizenship, to the ultimate detriment of the republic. If, however, we take a more pluralistic, localized perspective on citizenship in its multiple meanings for different student constituencies, we can come to see service learning as a rich source for connecting our students—most of whom, I will agree, are disengaged from electoral politics—to the larger public world.

For example, I have students who choose not to vote in off-year or primary elections, but who are working with a local community center to organize a neighborhood congress, whereby local citizens—especially those previously disenfranchised—will have an opportunity to place their issues on the political agenda. Still others have moved from earlier forms of direct service with local agencies to doing issue research for advocacy groups attempting to change government policy in the areas of welfare and educational reform and low-income housing. Traditional measures of political activity will not get at these kinds of civic engagement on the part of students in service learning settings.

I want to focus my attention on the specific practical and intellectual civic skills that service learning can teach. But before I can do this I need to elaborate on the different "models" or understandings of citizenship that emerge from student reflections on community service connected to a civic education-based curriculum. We cannot hope to engage our students as citizens until we find out what kind of civic language resonates with them. Students' written reflections are a rich resource in thinking about the variety of connections that can be made between *service* and *citizenship*. References to student reflections will be made, then, both to make concrete my students' understandings of the civic meaning of service and to draw out the implications for our own practice as educators seeking to connect service to engaged citizenship. For I agree with Dewey that experience alone—in this case, a service experience—does not translate into learning; it is only "the discipline of experience subjected to the tests of intelligent development and direction" that is educative (Dewey 1938). As the excerpts from my students will show, how we as faculty and program administrators subject service experiences to intelligent direction depends upon what perspective of citizenship the student brings to his or her work.

In service learning courses that I've taught over the past seven years, I have gleaned from my students a wide variety of civic attitudes and perspectives, or at least understandings, about themselves in relationship to various communities that I choose to name as *civic*. Here, I will examine four different, but I think related, perspectives that I have found consistently stated in journal and other written reflections. Other civic themes emerge from student writings over this period, but I choose to focus on these four in particular.

## Theme I: Citizenship as Better Knowledge of the Community of Which the Institution of Higher Education Is a Part

Our colleges and universities are often disconnected, intentionally in many cases, from the neighborhoods of which they are immediately a part. For students attending urban institutions, especially noncommuters, the town-gown disconnect is quite clear, as these representative observations from Rutgers University students at the beginning of their service learning class indicate:

*In between [campuses] lies a more harsh neighborhood of New Brunswick. Although the students ride through this area daily to and from [the campuses] . . . it may as well be on another planet. The University community barely acknowledges the existence of this area, as well as many others in New Brunswick, I'm sure. It's very sad, but I am as guilty as anyone. When riding that route I barely give this area a thought. It never occurs to me that I live two minutes from this area—and yet I think of this place as another world.*

*[Our] school is located in the city of New Brunswick but there is little connection between the two. If community includes geographic area then the school should be interacting with the city but unfortunately it doesn't. In fact, most students are afraid of any citizen of New Brunswick who walks by and every girl seems to be carrying mace. Crime is a definite fear but it inhibits Rutgers students from talking and connecting to New Brunswick people especially since there seems to be an economic distinction.*

I've found that one of the more important outcomes of my service learning courses for students who are not local residents is that they get to know the metropolitan area and its citizens in a way they would never have without service learning. Two different seniors reported that for the first time in their college careers they were able to "get to know [their] neighbors in the larger community." Another student wrote that his experiences made him comfortable walking, jogging, and shopping in and around housing projects that bordered the campus, greeting people he was working with on site, putting a lie to the

message of the campus orientation program: "don't leave the campus."
The written reflections of three students add to this dimension of learning about citizenship:

> *When I went on the neighborhood walk during the first week of class, I remember thinking that many of the houses were somewhat run down and they reminded me a lot of the low income housing projects that were in my town. I look back on that experience and think how wrong I was. Now that I've been in this service learning class, I go into those same neighborhoods many times during the week to go to the store and meet many of the people who live in the neighborhood. For me it all relates back to what Dr. King said, that you have to look past the religion or color of the person in order to see the true person.*

> *I think I truly learned more clearly to understand the development of the neighborhood and its present-day condition. I have never learned so much history packed into one neighborhood. I was glad to have had the opportunity to "walk through history" and gain an appreciation of what there is around me at [the college]. I now do not see it as a "bad section" neighborhood but rather a piece of history that should have been preserved and maintained so that it does not lose its historical environment.*

> *I recall my freshman year, when I first passed by the downtown section of the city. I got lost with my family, and we found ourselves driving around an unfamiliar neighborhood. That section of the town was only a block away from the well-developed part of downtown, but it looked like a totally different place . . . my parents warned me not to be around this place. I just ignored their comments as prejudiced, but I did find myself a little surprised at seeing such a different world a few blocks away from the campus. When I read Katherine Mansfield's "The Garden Party" for this class and began my service work, I started seeing the correlation between this fiction and the reality around me, and remembered my earliest impressions of the local community. Here we are, in one of the finest educational institutions, living in the richness of intellect and social contact with other people. We don't realize that there is a different world outside the campus, unless we are taken outside the campus, which is only 2–3 blocks or less away from us. Just like the rich people in Laura's world who continued to have the party right next to the neighborhood where one of their own workers had died, we simply don't see the seriousness of this depravity of others and the communal separation that resulted from it . . . [T]he service I have just begun should not be just hanging around outside the doors of the people of New Brunswick. It shouldn't be just "giving them what they need and leaving." Service would only be meaningful when I really get involved with the people from the other side of town, to feel what they feel. We all have to see that we exist with them within the same neighborhood, within a short distance from one another.*

For those students who come from the surrounding metropolitan communities, service learning can give them a better knowledge of the community with which they identify but of which they are not nearly as knowledgeable as they originally thought. One Salvadoran student I taught last year wrote that the service learning course she took made her more aware of her own community: "Even though I'm from Providence, I learned I didn't know the community as well as I thought I did, especially the needs of racial and ethnic minorities other than my own." An African American woman at Rutgers testified powerfully about how, though she was from an urban area and was working with younger African American students in a "Girls Club rap session" as part of an after-school program, she was unaware until she participated in service of the differences these girls' generation faced from the ones she did, especially with respect to issues around violence and sexuality:

> *Many of the girls . . . have brought up the topic of sex. They come in with many questions and beliefs, misconstrued at times. . . . I tried to correct their misunderstandings, to teach them to respect themselves and others, . . . to teach them self-reliance and self-sufficiency, but found myself ineffective because my own situation as a teenager was so different from that of these girls. . . . I feel I owe it to my race and my culture to reach out and try to help the children of the future become better able to survive in this world, and now I know better what young African-American girls face in the world.*

So whether students come from the community of which the university is a part or reside there during their college years, citizenship-based service learning courses can teach them more about the metropolitan community, and will make them better neighbors. Is citizenship about being a good neighbor? I think the following journal entries from Providence College students tell the story:

> *I realized that my only responsibilities at my college aren't school related. I also have the responsibility of being a good neighbor to those around us. If everyone involved in this community comes to realize that everyone is their neighbor, then the community may start to function a little bit better. The better the community functions, the better life everyone in it will have.*

> *The key to truly being a good neighbor and helping the community of neighbors outside of the college community is to see them as people, and not as simply things that add to the Providence landscape. If we considered the fact that these neighbors had families, lives, tragedies, feelings, and emotions, and could get*

*beyond our prejudices, reach out to them, and benefit the whole community of neighbors.*

## Theme II: Citizenship as Self in Relationship with Others, "Community"

A related perspective that constantly emerges from student reflections on the civic meaning of their service work is that of the good citizen as an individual self in relation to others. Students report that one of the most important things they have gained from a service learning class is this sense of self in relation with and responsible to others:

*I've come to think of myself as a part of the community more than previously. I've learned that the community is me; I'm a part of it. I need to look around me more and look at what I'm doing, what kind of positive or negative impact it has on the larger community.*

*I've learned about myself and my relationship with other people, what my part is, what my commitment to them is. I've learned what a community is, where I fit in; I can now place myself in communities, and have actually found myself identified with communities. . . .*

These student testimonials provide evidence that campus-based community service can develop a deep understanding of what it means to be in relationship with other citizens in a community. But service alone will not produce that result. A campus must create a structure that supports such learning opportunities. It means that I as a teacher consciously create in my classroom, in reading and written assignments and in class discussions, an environment that is conducive to serious reflection on the question of what it means to be in relationship with others, to be a good neighbor. It also means that I must pay attention to the kinds of service sites and service work that students are offered as part of the course, and that the students are adequately prepared to do their service work, in light of the civic themes upon which I want to encourage reflection.

But paying attention to how we structure service learning goes beyond the structure of the curriculum or an individual class itself. If students are to think about citizenship as knowing their geographic neighbors and being in a committed and just relationship with others—neighbors—in community, the structure of the campus service learning program as a whole needs to mirror these principles. What a properly devised service learning program can do is to communicate that the campus-community partnership involved is one of mutual interest and equal power. Students—through their service—provide a valuable resource for communities attempting to improve the lives of their people, while community partners—through their interaction with students—provide an equally valuable resource to students in their own learning.

This acknowledgment of equality in the campus-community relationship that I believe is implied in quality service learning can go a long way toward providing an overall campus structure through which students can learn lessons of democratic citizenship. But we must also work toward making our institutions of higher education better citizens in the larger community. Much of the disconnect between town and gown that students feel comes not from themselves or from the larger community, but from the apathetic citizenship of the university or college, which is not engaged in the life of the surrounding neighborhoods. Here at Providence College, where we have established a new liberal arts major and minor in public and community service studies, we have found that the more our students get involved in the community as part of their academic curriculum, the more the explicit message of our campus program—that of the connection of service to civic engagement—pushes an implicit message on the college itself to be a better institutional citizen (in return for the community's role in helping to educate our students). For example, we have been asked by our community partners to provide space for a community garden and for community education classes—which we have done—and are being asked to participate actively in neighborhood plans for housing and economic development. As we work with low-income youth in a variety of projects, we are being asked whether Providence College will be an inviting place for them when they graduate from high school. As our community partners ask us to be better institutional citizens, we ask them to participate more fully in the education of our students, by coming into the classroom as advisers and "co-faculty." This mutual relationship between campus and community not only models democratic citizenship and "neighborliness"; we have found that it also makes it easier for our students to connect their actions to those of citizens in the larger urban community, to join in common cause, and to learn about their neighbors and the possible solutions to their concerns.

# Theme III: Identity, Diversity, Pluralistic Citizenship

One of the most important challenges in preparing students to be engaged in American public life into the next century is to get them to explore questions concerning their place as citizens in a multicultural democracy. I have written elsewhere about the powerful insights connecting democracy and diversity that can come in a curriculum incorporating community service involvement (Battistoni 1995). Listen to the words of a variety of students that reveal the possibility of learning about citizenship in a pluralistic society through service learning:

*I do not come from a diverse background. My contacts and friendships have always been with people very similar to myself. [M]y service is helping me become a more diverse person . . . [by] coming into contact with people of cultures different than my own.*

*My images of race come from the media and movies mainly—unfortunately. Dealing with different races [through community service] provides alternative images of other races than what is fed to us on the news or in movies. At [my service site] I am able to interact with all different races who are positive people/ role models for the community. Probably being involved in service could improve race relations in the general public. Those being helped and those who help get alternative images of different races. Not to say that all students [at my site] are minorities or all tutors, teachers, volunteers are white: it is just the opposite; all races occupy all roles and provide an alternative to classification and stereotyping.*

*The structure of this course . . . has helped me to think. [D]ifference and racism . . . are issues very close to me, and yet at times so distant. [A]s a student of Indian origin, I have often been at the receiving end of racial prejudice. Despite this fact, I am not too knowledgeable on this issue, for in order to know an issue well, one has to be able to discuss both sides of it. I often treat it as a closed issue, seeing myself as a victim and the rest of American society as oppressive. I see this problem amplified several times in my father and his Indian friends. I listen to the way that my father and other adult friends talk about such issues. The unfortunate thing is that such talk often influences my thinking and results in a polarization of myself into my private and public selves. In public I may at times hide my particular biases, in order to appease the other ethnic groups. But then in private, I see myself often as trying to justify my biases through my friends, family, and the Indian community. Why do I have this problem? Because I don't think about the issue in depth. I recognize the issues like prejudice and racism in conversations and while watching TV. But I do not pick apart these issues often. I store them away in the cobwebs of my brain. So, I feel that by making me reflect deeply on such issues through class discussion, various readings and journals,*

*and in my community service, where I work with African-American and His-
panic youth corps members with backgrounds and lifestyles very different from
my own, it has helped me to some extent in unifying my two selves.*

As you can see from this last quote, the images of diversity and difference that emerge in service learning curricula are not simple or un-
problematic. For students of color or those whose background or status
places them in an "oppressed minority" status, community experiences can be enriching but also the source of deep conflict. I have
worked with a number of African American students for whom the
language of citizenship connected to service had great power, but it
was understood first as "cultural citizenship," a way of explaining
how and why "I can contribute or give something back to *my* community." It also prompted them to challenge white students doing work
in communities of color, and to make observations about the segrega-
tion of students on campus, especially in the dining halls.

For those of us interested in pursuing the connections between citizenship and diversity, we must not diminish the difficult conflicts that
may emerge, for both teachers and students. One African American
student whose family had once received public assistance and who
was in college on full financial aid was challenged as one of the privileged elite by the high school dropouts with whom he was working at
his service site. A Korean woman had to courageously deal with the
racism of her family as they tried to forbid her from participating in a
service learning class. A Latino student spoke eloquently, both in class
and in this journal entry, about how his service work brought his own
personal story to light:

*I am a Hispanic minority. [M]y parents worked hard and made enough money
for us to live comfortably in an upper middle class neighborhood. My memories
of living in an urban neighborhood in an apartment building are so vague in my
mind they seem as almost a movie I watched years ago. I feel distanced from the
experience. Working at [my service site] brought back these old experiences and
made them a reality. It did occur to me it was not all a bad dream. I escaped; in
this sense I am truly a minority because the majority of these people do not
escape. It's a perpetual cycle of degradation.*

And a gay student was forced to confront and overcome the homopho-
bia of minority children in an urban after-school enrichment program:

*I wear two earrings in my left ear, and one in my right ear. In the first 15
minutes I had a swarm of kids around me asking me why I had earrings in both*

*ears, because only "gays" did that. They said I looked like a girl and actually demanded that I remove two of the three earrings. First, I am gay, and it made me feel very uncomfortable having that be an issue in my first 15 minutes on the job. I felt awkward. Also the kids threw the word "faggot" around like it was nothing. This was very hurtful for me, but I swallowed it, removed the earrings and pressed on. It was not how I anticipated the start of my volunteer work. It got better though. The spirit, enthusiasm, and openness of the kids swept me away. I could not believe how friendly and forward they were, virtually fighting over me to check their homework. It was really great.*

Too few educators pay attention to service learning as a powerful way of teaching and learning about citizenship within a pluralistic society, or to how service learning might be tied to other campus initiatives around diversity and multiculturalism. But to make these connections requires extensive coordination and class preparation.

## Theme IV: Democratic Citizenship and the Service Learning Classroom Itself

*Usually, my classes consist of reading the text then being lectured on the material the next day. Although I do learn from this I don't feel involved or integrated with the class and material we are covering. So, this course was a new experience for me. In this course I get the chance to express my views and experiences to the rest of the class. I also hear my classmates' opinions and views on certain topics. I enjoy this because I often don't talk to my peers about social prejudices, community service or democracy even though these are big concerns of modern times. By hearing other college students' beliefs on these topics it helps me understand my own feelings and come to terms with them. By having a discussion type of format . . . it also forces me to relate the topic we are covering to my own life and experiences. Many times I've thought of incidents I haven't thought of in years and this has helped me understand myself and the subject more.*

So far, my discussion of the different perspectives on democratic citizenship that emerge from students engaged in education-based community service has focused on the content of civic lessons learned. But equally important for my students has been the impact created by the nature of the classroom interaction. When the service learning classroom is itself a democratic community, where equal participation and voice is invited and expected, students and faculty gain a better sense of the civic meaning of group responsibility, reciprocity, interdependence, and intercultural cooperation (or conflict!). Hear again the voices of my students on this matter:

*[The classroom] format is extremely beneficial to each of us because we are encouraged to express our thoughts, opinions, and beliefs as a group. It helps us to create a community within the classroom. We all come together as a unit responding to all of the issues we face relating to community.*

*[D]emocracy is key in understanding the work that is performed by the participants of [service learning] classes. . . . The class itself is considered a small group community whose goal it is to bring about a sense of friendship and trust within its participants. In my [service learning course] I became directly involved with my classmates in open discussions on past experiences in different styles of community. This free class structure is conducive to interactive learning with my peers. For a semester I was involved in class discussions which tended to continue outside of the classroom. The issues which are discussed are everyday occurrences which all who serve encounter. In one particular instance, my service group was experiencing difficulties with the staff at our service site. The class dynamic, which is relaxed and non-judgmental, changed to accommodate the needs of my small group to discuss the difficulties and work at a solution. . . . As in a functioning community, all members came together to help sort out a problem and offer varied views on an approach. This openness with class members provides for a friendly environment [and] encourages the building of class community.*

The creation of a democratic service learning classroom is not an automatic consequence of service learning: too often even the service learning classroom mirrors the hierarchy of what Paolo Freire (1970) called the "banking model of education." To create a democratic classroom involves much greater time and effort in coordinating and structuring activities and class discussions, and much more attention to "process" than does a "traditional" classroom. Additionally, when successful, a democratic service learning class may cause students cognitive dissonance, especially if a democratic pedagogy conflicts with the school's institutional or academic culture.

## Beyond Theory: The Practical Skills of Engaged Citizenship

My extensive use of students' excerpted written reflections should demonstrate the power that service learning can have for one's perspective on citizenship, especially if we broaden our notion of what democratic citizenship means. But we must move beyond abstract notions of citizenship if we are to make a strong case about the connections between service learning and an empowered citizenry. We must be able to show that service learning, in a unique way, builds our students' concrete civic skills. Here I will focus on three general areas:

intellectual understanding, communication and public problem solving, and the development of civic attitudes of judgment and imagination.

## Intellectual Understanding

As with other areas of the curriculum, intellectual understanding comes first. Since 1893, when a "Committee of Ten" leading American educators produced a report that said the chief purpose of education was "to train the mind," the main thrust of American education at all levels has been cognitive development. The "thinking certain" is certainly an important aim of civic education. We want to develop citizens who can use a variety of methods, theories, and models to examine the world and evaluate facts, in order to reach conclusions. Service learning can enhance the development of students' critical thinking skills, and experiences in the community can reveal challenges to their working cognitive assumptions regarding human nature, society, and justice. As the numerous excerpts quoted above should indicate, students' abilities to analyze critically are enhanced by confronting ideas and theories with the actual realities in the world surrounding them. As an added example here, I've placed students in service experiences working with guests in homeless shelters, and they have reported that they were able both to put a face on "the poor" and to test their own and others' theories about poverty, public policy, and democracy against their actual observations and the real-life stories of those with whom they interact in the shelters.

## Communication and Problem Solving

Intellectual understanding, while essential to democratic citizenship, must be accompanied by what I would call participation skills—those of communication and problem solving—that can be developed through service learning. Alexis de Tocqueville laid out most clearly the argument for participation in community-based organizations as essential to maintaining democratic institutions and to educating people for citizenship. He argued that in democracies, "all the citizens are independent and feeble; they can do hardly anything by themselves, and none of them can oblige [others] to lend their assistance. They all therefore become powerless if they do not learn voluntarily to help one another." Participation in civic associations educates people to overcome this powerlessness and isolation, since through this participation members of associations learn "the art of pursuing in common the object of their common desires" and of "proposing a common object for the exertions of a great many and inducing them voluntarily to pursue it" (Tocqueville 1945, 115). More recently, Robert Putnam (1995) echoes Tocqueville's argument, lamenting the decline in voluntary associations and the subsequent loss of "social capital," the foundation of our democracy.

Communication skills are essential for effective civic participation. In addition to clear thinking about public matters, democratic citizenship involves the communication of our thoughts and actions, both vertically, to our leaders and representatives, and horizontally, with our fellow citizens. Speech, argument, and persuasive communication are all important elements of democratic literacy. Perhaps even more important is the lost art of listening. In a democracy, citizens need to be able to listen to each other, to understand the places and interests of others in the community, and to achieve compromises and solve problems when conflict occurs. The overriding images of our democratic culture tend to involve talkers: great communicators like Thomas Jefferson, Daniel Webster, Martin Luther King Jr., and Ronald Reagan; representatives giving speeches or talking on C-SPAN; or lawyers arguing persuasively in the courtroom. Perhaps the truer image of democracy exists on the other side of the courtroom, among the members of the jury, listening both to the arguments and testimony and to each other in deliberation. An effective congressional representative delivers persuasive speeches on the House floor yet also listens carefully to constituents at public hearings. Effective civic education must involve the development of the ability to listen as part of communication skills.

Service learning programs that employ appropriate and varied reflection strategies heighten students' communicative abilities. Through reflecting on their service experiences, students are called upon to give an account of themselves and their thoughts in classroom discussions, in oral or artistic presentations, and in their writings. Two brief excerpts from Rutgers student journals demonstrate the importance of in-class reflections on service in enhancing the students' speaking and listening skills, all as part of their civic education:

*Not all things can be learned from going to [a service site] only once a week. We must be willing to talk to each other, tell each other our lives and stories, and believe each other so to tear down that wall which seems to separate all cultures— ignorance.*

> *I think that the university should be civic as well as academic and social. Many people from various backgrounds enter into the university with sometimes negative and/or ignorant perceptions of people. If the university were to be civic, we could change these views through practice. Also, such change would no longer promote individualism and would allow students to relate to themselves in the context of the larger society in order to promote democracy. . . . [F]or this to happen, we need a model for listening and speaking. This has been my experience in the classroom. Because of that, multiculturalism is a reality for me. In listening, I also tell my stories and realities so that people can become aware of what black and other people experience.*

In addition, as many of my students' writings indicate, the community service experience itself also teaches students to listen to the stories and needs of others. When tutoring, visiting an elderly person, serving overnight in a homeless shelter, or doing an oral history, our students learn, in a tangible way, the art of listening. But once again, for these skills to be most effectively developed, time and effort must be spent in structuring both the service experience and that of the classroom to maximize student dialogue and listening opportunities.

The other "participation skill" I want to focus upon is the ability to identify and solve public problems. I mention identifying public problems as important because too often community service and service learning programs overemphasize the service activity, leading students to conclude that their service is both the problem (what service to perform, how to organize it) and the solution (to larger social problems). The infamous example of the student who told her service learning director that her service experience was so meaningful that she hoped her children would have the opportunity to work in homeless shelters should remind us that service is not an end in itself. Only when service leads students to examine the underlying issues beneath their community work to identify concerns/problems, and then explore with fellow citizens possible solutions to these public problems, have we done our best to make service an education for citizenship. A Rutgers student makes this point clearly:

> *Community service is nothing new to me. I've always done it wholeheartedly and thought of it as something useful and necessary. However, [in this class] I began to realize that helping individuals is only part of the solution. The scope of the problem was wider social problems, economic problems, social neglect and apathy, political neglect, and without addressing these, nothing could fix the problems individuals face. . . .*

Not only can service learning help students *identify* the problems that underlie the need for service, but it can enhance their ability to solve public problems. In my experience, students have learned public problem-solving skills in the context of working together to make their service placement more meaningful and/or more aligned with their abilities and interests. That is, in countless situations, I have witnessed students, working in teams, having to work through problems at their service sites, problems of organization, effective use of their time, or creative programming. For example, students working in an after-school program complaining about their relationships with site staff and their "not being effectively used" had to meet with the program director and develop an alternative structure that would allow them to interact more with program staff and to creatively plan after-school activities of their own for the children. I am certain that this experience in problem solving at their community service site enhanced not only their work that semester, but also their civic capacity. Other students have learned similar lessons about problem solving through "participant observation," i.e., through watching others at their placement sites work together to solve common concerns:

> *Service allows you to work closely with people towards a common, respectable goal. When a group works together towards a common good, it inevitably becomes closer, even if the group is diverse. Working at [my service site], I've seen people of all ages, all races, religions and financial status befriend each other and work successfully together. . . .*

Once again, for this to happen, both the service activities and the service learning program need to be organized so that public problem solving will be one of the outcomes. This is best done by organizing students into service "teams," as opposed to individual placements, and by giving students an active role in the design and structure of the campus service learning program itself (see Barber and Battistoni 1993; Battistoni 1996).

## Civic Attitudes: Judgment and Imagination

A service learning program aimed at civic education should also develop students' moral dispositions of civic judgment and imagination. By civic judgment I mean the ability to use publicly defensible moral standards in application to the actual life and history of a community. A citizenship-oriented service learning program can develop capacities for public judgment, because the practical experience students gain through their community involvement allows them to set and reset their standards of judgment, and it may cause them to modify their political judgments in reaction to the world they observe and the people with whom they interact:

> *I think this class has really opened a lot of people's eyes to what they are like, and what their communities are like. I also think it has made people more aware of the different perspectives we all have. . . . It is an incredible feeling to be able to see things from a different perspective.*

> *I learned a lot more about the views which I differ from. And in fact I have changed some of my previous beliefs after reading, hearing, and experiencing the "other side."*

These two excerpts suggest that students emerge from a quality service learning experience more open and tolerant. There is evidence, once again from the Whitman Center's Measuring Citizenship Project (1996), that college service learning programs (where student learning is focused on education for citizenship) show desirable changes in mean scores for religious and racial tolerance. But beyond enhancing traditional measures of openness and toleration, service learning can encourage the crucial civic competence of imagination. Imagination involves the ability to think creatively about public problems. Moreover, to truly put oneself in the place of others requires more than mere tolerance: it requires imagination. Imagination is also present in the ability to project and embrace a vision for the future, to think about oneself and one's community in ways not tied to the past; to "dream things that never were and say, 'Why not?'" as George Bernard Shaw put it. Students' imaginative abilities can be enhanced through service learning, by enlarging their sense of who they are and enabling them to use their imagination to join together in working toward a common goal with people who have different backgrounds, values, and life stories.

## Conclusion: Making the Connections between Service and Citizenship

I have attempted to demonstrate that service learning can be a powerful method of citizen education, but only if we understand the two conditions I have laid out here. The first is that we must assume a diversity of perspectives about what it means to be a democratic citizen. Narrow or rhetorical definitions of service and citizenship are inadequate to the task of reinvigorating public life, or inviting into public dialogue the people, such as college students, who have walked away. As I have tried to do in laying out different understandings of citizenship that I see emerging from "service learners," we must make room in our practices and in our service learning curriculum for a conversation where people name for themselves what it is they are doing and its connection to community, citizenship, and democratic society. Additionally, we must develop new ways to measure "civic impact" on service learning participants, using these new definitions of citizenship.

The second point is that service alone does not automatically lead to engaged citizenship; only if we consciously construct our programs with the education of democratic citizens—in the broadest sense—in mind can service learning be the vehicle by which we educate for citizenship and reinvigorate our rapidly deteriorating public life. In addition to the suggestions I have offered, other essays in this volume give examples of how to encourage citizenship in our teaching practices.

## Notes

The selections excerpted here truly reflect all of the students I have taught in service learning classes over the past six years, not a select few. Over two dozen different student reflections are quoted throughout the essay, and the ones I chose to include here just as easily could have come from several dozen other student journals or written assignments. I *have* restricted my use of student written work to those classes from whom I obtained permission; as a result, some students whose perspectives would otherwise be included are not. All specific references to particular service sites have been excluded: in all cases I replaced the specific site mentioned in the student's writing with a bracketed general reference (e.g., [at my service site]).

3

# The Urban Agenda Project

Otto Feinstein and James D. Chesney

Our project deals directly with the *ways* people learn about *citizenship in higher education* and how this relates to education for citizenship in other learning environments. We have called the project "Civic Literacy: The Urban Agenda" and have implemented it, with a number of revisions, over the past ten years at Wayne State University in Detroit.

Civic literacy is the collection of knowledge and skills a citizen must have in order to participate fully in a democratic, civil society. This knowledge and these skills deal with both thought and action, and how to combine the two. The desired outcome of education for citizenship is civic literacy. Book VII of Plato's *Republic*, written some 2,400 years ago, indicates the intrinsic relation between education and the operation of a wise and just system of governance, of civic literacy.

Wayne State University is an urban institution serving 35,000 to 40,000 students, principally commuters, in a full undergraduate, professional, and graduate program. More than 150,000 of its graduates continue to live in southeastern Michigan, a region with a population of 4,200,000 people. The civic literacy and citizenship participation of these students and graduates would seem essential for the existence of a civil society in our region.

Since the founding of the American republic, the establishment of this country's educational system, from Head Start to Ph.D. programs, has been based on two main objectives: preparing a new generation for work (the economic system) and preparing it for citizenship (the political system). The history of this struggle has given us a massive system of teachers, departments, and research institutions dedicated to civic

51

literacy at all levels of the educational system. This system is much larger today than it was historically, or even thirty years ago. It is represented at all public universities (and nearly every other postsecondary institution) by required courses and faculty who teach them. With such an extensive system and budget available, why do we have the feeling expressed generally throughout this book: that education is not meeting the needs for citizenship?

In our civic literacy project, we have focused on two explanations for this phenomenon. We believe that our project attempts to respond to both of them. The first explanation deals with the massive growth of knowledge about the political system and the rapid increase of major issues that it is designed to address. In order to accommodate this massive increase in information and knowledge, civics and government courses and the texts they use are left with no (or very little) space for teaching the skills of civic literacy. Teaching and learning in these courses focuses on political structures and policy making, with limited attention to the skills required for becoming involved in the political process. Our study of high school and college texts clearly lends substance to this explanation.

Our second explanation deals with the massive cultural changes in modern society, including the role of the mass media in political communications and the changing institutional structures brought on by the success of the welfare state: more complex class structures, suburbanization, political parties, and so on. These cultural changes require new types of participatory structures, which in most places have not yet been invented. Decline in voter turnout, the absence of efforts to recruit students into political parties, and the vacancy rate in precinct delegate positions (the lowest level of elected party officials in Michigan) are all factors that led us to this explanation.

In connection with our project, we have visited classrooms in more than eighty middle schools, high schools, and postsecondary institutions. In every classroom we have visited, the vast majority of students had opinions on some key political issues. The common denominator among these students is not apathy but rather a feeling, across class, ethnic, and gender lines, that *their opinions do not matter*, that nobody cares what they think. Some students have even gone so far as to state that the problem is not an X-generation but X-institutions, not apathetic youths but institutions that do not need them.

The two explanations and our related observations give us the following perspectives on education and citizenship.

1. The *crisis in education* is the result of a gap between the massive increase in knowledge over the past thirty years and the resultant need for *new ways* of teaching so that America does not fall behind its peer nations;
2. The sense of *crisis in political citizenship* is the outcome of basic cultural changes that resulted from the success of the welfare state as well as from the rise of the consumer/information society and the resultant need for *new ways* for citizens to participate in civil society;
3. The existing civic literacy infrastructure, the interest of younger people in expressing their views, and the knowledge we have acquired in civic literacy and community service education provide a sufficient base for the development of these *new ways*.

## The Civic Literacy Module in Political Science 101

At Wayne State University we offer a course called the Introduction to American Government (Political Science 101), a four-credit hour (semester) course required of nearly all students. Thousands of students, from freshmen to seniors, with majors ranging from political science to engineering, take this course every year. Nearly all of them have taken civics or government courses in high school, as well as courses dealing with community and history in primary and middle schools. The course is taught in large classes of between 250 and 400 students, by a senior professor and graduate teaching assistants. Normally, the professor presents three lectures a week (for fourteen to fifteen weeks); one hour a week is reserved for small group discussions (or quiz preparation sections) led by the graduate teaching assistants. The course uses a standard textbook in all its sections. Individual instructors make up their exams and additional class assignments. The teaching assistants are enrolled in graduate courses and working on their M.A. or Ph.D. degrees.

In 1986 we introduced a civic literacy module into the traditional, textbook-based Political Science 101 course taught by Professor Feinstein. The module had three components: (1) theory building for civic literacy; (2) creating an urban agenda: deliberation and study; and (3) civic participation: voter registration, education, participation, designed to promote experience.

As Plato pointed out in Book VII of the *Republic*, human beings have three ways of defining and dealing with reality: experience, thought, and theory. These three ways need to be connected by an educational process relating thought to action, in what Plato called the dialectic, the basic methodology of science, or what we call systems analysis. It is this methodology that allows us to use the symbols necessary for communication, without becoming prisoners of the symbols (shadows) as we try to ascertain and act on reality (the light).

The civic literacy module has accounted for 25 to 40 percent of the course grade, depending on the extent of civic participation activity during the particular semester. The remaining 75 to 60 percent of the grade is based on written examinations that focus on the basic textbook and on the readings related to the civic literacy module.

## Theory Building for Civic Literacy: The Needs to Demands Resulting in Response Model

In order for students to develop civic literacy they must to be able to develop their own theoretical model of politics and political power. To help them do this, we point out that the concept of politics derives from the Greek word *polis,* referring to the many cultures residing in an urban environment. We define "power" as the ability to do something, in both verb and noun forms. As the process of modernization creates environments that bring different peoples (cultures) into continuous contact with each other, power and governance can no longer be based on traditional customary law. Written laws and the process for constructing them (constitutions) are introduced into society, and thus politics, as we understand it, begins.

The concept of theory building is introduced by a series of readings and small-group discussions on how to use them to help build each student's own theoretical tools. The theoretical model we introduce is the relation of needs to demands to response—*Needs to Demands resulting in Response*—within the individual, institutional, community, social, and cultural contexts.

The readings and discussions start with an introduction to the module: *The Relation of Civic Literacy and Adult Education to the Voluntary Sector: A Case Study of Detroit's Urban Agenda,* by Otto Feinstein. The introduction states that at this stage of the process of modernization, the development of a civic society requires an autonomous voluntary sector, independent of but related to the private and public sectors. The development and functioning of such a voluntary sector requires civic literacy (the knowledge of how to affect the modern political/civic system), and that civic literacy is the task of adult education.

The second of the readings is *Great Dialogues of Plato: Book VII of the Republic* (translated by W. H. D. Rouse), a work that has dealt with the role of education in the wise and just governance of a changing society. In the first section of Book VII, Socrates explains how human beings perceive reality. He presents humanity as a cultural species, surviving on the basis of our knowledge (culture), that uses symbols in order to understand and act on reality. Symbols are our means of retrieving necessary knowledge from the existing cultural database and placing new knowledge into that cultural database. The inherent weakness in this process is our dependence and attachment to the symbols (shadows) and our inherent difficulty in dealing with reality (the light). The means for dealing with this *inherent weakness* is education. In the second section of Book VII, Socrates presents his educational curriculum that uses the three human capacities for dealing with reality (the light): experience, which leads to thought; thought, which leads to theory; and theory, which enlightens experience. This cycle may be represented as *Experience and Thought resulting in Theory* (the dialectic). The educational curriculum continuously links these three human capacities in a process that lasts until a person reaches the age of fifty. The ability of decision makers in a given society to use the dialectic is what makes possible the governance of society (and change) with wisdom and justice.

The third reading is *The Body Ritual among the Nacirema*, by Horace Miner (first published in *The American Anthropologist*, vol. 58, 1956). It introduces the concept of cultural meaning into the understanding of politics and the differing interpretations of reality. Miner spells out the most effective methods for listing experience and their relational impacts. He then demonstrates that if one fails to look at the meanings of events and their relational impacts, one cannot understand the reality at hand. We call this the relation of *Meaning to Reality*.

The fourth reading is *Two Concepts of Authority*, by Walter B. Miller (first published in *The American Anthropologist*, vol. 57, 1955). It provides an alternate model of decision making (authority-power) in human experience, which is necessary for understanding both pluralism and hegemony. Within this context, the article reviews basic political concepts that the students must learn.

The fifth reading is *Colonialism: Classic and Internal*, by Robert K. Thomas (first published in *New University Thought*, vol. IV, no. 1, 1967). This article looks at the consequences of an unequal allocation of power on the ability of the powerless to deal with changing reality and at the impact on their decision-making structures and personal relations. It argues that colonialism is the inability of people to act on their own experience, and that internal colonialism raises the question of access to power for people living in highly bureaucratized societies. Out of this reading emerges the theoretical model of *Experience in the Relational Context results in Meaning*, the ability to use symbols for dealing with reality.

The sixth reading is *Why Ethnicity?* by Otto Feinstein (in Judith Gardner and Richard McMann, eds., *Culture, Community and Identity*). This work discusses the importance of understanding the cultural composition of American society and looking at peoples first before beginning to evaluate the problems.

The seventh set of readings includes Martin Luther King Jr., *Letter from the Birmingham Jail*; an essay by Mark Suprin and Otto Feinstein on *Auschwitz*; and a video with lesson plans from David Hackett Fischer's *Albion's Seed*. Discussion of these readings raises the issue that a political (urban) agenda occurs in a multicultural society and depends on norms and values in a scientific and technological world.

## Creating an Urban Agenda: Deliberation and Study (Thought)

The second part of the module deals with the formulation of political strategies, of political thought using both theoretical tools and the participants' experience. The actions undertaken and then evaluated in this part of the module are called the *Urban Agenda Process and Convention*. The process starts in discussion sections, with small groups of three to five students building their own urban agenda comprising up to ten agenda items. Once the issues have been articulated and the agenda agreed to by the small group, the entire discussion group of fifteen to thirty students works to create its urban agenda. When this stage is complete, each graduate teaching assistant convenes all the discussion sections that he or she teaches, usually about a hundred students, to formulate a ten-item agenda. At this point the process of *direct democracy* becomes a *representative democracy* involving three hundred to five hundred students.

Each discussion section elects its own spokesperson to negotiate a common urban agenda to be presented and voted on at the Urban Agenda Convention attended by all the students, their guests, and potential urban agenda coalition partners. The negotiators meet several times to agree on a proposed agenda, and they take this back to the individual discussion groups for amendments and eventual adoption.

The majority urban agenda resolution is then presented at the Urban Agenda Convention for amendment and ratification.

The core of the Urban Agenda Convention lasts four hours. In the first hour, a plenary session, the rules for the convention are proposed and adopted, the majority resolution is presented by different students, and the convention is addressed by elected officials and community leaders who are committed to supporting the effort. During the second hour, students convene in small-group (ten to thirty students) discussions that focus on the specific issue in which they are most interested. In this context they can formulate changes for the agenda to be voted on and can also agree to activities they would like to engage in after the convention is over. During the third hour, they convene in their term-long, small discussion groups to formulate voting and convention strategies. Those concerned with specific issues can lobby the discussion groups for their vote or active support. During the fourth hour, also a plenary, all the students meet again. First they put in motion, amend, discuss, and vote on the urban agenda resolution, and when that is completed they endorse various activities proposed by their fellow students. At the end of this process, between one and three key public officials receive the Urban Agenda and agree to circulate it to all elected officials (local, state, and national) from southeastern Michigan. The number of participants and their guests varies from convention to convention, between five hundred and fifteen hundred persons.

In the past few years, entire conventions have been videotaped and presented on local cable systems, sometimes live and sometimes prerecorded. Other video components have included interviews with various experts on the key issues making up the urban agenda and presentations on how to organize the urban agenda process and other elements of the curriculum.

After the convention, the educational and political results are reviewed in the small discussion groups. These are presented at one of the weekly lectures before the end of the semester. From time to time, survey research procedures have been used for this evaluation process. Some of the graduate teaching assistants also have required their students to write short essays evaluating this learning experience.

Sometimes when the conventions are held early enough in the semester, students take their urban agenda to community organizations and to elected officials in southeastern Michigan for individual or institutional support. The students collect these resolutions and forward them to the community organizations and elected officials they pre-

viously contacted. In some years, time permitting, this is done in coop-
eration with the Michigan Municipal League, the National League of
Cities, the U.S. Conference of Mayors, and the American Assembly
(Columbia University).

At the theoretical level the students have used the $N + D = R$ (needs
to demands to response) cycle first among themselves, next with community leaders and elected officials, and then with the general public
through cable television. They have used the $E + T = Th$ (experience
to thought to theory) cycle from the dialectic in Book VII of the *Republic*
to formulate the agenda. Given the differentiated cultural, class, gender, and ethnic composition of our students and the urban communities in which they live, they will also have to deal with the $E + R = M$
(experience in a relational system leads to meaning) model. This process is designed to strengthen the students' analytical and communicative skills.

In addition to building an urban agenda, the students are engaged
in a series of readings and discussions regarding the status of an urban
agenda in current American politics. The readings and discussions
start with Otto Feinstein's *America's Urban Agenda: Quo Vadis* (first published in *The Journal of Ethno-Development*, vol. III, no. 2, 1965), which
looks at the way the 1988 and 1992 elections dealt with urban issues
and urban constituencies.

This is followed by two articles that evaluate the role of universities
and political science introductory courses in dealing with urban civic
literacy: Sheldon Hackney, *The University and Its Community: Past and
Present* (first published in the *Annals of the American Academy*, AAPSS
488, November 1986), which discusses the role of American universities in relation to urban life; and James Chesney and Otto Feinstein,
*Making Political Activity a Requirement in Introductory Political Science
Courses* (first published in *PS*, Fall 1993).

A selection of readings presents other ways of articulating an urban
agenda. These readings include *Investing in Hometown America: Ten Is-
sues for the 1988 Elections* (first published by the National League of
Cities); *The United States Conference of Mayors: Memo and News; The Final
Report of the 82nd American Assembly*, which was convened at Columbia
University on urban policies for America; *Interwoven Destinies: Cities
and the Nation* (first published by Henry Cisneros); *Congress Fiddles as
Cities Burn*, by Carter Harris, in the Detroit-area *Metro-Times; A Funding
Analysis of Select Key Urban Programs;* and a selection of newspaper and
periodical articles. In the second component of the module, students
are asked to write short reports on their chosen urban agenda using
these readings with the Urban Agenda Convention and Process.

## Civic Participation: Voter Registration, Education, Participation (Experience)

The third component of the module deals directly with students' political experience and their evaluation of it, i.e., voter registration, voter education, and voter participation. Each student who is a U.S. citizen is asked to register ten new voters.

Some students have chosen to organize voter registration drives at the university, in high schools, at other postsecondary institutions, churches, banks, shopping malls, and so on. Before passage of the motor-voter legislation, hundreds of students were trained and sworn in as county deputy voter registrars. The legislation permitting county voter registrars was partially the result of our previous registration efforts at the university. These efforts were made difficult by rules that required that deputy registrars be from the city of Detroit, and the requirement that there be at least twenty registrars at each site. Each semester this activity results in thousands of new voter registrations. In 1992 we registered 15,000 new voters. This experience makes the Urban Agenda Convention and Process real in the eyes of the students and the community; it also requires students to address the reluctance of many of their peers to register and vote.

Students may take part in activities other than organizing voter registration campaigns. They can participate in survey research on youth voter registration and participation; develop cable television programming on voter registration, voting, and the urban agenda; undertake internships in related activities sponsored by other institutions and organizations; train volunteers from community groups to enact their own urban agenda and voter registration process; or help ethnic organizations with citizenship education. Out of these alternative activities and their evaluation have emerged major new activities: the Candidate Job Interview, the Youth Urban Agenda (middle school, high school, adult education), Project Go Vote, and Research on Youth Civic Literacy.

In 1988 a group of students suggested that they would like to use the urban agenda to interview candidates seeking to be nominated for president by their political parties in Michigan. They saw this as a natural outcome of civic literacy and citizenship training. Through Wayne State University, we had access to many regional cable systems and could thus make the interviews public. Furthermore, it would be an innovative use of the media. Like most of the U.S. population, nearly every Wayne State University student seeking a job has to be interviewed by potential employers. Why shouldn't it be the same for people competing for public office? Job interviews by the students (the citizens) would take the place of speeches, debates, sound bites, and the rest. All candidates in the 1988 primaries were contacted. Paul Simon, U.S. senator from Illinois, accepted. The first Candidate Job Interview took place and was cable-cast in southeastern Michigan. By 1992 every candidate for president in the Michigan Democratic primary agreed to separate Job Interviews. Paul Tsongas and Jerry Brown—two of the three people running in the primary—were interviewed. The technique spread to the primary elections for governor and U.S. senator and then to the election of federal and county officials in Wayne County. The interviewers were students, and they used the urban agenda as the basis of the interview.

In 1995 Wayne State University decided to suspend classes to commemorate Martin Luther King's birthday. A group of students and our Political Science 101 class organized a meeting to discuss the significance of the day and what observances were appropriate. At the end of a four-hour meeting, the students agreed that they would take the urban agenda to other colleges, middle schools, and high schools. Other colleges were contacted through friends of the students, the Michigan Campus Compact, a Kellogg Foundation–funded community service project for Michigan postsecondary institutions, SEMTEC (the South East Michigan Television Education Consortium), and the Michigan Political Science Association. Middle and high schools were contacted by Political Science 101 students and by graduate students in the College of Education. In the winter semester of 1996, four urban agenda conventions were held: one each for middle schools, high schools, adult education schools, and Wayne State University. As part of this process, classes in some eighty institutions were visited by our students and faculty. Participation in the Urban Agenda Convention involves a minimum of three preconvention, in-school sessions, with each class using our students working as facilitators alongside the classroom teachers. Some financial support (including bus transportation and curricular materials) was received from the Wayne County Clerk, the Michigan Campus Compact, New Detroit Inc., and units of Wayne State University.

In the fall of 1995 the City Clerk of Detroit invited the Wayne County Extension Service (Michigan State University) and the Urban Agenda to join with them and others in a major effort called Project GO VOTE. The mission of the project was:

- To educate local youth about the democratic process.
- To encourage voter participation.
- To educate citizens on the importance of voting.

The issues to be addressed were:

- The need to actively educate local youth about the political process.
- The lack of information about the importance of voting.
- The need for increased voter participation.

To carry out this mission, participants agreed to implement the Urban Agenda Process and Convention within their own organizations. In 1995–96 they would observe our approach in detail and start to implement it in 1996–97.

The involvement of graduate students from the Department of Political Science and the College of Education, combined with encouragement from a number of faculty members, raised the issue of using the urban agenda as a research subject for term papers, master's theses, and Ph.D. dissertations.

The growing interest in political science in civic literacy as well as in sociology and education in community service learning has encouraged these activities. A preliminary study on political socialization and civic literacy was undertaken in the summer of 1996. A seminar was organized for the fall. A presentation was made at the 1996 APSA meetings and a book on the experience has been published (see Chesney and Feinstein 1997).

The invention of these new activities and the spread of the concept into other environments show strong evidence of the vitality of the process. The project clearly encourages communications and relationships across class, gender, race, and ethnic boundaries of the region. The student body at Wayne State University (as at many other urban commuter universities) has undergraduate, graduate, and professional students from every class, gender, racial, and ethnic community in the region. The middle schools, high schools, adult education centers, community colleges, and other universities are more limited in the composition of their student bodies, but by participating in the Urban Agenda and Youth Urban Agenda processes and conventions at Wayne State University, these basic social boundaries can be crossed. The agenda that is produced requires this crossing of boundaries by deliberation rather than confrontation. By using the voter registration/education activities and the media, the participants also achieve a reality-based feeling *that their voice can be heard.*

The combination of activities—along with the ability of students to choose among them and to initiate new ones—makes the project real. It has an impact on individuals, their friends, and their families. It affects the class, the school, the locality, the urban region, the nation, and the world. It presents systems solutions for systems problems by means available to the individual, to the potential citizen.

From our observations and surveys we know that 100 percent of students who are U.S. citizens without contrary religious obligations are registered voters. We know that over 80 percent have registered other people to vote. A number of the students have run for and have been elected to a variety of elective positions. On the basis of short-term surveys we are informed by the students that they have a much greater interest in citizenship, government, and politics. We are attempting to obtain grants for a long-term study of the civic literacy project on citizenship and participation.

## Some Concluding Thoughts

We believe that the Civic Literacy: The Urban Agenda project addresses the basic issue raised by the editors of this book: that *citizenship education* is not basically *what* students should be learning but rather the *ways* in which they learn. We think that the project has addressed some aspect of each of the questions the editors pose:

1. How do we (as educators) adapt to changing realities of higher education?
2. What are some active and innovative teaching techniques for active citizenship?
3. How can higher education be a connective tissue between the individual and the public realm?
4. How can teaching for citizenship contribute to analytic and action skills?

We also believe that the project has raised these questions in the tradition of Book VII of the *Republic* applied to current times. We are hopeful that the publication and circulation of this book will encourage cooperation within political science and within higher education to further these goals.

**4**

# Citizenship Courses as Life-Changing Experiences

*William D. Coplin*

A course that claims to help prepare good citizens seeks as its primary goal the transformation of students from self-interested and apathetic individuals into adults who want to shape government actions to serve both their own needs and the public interest. Such a transformation cannot be accomplished by a single course or even a group of courses. It occurs only as part of the total set of any individual's experiences. However, courses in political science need to play a major role in this transformation if "liberal arts" is to be anything more than a sales gimmick to provide jobs for college teachers whose interest in their specialized subjects exceeds their commitment to their students and the public good.

After taking a course aimed at citizenship education, students must have an increased capacity and willingness to work for a better society through social and political institutions. This requires instructors to think strategically about the skills, attitudes, and knowledge objectives of their courses. This chapter describes a lower-division course, but the techniques and underlying philosophy can be applied to courses at any level. Readers are encouraged to take what appears useful. They need not teach the entire course.

The course is Public Affairs 101: Introduction to the Analysis of Public Policy. It is one of more than one hundred courses that satisfy the social science distribution in liberal arts requirements at Syracuse University. Averaging 125 students a semester, the course meets three times a week. Students complete five papers on a local, state, or federal

63

public policy problem of their choice. Class meetings are used for a variety of purposes, but most students view them as preparation for the papers. Students practice policy skills on university problems in class exercises designed to help them write their papers. The textbook *Public Policy Skills*, which I co-authored with Michael K. O'Leary (1992), introduces the skills and assignments for the course.

## Citizenship Education as Experience

In developing courses intended to transform individuals into citizens, we need to recognize that students learn as individuals and that the learning process is multicausal and nonlinear. The "individuality of the learner" is similar to the individuality of the priesthood that was the conceptual heart of the Protestant Reformation. The concept of the individuality of the priesthood requires that the church provide experiences that help the individual gain religious meaning. The idea of the individuality of the learner suggests that schools should provide experiences that help learners develop themselves into good citizens.

Because the world is multicausal and nonlinear, every event or condition is shaped by many factors that interact in different sequences. This same pattern holds for the way any given individual learns. Many factors, both within and outside formal schooling, and in sequences that appear to be almost random, affect how quickly and how much anyone learns. Therefore, a course is only one set of experiences, greatly limited by time and context, that can influence the learner's path to becoming a good citizen.

If we accept the notions that learning is an individualized process shaped by many factors in a nonlinear way, the purpose of all education, whether offered through school, provided through other institutions, or self-initiated, is to provide learners with experiences that change them in some way. Teachers, under this definition, are people who help the student along the path toward whatever goal they have for the student, and they do this by exposing the student to experiences. As John Dewey said, "education is of, by, and for experience" (1938, 29). For transforming people into citizens, the role of the teacher is to create or encourage a set of experiences that helps the students become effective and responsible citizens.

This view of the teacher conflicts with the current educational practices of most college professors of the social sciences who value learning that

> appeals for the most part simply to the intellectual aspect of our natures, our desire to learn, to accumulate information, and to get control of the symbols of learning; not to our impulses and tendencies to make, to do, to create, to produce, whether in the form of utility or of art. (Dewey, 1899, 18)

The expectations of the overwhelming majority of our students when it comes to citizenship education (and most of their education) are making, doing, creating, and producing. They want to learn how to understand and take action, but most college professors want to teach them how to accumulate information and explore and (but not necessarily) apply theoretical perspectives. The considerable mismatch between the goals of the two groups creates complaints by students that courses are irrelevant and by professors that the students are lazy and distant.

Professors require students to spend their time reading great thinkers, studying political theory, and engaging in sophisticated discussions. They assume that such intellectual activity will transform the majority of apathetic, selfish, and uninformed adolescents into a generation that takes responsibility for society in a constructive way. A few might be transformed through such discourse, but many more will not be, and too many more will have their underdeveloped desire to become good citizens destroyed by abstractions that they cannot connect to their reality.

The blind commitment to the value of intellectual discourse as the way to create future citizens has led many academics to define good citizenship as the willingness and ability of students to participate in enlightened discourse. These academics have convinced themselves that we would have much better public policy if only the quality of intellectual exchange over policy issues could be enhanced. The law of the hammer is at work here. Academics are good at intellectual discourse, and seek to make their students good at it, and then argue that the world will be saved through improved discourse. University politics, which enjoys, if nothing else, plenty of intellectual discourse, demonstrates clearly that discourse by intellectuals does not lead to good public policy. Dare we say, "quite the opposite?" Rational discourse is only a small ingredient of any policy-making process, good or bad.

Processing symbols of democracy and recalling historical examples are only part of the path that leads to effective citizenship. They are one of many types of experiences that may have an impact on a student's learning. Students can learn from experiences like reading, listening, talking, and writing about what others have said or what has happened in the past, but they also learn from all other possible experiences, like tutoring in an inner-city school, changing a policy that affects their lives, or interning in the mayor's office. Book-lecture-discussion-testing of traditional intellectual material is actually a subset of experiential learning.

This is much more than an argument for internships and community service, because it asserts that everything connected with the course is part of the experience that the professor shapes for the purpose of learning. What happens in the classroom outside the conventional reading, lecturing, discussion, and testing can have as big an impact, if not bigger, on what the students learn. Professors who are caring and competent in delivering the services agreed to in their tacit contract with the members of the class are doing more in nurturing citizenship than the most spellbinding lecturer who refuses to hold adequate office hours or who bases grades on the repression of multiple-guess tests. Unless students report the lecturer to the university president, and Dr. Spellbinder begins to treat students like human beings, such a lecturer teaches that "you can't fight city hall."

There is a false dichotomy between book-lecture-discussion-testing and experiential learning. The former should be viewed as a subset of the latter; not the other way around. Unfortunately, even proponents of experiential learning have failed to directly challenge the primacy of traditional classroom activities. They talk about integrating service learning experience with traditional educational material for reasons that run the range from academic camouflage to a genuine belief that intellectual activity is the highest form of learning. They fail to recognize that application is the highest form of learning, just as experiential application is the highest form of teaching. As a very well known sociologist told me when his study had a major impact on public policy, academic writings and conference presentations are like minor league practices for the public policy big league.

If you accept Dewey's view that education is "of, by, and for" experience, the question then becomes, what experiences will put students on the path to becoming effective citizens? Is reading a textbook description of how legislation develops preferred to interviewing a member of a senator's staff or to a legislative simulation? Given the principles of the individuality of the learner and the multicausal and nonlinear nature of the learning process, such questions must always be answered in the context of the student and the course. However, given time and given resource constraints on both the student and instructor, a strategic trade-off among the various forms of experience must be made. Because most college instructors naturally think students learn more from reading, taking tests, writing papers, and listening to lectures, they should err on the side of the nontraditional.

This is especially true at the introductory level. Students need to start within the realm of their own experience, which means more hands-on activity and less exposure to the thoughts of third parties. As students develop their interest in and capacity for becoming citizens, the concepts and wisdom of others could play a larger role, depending upon the student.

PAF 101 is my approach to creating life-changing experiences to help students become individuals who seek to improve society through their actions as individuals, workers, members of groups, and, in some cases, players in the political process. As a life-changing experience, PAF 101 has four goals:

1. To awaken students to the connection between their lives and public policy.
2. To provide an introduction to the range of skills needed to be an effective citizen.
3. To generate a capacity for caring about society.
4. To acquire some understanding of how policy is made.

I have organized my description of PAF 101 around the first three goals. The fourth goal—acquiring an understanding of the policy-making process—results from many of the experiences described under the first three, as should become obvious, and also from the research conducted by each student individually. Where I have placed descriptions of class activities is somewhat arbitrary. An activity may awaken one student, provide an introduction to a skill for another student, and convince a third that he or she needs to care more for society. Because learning is multicausal, nonlinear, and dependent upon the previous and future experiences of the individual, it is inevitable that the categories serve only a heuristic purpose.

To illustrate my basic contention that education is experience created by the teacher, let us suppose for a moment that I as the author of this chapter am a teacher and you, the reader, are a student. This essay is intended to create a life-changing experience for you as a teacher and learner but only if you test the ideas given here. Until you try one or more of the techniques described below, you will have learned very little. You will note, however, that I began this chapter with a theoretical discussion to put you in your comfort zone and, therefore, make you more open to seriously considering the suggested techniques. In other words, I started where you live, just as all good teachers should start within the experiences of their students.

## The Awakening

I do several things to make sure that the students understand that this is an action course that is directly relevant to their lives. Almost every class meeting forces students to take a position about an issue that has meaning to them. Most examples are often drawn from university policies to ensure a common experiential base for the discussion. A few are drawn from societal problem areas that I can assume most students are interested in (e.g., criminal justice, gender discrimination in the workplace, and health care). The use of examples close to the students' experience and interest is vital so that the content of the examples is not off-putting and does not require a major effort in setting the context.

### The Wallet as a Window into Public Policy

I begin the class by asking the students to define a public policy. After some discussion, I ask students to identify something in their wallet relevant to a public policy. My handling their wallets ten minutes into the course is itself a way of forcing them to act. The contents of their wallet define them as it appears to define us all as members of society. Students offer their Social Security card, money, and driver license. A shill then hands me an ID which indicates he (just as frequently she) is close to twenty-five years old. I ask if it is a false ID to which he responds "yes." I pull out a pair of large scissors and cut it in half. Then, he says a few disrespectful words as he leaves the room.

Several students then tell me I had no right to do such a thing, and the twenty-one-year-old drinking age is a bad idea. I respond by saying, "It is my responsibility as a good citizen, because I care about law and our society, and obviously most of this class only cares about their own self-interest, which in this case requires breaking the law."

This stunt creates an experience that indicates this class is intrusive to the core of their being and demonstrates that the professor is teaching by acting as well as talking. The wallet activity is the first of many experiences to illustrate that their own self-interest, and the degree to which it relates to the public good, is on trial in everything they do.

## Grading America

In the second and third class meetings, I suggest that life, liberty, and the pursuit of happiness provide three general criteria against which we can judge the United States. Each of the three categories is divided into two subcategories, providing six criteria against which to judge societal conditions in the United States and, by implication, the effectiveness of our political system. The six criteria are:

| LIFE | LIBERTY | HAPPINESS |
|---|---|---|
| 1. Personal Safety | 3. Free Speech | 5. Economic Opportunity |
| 2. Health | 4. Free Choice | 6. Clean Environment |

I point out that we need to think about level of performance as well as how equally distributed the performance is throughout the society. I ask the students to come to the next class with evidence from their almanacs supporting how they would grade the United States, A to F, on these six criteria with respect to both absolute level and distribution.

In the next class, students participate in a serious discussion that leads to votes on grades for the United States on each of the six criteria. The clash between self-interest and public interest becomes paramount in the discussion as most agree that the United States ranks relatively high on level of performance, but does very poorly on distribution. I tell them that we will return to these grades at the end of the course. The activities allow the student to think seriously about conditions in the United States and to observe how other members of the class apply the criteria. The grading activity awakens the students to the need to make critical judgments about society from their own perspective.

A point to note about this exercise is that the students are not given any conceptual material beyond the two pages in the textbook concerning the values used for criteria. Some professors might have a problem with the six criteria listed for the exercise as being too poorly defined and too coarse to be useful. I recognize that the criteria are somewhat imprecise, overlapping, and simplistic. However, what is the alternative? To have them read about what American democracy is all about, or to have them come up with their own criteria? Either of these two approaches runs the risk of putting the students to sleep or only entertaining them with semantic gymnastics.

## Community Experience

Despite a heavy workload of required class attendance and papers every two and a half weeks, I also require a five-hour community service experience by the end of the ninth week. This ungraded requirement (students can only lose points that amount to one-half of a letter grade) exists to make sure every student has performed a service for someone in the community surrounding Syracuse University. The university's Center for Public and Community Service facilitates the placement, and the undergraduate teaching assistants take care of the rest of the administrative problems. Students often tutor at a local elementary school or an afternoon program at a community center, but sometimes they work on projects for organizations such as the Food Bank and Habitat for Humanity. About 30 percent of the students work more than the five-hour requirement as a result of their rewarding experience, while about 30 percent of the students were already doing volunteer work. The remaining 40 percent seem relatively unaffected by the experience. This limited use of community experience has as its only purpose the awakening of students to the community that surrounds the university.

## The Grading Exercise

The final approach in developing the awakening process is an exercise I developed in the early 1980s. I adapted it from a philosophy professor who decided to wake up his class, some members of which were literally asleep, by announcing that he would give everyone in the class an A if they wanted him to. The offer resulted in a rejuvenation of the class and a rejection of his offer. The exercise that I used provides students with the opportunity to change the grading structure from a traditional system—in which 90–100 is an A; 80–89 is a B; and so forth—to one of two other systems: (1) a conservative system in which 35 percent of the class is guaranteed an A or (2) a socialist system in which 80 percent of the class is guaranteed at least a B. A full explanation of this appears in the course textbook (Coplin and O'Leary, 1992, 69–72).

The rules require that in order to change to either the conservative or socialist system, the students must unanimously agree on the change or, failing that, unanimously agree on the voting procedure to make the change. If the class cannot make the decision after thirty-five minutes, the traditional system remains by default.

This event gives students an opportunity to decide on a policy of actual importance to their lives and, therefore, is an experience in collective decision making with real consequences. I agree to implement the decision they make. Because those who opt for the traditional system have in effect a veto power and the students have thirty-five minutes to make the decision, the interchange becomes extremely tense. Students speak honestly and emotionally, but very few have a strategic purpose for what they say or provide a coherent rationale on how the system they support will serve the public good. Eventually, a few start to take strategic actions like saying "time is running out so vote for my position, now." In about a third of the cases, the traditional system is maintained, while the rest of the time is evenly divided between the conservative system and the socialist system.

Immediately following the exercise, I conduct a debriefing designed to awaken the students to the importance of responsible participation. I try to lead them to the conclusion that what happens in class is similar to what happens in the real world, and the lack of rules and the lack of mutual respect among members of the class led to the chaotic conditions during the exercise. The point I try to make is that there is no reason that just because the politics of policy making is messy, frustrating, and likely to completely satisfy no one, abstention is not a viable option if you want to improve yourself and society.

## Helping Develop Skills

The course is designed to introduce students to key skills needed to identify societal problems and to develop an action orientation to solve those problems. This is done primarily through written exercises and through the classroom activities to prepare students to complete those exercises. The types of skills developed include but are not limited to (1) using a problem-solving framework, (2) gathering information, and (3) using models to relate the information to the problems and their

solutions. After discussing these three skill areas, I will describe some
of the methods used to develop the students' skills.


## Using a Problem-Solving Framework

The framework presented in the textbook, the lectures, and the required exercise is a familiar problem-solving exercise. It consists of the
following steps:

1. Identify societal problems (defined as undesirable social conditions).
2. Provide evidence of the existence of the problem.
3. Discuss the causes of the problem.
4. Identify and select a public policy alternative.
5. Evaluate the potential benefits and costs of the preferred policy.
6. Forecast the impact of a proposed policy.
7. Analyze the political feasibility of the policy and what might be
   done to increase its likelihood.


Students write papers on a topic of their choice going through these
steps. They also critique newspaper articles and editorials for each of
these steps.


## Information Gathering

Students are introduced to the three major sources of information:
the library (including electronic sources), surveys, and knowledgeable
observers/players. They are given exercises to complete on the topic of
their choice. Starting in the third week of the course, they select their
topic and are encouraged to become "experts."
With respect to the library and Internet, the students are introduced
to information searching in two waves. First, they complete a series of
exercises that require them to find pieces of information that have some
relevance to their topic. They are required to use the catalog system,
abstracts and indexes, including the American Statistical Index, the
Monthly Catalogue of U. S. Government Publications, the World Wide
Web, and whatever else the librarians and I think is important. In fact,
the university reference librarian wrote the research chapter in the textbook. While the first foray into the library and Internet is like a general
scavenger hunt, where the item must have only some general relevance

to the student's topic, the second is a more focused search that students undertake in finding specific information for their papers.

Survey research is introduced through an exercise requiring students to design but not conduct a survey. The purpose of this exercise is to introduce the uses and misuses of surveys, enough for a course of this scope. In addition to the traditional topics of survey design like target population, sample selection, and the wording of questions, students are required to identify a potential client and defend the survey on grounds that it will help the client. They are also asked to estimate the costs of the survey. These two tasks help the student think about the actual use and implementation of a survey. The idea is to introduce the skill of survey research so that students can place additional training on their educational agendas.

Finding and calling knowledgeable experts is also a requirement of the course. Students must write to at least one expert and identify others. Students learn that knowledgeable people, whether scholars, journalists, or actual players, can provide the quickest and most focused way to get critical information. They also learn that they need multiple sources of information to check for accuracy. Frequently, students get involved in a meaningful dialogue because the experts are sometimes players who are looking for support. For many students, it is the first time that they have had a conversation with an adult who may be a player. Although many students initially resist the interaction, once they find out how useful it can be, they gain the confidence they need to approach people on policy issues. They also learn how to use the phone and how to communicate with adults who are not members of their family or their teachers.

## Using Models: The Prince Model

Students are required to estimate the likelihood that their policy proposal would be implemented. In order to organize their thinking on this topic, they are introduced to the Prince system, a paper-and-pencil model Michael O'Leary and I developed in the early 1970s. The model requires that (1) a specific policy action be identified and that the players, who determine whether the policy is implemented, be listed; (2) numerical values be assigned to the players' position, power, and priority on the issue; and (3) a probability of the likelihood of the policy's implementation be calculated. The form provided below is used by students in their papers. It will also serve as a summary explanation of the system. The most concise introduction to the Prince system can be found in the course textbook (Coplin and O'Leary 1992, 101–125).

*Players*

| | Issue | | | | | | |
|---|---|---|---|---|---|---|---|
| | Position | × | Power | × | Priority | = | Score |
| | (-5 to +5)* | | (1 to 5) | | (1 to 5) | | |
| 1 ___________ | _____ | × | _____ | × | _____ | = | _____ |
| 2 ___________ | _____ | × | _____ | × | _____ | = | _____ |
| 3 ___________ | _____ | × | _____ | × | _____ | = | _____ |
| 4 ___________ | _____ | × | _____ | × | _____ | = | _____ |
| 5 ___________ | _____ | × | _____ | × | _____ | = | _____ |

Sum of all positive scores plus 1/2 neutral scores = _______*
Sum of all scores ignoring signs and parentheses = _______
Probability of support = Calculation 2 divided by Calculation 3 = _______

** Issue positions of "0" can be assigned to players as a position of "neutral." Multiply scores across without multiplying by zero, recording them with parentheses around the score.*

The Prince system requires an understanding of the political system much beyond what can be expected of a first-year student, or even a college graduate. Students are forced to scramble to get the information, which in some cases requires them to read about how a bill becomes a law, and to educate themselves quickly on the political process. Most students have had American government courses, but as we all know, that is frequently not a life-changing educational experience. The Prince system requires that students grasp the workings of the political system in order to make a structured forecast. The system also provides a framework for developing a strategy in the contexts of the analysis they have performed. Students finish the assignment realizing that political forecasting requires precise, accurate, and up-to-date information, which is very hard to obtain.

## Developing the Skills

Although the description has been brief, it is should be clear that the course has ambitious objectives that may be the same as those expected of an M.P.A. program or even a Ph.D. in policy analysis or, better yet, the skills expected of a professional lobbyist, politician, or civil servant. The goal is not to make students proficient in these skills, but to start them on the road to acquiring enough of them to be effective citizens.

The techniques described below are designed to achieve this rudimentary objective and must be viewed in that context.

### *(1)  Community Link Team Approach*

The problem-solving framework, which constitutes a set of skills that students begin to develop in the course, is introduced in the second week through an exercise in which teams of students prepare policy memorandums for a player on campus. The player may be the head of financial aid, or the leader of a task force on substance abuse on campus, or the head of the computer center, trying to figure out how to get Internet junkies out of the computer clusters so that serious students can use the computers for academic work. The entire class listens to all the players, but each group of five students is assigned to help a specific player. In three working class sections, the groups prepare a policy memorandum using the general framework described above. The shortness of time, and the fact that the exercise comes at the beginning of the course, means that the policy memorandums are as a whole mediocre. They frequently have good content, but usually lack documentation and coherent argumentation.

The value of the exercise is to illustrate the need for a systematic approach to societal problem solving, and why the skills taught in the course are important. Students complain that I set them up for failure. My response is that failure is a good way to learn, and societal problems are very hard to solve. After the experience, they see the value of the skills, not only for societal problem solving, but for all decision making. Occasionally, the policy memorandums are very helpful to the players and are sometimes implemented. When this happens, all the students see that they can make a difference.

### *(2)  Exercises on Topics of the Students' Choice*

Students are encouraged to choose a topic they already know about or one for which they can easily acquire information. They are warned that following directions is as important as getting the right information. They are encouraged to become experts on their topic so as to answer questions in the exercise. This approach allows students to build on previous experiences in order to master skills. Many students have no interest or knowledge of any policy issue, which limits to some extent the effectiveness of this approach. However, allowing students to choose the subject helps to reduce the barriers to learning the skills for most students. It also increases the chances students will be motivated to work hard because they are studying what they choose to study.

One of my problems with letting students choose their topics is that the student may know more than I do, especially if he or she chooses something out of the ordinary, like a prison issue in a local county or a high-tech policy issue. My role, however, can only be to enforce the rules of the exercises and make guesses about the accuracy of the information provided by the student. This causes something of a role reversal that is as empowering to the student as it may be disquieting to professors who like control.

Ultimately, the role reversal makes a lot of sense, not just for a generalist like me, but for most faculty. The subject-matter expertise of faculty is what separates them from their students. By creating a course in which the student becomes the substantive expert, and the faculty member is a process expert, helping the student learn the required skills, there is less of a gulf between them. The increasingly easy access to information, both good and bad, requires that students learn how to find it and assess it on their own. The instructor is primarily a facilitator in that process.

### (3) Competition Groups

In each of the last four sections of this five-module course, I play a little game with the students for extra credit points. Each group of about ten students, led by an undergraduate teaching assistant, is allowed a class period to write the most difficult section of the paper on a university-based topic. The papers are given to the instructor for evaluation. In the next class, examples of good and bad work are displayed and all groups are asked to attack the group whose paper is displayed. Extra credit points are awarded to the best papers and group attacks. The points are very small so the impact on the final grade is negligible. This does not prevent the students from fighting for every point.

As a result of the competition, students practice the paper before they write it on their subject and then hear a thorough debriefing and evaluation from their peers and the instructor. Most students consider the competitions useful. I occasionally call a brief competition in class if I am not getting enough discussion. I might ask a factual question, or ask for ideas on a cause for a societal problem, and give the group who answers well a half-point. Even though the reward is minuscule, the competitive reflexes take over and the class becomes revitalized for the remainder of the period with no more "snacks."

## Caring for the Public Good

It is not enough to awaken students to the possibilities of citizenship and provide a window on the skills they need to become effective citizens. We must also convince students that while they are working for themselves they must donate some of their time and effort to the public good. Most of the techniques and material already described contributes to this. The wallet performance and the grading exercise show students that we cannot survive as a society unless we care about each other. The Prince system emphasizes the importance of consensus, compromise, and log-rolling in the development of public policy. The community service requirement shows that public service is crucial. Grading the United States shows students that how widespread the benefits of society are is a key consideration.

There are several other explicit activities I undertake to emphasize the need to commit to the public good. These include (1) using shame and guilt, (2) bringing in outside speakers, (3) talking about foolish freedom, and (4) ending the course with an oath.

### Using Shame and Guilt

A key element in motivating students to become players is to introduce a metaphor of "dogs" into the discussion. I point out early in the course that dogs are affected by but do not influence public policy. Dogs are affected by leash laws; they do not make them. I point out that people are dogs in the public policy-making process unless they join organizations or obtain authoritative positions. For example, with respect to the university's policy of raising tuition, students are dogs unless they work through the Student Government Association or some other entity. This is also true of the masses, taxpayers, welfare mothers, smokers, and any other group of people that are targeted by policy. They only become players when they organize and consciously seek to influence the political process.

The dog metaphor has a shaming impact. In subsequent discussions over whether policies will be implemented, students frequently talk about whether or not a given individual or group is a "dog." They are derisive about people who whine about policies but do not organize to do something about it. Presumably, the students do not like to see themselves as dogs and, therefore, the seeds have been planted for them to become players when they find themselves whining in the future.

Shaming students into wanting to become players rather than dogs is combined with a heavy dose of guilt that I lay on the students throughout the course. I want my students to be players who care about the public good and try to do this by emphasizing how lucky they are and how much they owe society.

After the ID-cutting episode, I make it a point to say that they are selfish and don't care about society, which is why they break the law in order to enjoy themselves. This theme is usually expressed by my frequently repeated refrain: "The class is disgusting." Although some students find the remark offensive (which may be justified for those who have performed community service or who work as a responsible player in the policy process), many students find the refrain a light-hearted reminder of their guilt.

I also remind the students that they are all in the top 1 percent of the entire world's economic class. This statement outrages many of them, since many feel they are downtrodden, even at Syracuse University. I only need to remind them of the more than 3.5 billion people in the world, a significant percentage of whom do not have electricity, and most of whom do not live in the industrialized world. By the middle of the term, they turn on me and ask why I wear designer label shirts and what kind of car I drive. I tell them that I am not perfect, but I devote some of my time and money to the public good, and that if they devoted as much as I do, the world would be much better. Most still consider me a hypocrite, which some realize is a projection of their own guilt.

## Bringing in Outside Speakers

I carefully select outside speakers who represent different social perspectives, but who also are individuals dedicated to the public good. These speakers discuss topics related to crime and poverty. They are often people who have taken PAF 101. I ask the speakers to talk about their backgrounds. This allows my students to meet people whom they might emulate, people who work for the public good and who also make a good living.

## Talking about Foolish Freedom

In the next-to-last class, I start off with a definition of "foolish freedom" as the pursuit of self-interest for its own sake with little concern for society. I then provide a list of things people in our society do that are foolishly free. These include:

- Not wearing seat belts.
- Throwing cigarette butts on the ground.
- Demanding cable TV with hundreds of channels.
- Failing to take care of their family.
- Calling for lower taxes and less government as a way of curing all societal problems.
- Having unprotected sex whenever, wherever, and with whomever they like.
- Whining for handouts and special treatment.

I go on to say that because of this foolish freedom, we have:

- A criminal justice system that does not work.
- Too many students for too few teachers.
- Empty commercial real estate everywhere.
- Federal and state governments that can't pass a budget on time.

I remind my students of the grades they gave the United States at the beginning of the course.

This talk leads to an interesting conversation, most of which concludes that I am correct in my diagnoses, but "what can we do about it?" At this point, I announce that "I have the solution, and I will present it in the final class."

## Ending with an Oath

After collecting the final papers and course evaluation forms, I tell my students that I have the answer. I ask them to follow me to a statue of George Washington in the foyer of Maxwell Hall. Behind Washington's statue is the Athenian Oath:

"We will ever strive for the ideals and sacred things of the city, both alone and with many; We will unceasingly seek to quicken the sense of public duty; We will revere and obey the city's laws;

We will transmit this city not only not less, but greater, better and more beautiful than it was transmitted to us."

I ask them to take the oath and act upon it. If they do that and others do that, we will have a much better society in which to live. They take the oath and say good-bye. I would like them to hold hands to enhance the experience, but my teaching assistants tell me that I am crazy. So far I have accepted their advice, in part because I want them to have the feeling that they are also players in the policies of my course, and in part because I fear a lack of compliance. Maybe some year I'll over-rule them, but you can bet that if I do, I'll make sure the teaching assistants facilitate the hand-holding process.

## Conclusion

The kinds of attitudes, skills, and knowledge that students obtain from PAF 101 are designed to provide experiences that will put them on a path to becoming active, competent, and caring citizens, who balance their own self-interest with a reasonable concern for the public good. Whether the students continue on that path depends on many factors over which only the student has some control. Certainly, neither I nor the rest of my colleagues can do any more than help students move along on the path. We must be humble in thinking what any given course, or even major, can do in making a better citizenry. What we need to do is to create the full range of experiences to awaken students, to provide rudimentary skills, and to promote a commitment to the public good. To do this we must choose those experiences carefully and with an eye to the reality that "education is of, by, and for experience."

5

# Public Affairs Internships:
# Coming of Age

*Glen A. Halva-Neubauer*

Placing political science students in public affairs internships has a long history in the discipline. William Pederson and Norman Provizer (1995, 233) report that Colgate University established a Washington semester program in 1935; the University of Minnesota supported fieldwork experiences in local government, campaigns and elections, and the state legislature beginning in the late 1950s (Internship Program 1996). The cry for more relevant education coming out of the 1960s brought significant expansion in the number of institutions supporting Washington internship programs. Much of this expansion has been made possible by the establishment of nonprofit organizations, such as the Washington Center for Internships and Academic Seminars and the Institute for Experiential Learning, which allows many colleges and universities to send students to the nation's capital without supporting a full-blown program. The 1970s, however, also saw more colleges and universities launching independent Washington semester programs (Pederson and Provizer 1995, 233). Internships at the state and local level, too, were established and expanded during that time (Ferguson and Winder 1981; Williams 1976).

The flowering of public affairs internships brought with it many issues regarding the management of internships, as well as broader curricular concerns (e.g., where internships should fit in a liberal arts curriculum). In one of the most thoughtful and balanced articles on the subject, James Alexander (1982) addresses many of these issues. First, many faculty resist giving credit for vocational-like experiences in liberal arts programs. Equally problematic is the challenge that internships present to traditional authority and knowledge. Truth in the traditional liberal arts college emanates from the professor who has won the right to profess because of superior knowledge, experience, and theoretical sophistication in a field. Conversely, proponents of experiential education argue that truth can be ascertained from a student's unique experiences (Alexander 1982, 128–129). The differences in how truth is derived lead to numerous problems.

Internships place students with practitioners, who often do not have the same academic credentials as the faculty member. Yet agency supervisors have knowledge that students presumably can gain from these individuals only, so agency supervisors are disseminating knowledge. What, then, is the appropriate role of the faculty member? Internships bear little relation to the traditional teacher-student role. To address this problem, Alexander states that many departments make internship requirements similar to classroom work (e.g., requiring papers and examinations) so the professor has something familiar to evaluate and grade.

Alexander (129–130) further notes that internships present staffing problems and change the role of the professor in the institution, especially recruiting agency mentors to supervise students. Professors who supervise internships often do so at considerable risk because of the time it takes to coordinate these programs. This may lead to hiring a full-time internship coordinator, which signals further detachment from the academic nature of the program. Recruitment of students is sometimes problematic because underachievers in the classroom often do well in internship settings, reinforcing their view of the futility of a liberal arts education. Given that most internships were adopted with a cursory understanding of the conceptual and structural difficulties underlying them, few analysts have been surprised to find that internships are marginalized in many political science departments. These structural difficulties frequently lead to students' receiving subpar learning experiences (Profughi and Warren 1978).

Now, however, internships and other forms of experiential learning are enjoying elevated status within the academy. Three trends are linked to this transformation. First is a growing recognition that higher education institutions must shift paradigms from one of providing instruction to one of producing learning (Barr and Tagg 1995). No longer can universities merely instruct students; they must produce students who are flexible and prepared to meet the challenges of a global economy (Bikson and Law 1994). In a world in which change is fast-paced and omnipresent, knowledge is less important than the ability to learn. Higher education, then, must respond to the demands of the learning society and prepare students to be lifelong learners (Cross 1994). And at its core, experiential education is dedicated to learning about learning.

Second, research shows that the lecture—that much-venerated convention of a liberal arts education—is not the best way for students to retain content. While lecturing lies at the heart of the instruction paradigm, research has shown that participating in an activity, rather than listening to a lecturer, results in greater information retention (Next Steps Team Training Manual n.d.). Other research suggests that state legislative interns have a more nuanced and sophisticated understanding of the political process than do students enrolled in a traditional legislative process course (Eyler and Halteman 1981). In addition, Roberta Johnson (1993) found that interns were more conversant in public administration theory as a result of their experiences in public agencies.

Third, and most central to the essays in this volume, is citizenship education. Citizenship training has been a central aim of a liberal arts education from its beginnings in the ancient world. An educated and informed citizenry remains essential to the functioning of a democratic polity. Yet, given the dreary statistics on voting participation, the popularity of talk radio and TV shows that offer simplistic solutions to complex social and economic problems, the ideological fervor that dominates much of American political discourse, and the growing cynicism among the electorate (especially the young), traditional avenues of educating citizens appear inadequate. As a result, citizenship education is an important item on the agenda of many education-related groups, including the American Political Science Association (Ostrom 1996). As with most educational initiatives, what constitutes citizenship and how to devise curricula to achieve these outcomes remain undecided. How this controversy relates to internships will be addressed later.

Experiential education in general and public affairs internships in particular teach students to learn about learning, involve real-world problems that assist them in retaining content, and provide opportunities to participate in democracy. No longer the stepchild of the curriculum, public affairs internships are gaining a prominent place in the university of the twenty-first century. Following a prolonged adolescence, internships are moving toward adulthood.

While coming of age is a significant breakthrough for experiential education, it does not guarantee success. In many ways, Alexander's essay is more relevant today than when he penned it fifteen years ago. Just because experiential education may be gaining respect does not mean it will transform the university from an instruction-oriented to a learning-oriented institution. As students of public policy know, a program's impact lies with its implementation.

Based on my experiences as director of the state and local public affairs internship program at Furman University, I will chronicle one case of successful implementation in this essay. After discussing the Furman environment, I address three factors that played a significant role in shaping Furman's program: experiential education theory, mechanics and resources, and outcomes. First, I review the theory underlying the central goal of Furman's internship program—producing more reflective thinkers. Next, I provide information on the program's mechanics, paying attention to the resources and support critical to program implementation. In the final section, I evaluate the success of this program in promoting more reflective thinking among Furman interns.

## The Furman Environment

Furman University is a private, selective, independent liberal arts college of twenty-five hundred students located in Greenville, South Carolina. Its students hail principally from southeastern and Middle Atlantic states; only a few are nontraditional (those outside the eighteen-to-twenty-two-year-old range). Furman operates under a term academic calendar: In the fall and spring, students take three courses for twelve weeks (all classes meet daily for fifty minutes); during the winter, students take two courses for eight weeks (all classes meet daily for seventy-five minutes).

Political science is one of the most popular majors, constituting more than 10 percent of each year's graduating class. The political science department has a strong commitment to experiential education, including study abroad opportunities, in-class simulations, and participation in national simulations, notably Organization of African Unity and Mock Trial. Internship programs, however, lie at the core of its experiential education commitment. In 1979, the department established a Washington program in cooperation with the Washington Center for Internships and Academic Seminars, the first credit-bearing internship program at Furman. Building on its success in Washington, in 1991 the department began offering a second internship program, in state and local public affairs (the primary subject of this essay). Since that time, one hundred students have participated in this program.

The public affairs program operates during the winter term in Greenville. Furman's calendar is conducive to an immersion philosophy: Students work twenty-five hours per week and participate in a seminar each Thursday evening for three and a half hours. Students are encouraged, though not required, to enroll in Urban Politics as their second winter course.

The department has developed guiding principles for its internship experiences. Both programs include significant reflection components. Internship courses are graded like traditional classroom courses, and they count in the student's major. The department is committed to a program that integrates academic theory with the student's internship, develops citizenship skills, and provides students with insights into their own learning styles as well as promoting their affective development. To achieve these goals requires grounding in experiential education theory.

## Toward Reflective Thinking

A sound program of experiential education is built on a solid theoretical foundation. Furman's state and local public affairs program has been enriched by its grounding in experiential education theory, but true to the experiential philosophy, it is a work in progress. Not only are interns learning from their experiences, but so, too, am I. Furman's state and local public affairs internship program has taken many shapes not only because of my propensity to modify it yearly, but also because of the multiple goals (and theories that support them) of experiential education. As a program existing within a liberal arts college, the internship also had to fit within the broader context of this tradition. Throughout its short existence, the program has remained committed to improving the reflective thinking capacities of its interns. To better understand the importance of reflection, a brief introduction to John Dewey's classical theory of experiential education is in order.

### Dewey's Experiential Education Theory

The experiential education movement is based on a straightforward premise: Students as well as teachers learn through experience. This idea is neither profound nor new; vocational educators and those involved in professional education (especially medical personnel) have long been trained through apprenticeships, internships, and residencies. While the role of experience is accepted as essential to vocational and professional education, many educators find it difficult to discern the relationship between experience and learning in a liberal arts setting. Such was not the case with John Dewey, one of the foremost philosophers of American education and dean of the experiential education perspective. For Dewey, theoretical understanding was not fully developed until it was applied; similarly, purely vocational training was less than complete without a full understanding of methods of inquiry (Heinemann and De Falco 1990, 41). Dewey viewed the university as a laboratory where theories studied in the classroom could be tested through real-world experience, and he believed the connections made between school and work would make education more vital and powerful. Ultimately, Dewey saw this marriage of the world of ideas and the world of work as essential for creating an educated citizenry, one that would sustain democratic practices (41).

Despite Dewey's enthusiasm for learning through experience, he did not think that all experiences resulted in learning. Ormond Smythe (1990, 298) notes that Dewey believed learning occurred only when a connection was made between an action and its consequence. Consequently, for experiences to yield learning, they needed to be modeled after laboratory experiments; experiences must have a purpose, and connection must be made between the activity and its results; otherwise, no learning has taken place. Smythe contends that Dewey's formulation was too rigid and that learning through experience can transpire under conditions less structured than a laboratory experiment (298–99). Despite this important caveat, experiential educators realize that while learning through experience can occur under numerous conditions, it usually requires careful planning and purpose. Dewey's work, especially its discussion of planning and purpose and the place of experience in a liberal arts education, has found expression among several contemporary writers.

## Contemporary Theories

True to Dewey, Pat Hutchings and Allen Wutzdorff (1988) argue that liberal arts students should progress toward a greater integration of knowing and doing during their undergraduate careers. For instance, students should not treat the content of an English course as discrete information applicable neither to one's life nor to another class. To help students integrate knowledge, faculty must decide what it means to be a philosopher or a political scientist—not only what knowledge one should possess, but what it means to practice a discipline (Hutchings and Wutzdorff 1988, 9). To accomplish such integration between knowing and doing (as called for in Dewey's theory of experiential education), Hutchings and Wutzdorff outline the principal elements of the Alverno College curriculum.

The Alverno curriculum integrates learning and knowing by making its curriculum concrete, involved, dissonant, and reflective. Faculty bring concrete activities to bear on the study of their respective subjects; for example, rather than simply lecture on social structure, the professor asks students to set up a group and decide which issues to consider. Problems that students confront in completing this exercise make the theoretical presentations on social structure discussed later in the course come alive. Involvement refers to Alverno's commitment to educating on all modalities. Of special relevance to this essay is the college's commitment to engaging the affective domain—attempting to evoke personal responses from students and allowing them to evaluate these within the context of courses. Knowing and doing also require dissonance: Finding out that what one knows does not always work in practice is an essential part of learning, and finding out how to revise theory and action to create a better balance is a significant element of learning. The final and perhaps most important element of the Alverno perspective, is reflection: making sense of one's experience, processing the dissonance that occurs between theory and reality, and taking time to understand the meaning of one's involvement in an activity. Hutchings and Wutzdorff argue that a more complete integration of knowing and doing occurs as Alverno students move through the curriculum (15–17).

The Alverno curriculum, Furman's program, and the experiential education field writ large are deeply indebted to the theorizing of David Kolb (1984). His four-stage theory of learning builds on the work of John Dewey, Kurt Lewin, and Jean Piaget. In Kolb's view, learning is comprised of concrete experience, reflective observation, abstract conceptualization, and active experimentation. The process begins with the learners performing a task, such as working at an internship site. From this concrete experience, learners move to the reflective observation stage, where they evaluate the meaning of their work. After reflecting, learners draw broad conclusions from their reflections; Kolb refers to this stage as abstract conceptualization. Having discovered general principles, learners apply them in a new situation (active experimentation). Robert McKenzie (1994, 22–23) employs the "ready, aim, fire" metaphor to describe Kolb's conceptualization of learning. Learners ready themselves during experience and reflective phases, aim as a result of abstract conceptualization, and fire their "weapons" during the active experimentation stage. While Kolb's theory reduces a complex phenomenon to its constituent elements and posits that learning is linear and sequential, his supporters acknowledge that the stages of learning often occur simultaneously.

Kolb's model also makes another important contribution to experiential education. He divides learning into two dimensions: the kind of information we rely on when making decisions (arrayed from concrete experience to abstract conceptualization—essentially, do we use feeling or thinking as our guide?) and how we use information (on a continuum from reflective observation to active experimentation—do we prefer to watch or to do?). Hence, Kolb identifies four learning styles: divergers, accommodators, assimilators, and convergers. Divergers learn by feeling and observing, accommodators by feeling and doing, assimilators by thinking and observing, and convergers by thinking and doing. Good internship programs attempt to place students where they can develop their particular learning style to the fullest. Carefully designed programs also expose students to activities that require a variety of learning styles, creating a more well-rounded individual (Svinicki and Dixon 1987).

At the heart of Kolb's theory is turning experience into learning through the process of reflection. Reflection is important in learning and retaining content derived from experience, and allows students to integrate theory and practice. By reflecting on their experiences, students find that the learning becomes deeper and the nuances and ambiguities of a particular phenomenon more ingrained in their thinking. Suddenly the world is not "just-the-facts" but complex, messy, and contradictory. Experience alone does not ensure learning; only with reflection can students take full stock of what an experience means.

Kolb's learning cycle holds important implications for how we understand citizenship education, particularly reflection. McKenzie (1996) believes that the learning cycle roughly comports to four established ways of teaching citizenship. The traditional classical liberal education model is built on abstract conceptualization, while service learning and internships teach citizenship through immersion in the concrete dimension. Proponents of teaching citizenship through democratizing the campus believe that students learn best through active experimentation; democratic citizenship is learned behavior, and so it must be practiced. Finally, theorists who believe that citizens have lost the ability to deliberate collectively about public policy wish to teach citizenship through reflection. While McKenzie is very invested in teaching deliberative skills and views reflection as linking the other parts of the learning cycle, he recognizes the need for all traditions of citizenship education to be represented in the curriculum.

In earlier work, McKenzie (1994) notes another application of learning theory to citizen development. He argues that most of what is classified as democratic politics (voting, lobbying, campaigning) is due to a strong preference for using the experimentation phase of the learning cycle to process our understanding of reality. McKenzie is a passionate advocate for public politics, which stresses deliberation. Public politics is defined as listening, making connections between issues, and understanding all dimensions of a public policy issue. Obviously, deliberative politics shows a strong preference for understanding reality through reflective learning.

From Dewey to the recent theorizing of McKenzie, reflection remains key in transforming experience into learning. Kolb's learning cycle represents a major breakthrough in our understanding of how people learn. His theorizing has played an important role in the design of highly successful experiential education programs, notably Alverno College. Moreover, learning cycle theory has had a significant influence on how McKenzie conceptualizes citizenship education. The theorists reviewed in this section have had an influence on Furman's internship program as well.

## Integrating Knowing and Doing at Furman University

In this section, I provide information on the mechanics of Furman's state and local public affairs internship program. Special attention is given to the integration of experiential education theory into the program's curriculum and to the political environment in which the program operates. A sound internship program rests on the recruitment of able agency supervisors and students as well as an integrating seminar (complete with appropriate reflection exercises) and sufficient resources. Each of these dimensions of program management will be discussed.

Furman's program has evolved during its six years of existence, but a primary goal has always has been the integration of political science theory and practice. For students of state and local government, a hands-on experience provides them with the necessary perspective to understand and appreciate theories of subnational politics. What is often strange, distant, or unknown comes alive during the internship. For example, students who work in city or county government readily understand the limits of local governance and the importance of state legislative decisions as well as those rendered by Congress for the local government's economic health. Interns know why this is such a dominant theme in the literature after a few weeks in local government, while students in a traditional classroom setting may never fully grasp the concept. Students working in a local congressional office learn the importance of casework and representation, while those in grassroots organizations learn about the difficulty of holding such groups together.

## Agency Supervisors

Integrating theory and practice requires careful planning. First, one must secure agency supervisors willing to sponsor students. While some programs use a professional staff member to locate internship sites, the faculty member identifies the sponsoring agencies under the Furman model. Because I had no network to draw on during the program's first two years, I arranged on-site visits with potential agency supervisors. On-site visits have several advantages. They allow me to view the physical space available to the agency (oftentimes, agencies cannot accommodate an internship request because of limited space), obtain a sense of agency morale and culture, and make a personal connection between the internship coordinator and the agency supervisor. However, they are so time-consuming that I now write letters to potential supervisors and ascertain their interest in a follow-up phone call. The Furman program has been fortunate to have a dedicated set of internship supervisors, people who wish not merely to be supervisors but also are willing to play a significant role in ensuring that the internship is tailored to the student's needs.

I remind internship supervisors that the student is paying tuition for this experience and reasonably expects to learn something from it. Therefore, the work should be substantive. In addition, the internship supervisor is encouraged to include the intern in all staff meetings. Supervisors receive a tip sheet listing effective ways to communicate with the intern. Interns and supervisors complete an internship expectations sheet that outlines all aspects of the internship, from the office chain of command to the agency's confidentiality policies. Interns complete a learning agreement in cooperation with their supervisors. Midterm and final evaluations are required, and I also visit each site at the term's end. The final evaluation as well as the on-site assessment are geared toward discussing the degree to which the intern fulfilled his or her learning goals. By making the program expectations clear to agency supervisors, I have found that either supervisors are willing to work within the parameters of the program or they decline to participate.

Over time, I have identified several exemplary agency supervisors and sites, but the preferences of students change yearly, so each program is a combination of old and new supervisors. Building a stable network of agency supervisors is essential to the growth of an internship program. I use my contacts to foster support for the internship program, and my contacts mention additional people who may be willing to sponsor students. It is well worth the effort to cultivate support in the community for the program. Agency supervisors provide a crucial piece of the internship puzzle: a substantive experience, one that can serve as the basis for reflection.

## Students

Selecting students is another important component of an effective internship program. Furman's program chooses interns approximately three months before the beginning of the internship. To market the internship, I send a letter to all political science majors announcing the program as well as hold several informational meetings. Students complete an application that asks for their class standing, grade point average, previous coursework in political science, work and internship experience, travel abroad experiences, and the names of three references. I then meet with two colleagues to select program participants.

Most faculty believe that the integration of knowing and doing required by internships is best accomplished with advanced students (juniors and seniors). The Furman program adheres to this philosophy as well. Mature sophomores often are accepted, however, and they have been very successful interns. Most important in the selection process is a student's maturity and discipline as revealed by his or her references. Candidates who articulate their goals for the internship and demonstrate a willingness to work will be successful both at the work site and in the academic seminar.

After being selected, students prepare a dossier consisting of a four hundred word essay outlining three reasons why they wish to pursue a public affairs internship, three letters of recommendation, a transcript, and a resume. The dossier is sent to three or four internship agencies based on the student's interests. Students then complete in-person interviews. The process is competitive, and therefore several students may interview for the same position. Agency supervisors call me after the interviewing process is complete to tell me which student they have chosen. This process has worked very well to match students and internships. In addition, it has provided students with valuable interviewing skills. The application process already has begun to ask students what they wish to accomplish during the internship, and it makes them more self-directed learners.

Furman's program places students in a broad range of positions related to public affairs, from traditional internships in city and county government and local congressional offices to public relations departments of international corporations. Given students' strong interest in legal affairs, I have developed placements with the Solicitor's Office, Victim Witness Assistance, Public Defender's Office, Legal Services, and the Federal Probation Office. Each year, I also place students in media outlets. The diversity of placements creates a dynamic and exciting atmosphere for the weekly internship seminar.

## Internship Seminar and Reflection Activities

From the beginning, a weekly seminar was included in the internship program. Internship seminars take various shapes, and some excellent models of interdisciplinary seminars exist (Cromwell 1994). While Furman's seminar is focused on state and local public affairs, over time it has taken on a wide array of topics touched by the experiential education literature, including affective development, learning theory, and citizenship education. During the first three years, the seminar met for two hours weekly, but it has been lengthened to three and a half hours to accommodate an expanding agenda. The seminar was and remains the focal point of the internship seminar because it is here that the reflection component is added.

Reflection yields many results. The primary goal of the internship is to make students better political scientists by using their internships to examine political phenomena and to compare their own generalizations with those in the political science literature. Content, too, can be taught through internships and probably is retained well in internship settings because it has to be used daily. For example, the rules under which a bill comes to the floor take on a very different meaning for a House Rules Committee intern than for a student in a legislative process course. To assist my students in learning the rudimentary elements of local government, I assign a local government and politics text, and students complete a final exam covering the primary issues in the book. Many of them, however, routinely confront topics covered in the text, and the reading and experience reinforce each other.

The internship seminar is not dominated by lectures on local government. In fact, lecturing seldom occurs. Rather, interns share their activities from the past week with fellow interns. The purpose of these sessions is not merely to chronicle one's activities, but also to make sense of them. At the beginning of the internship, students complete a learning agreement that establishes learning goals for the term as well as strategies to reach those goals. Each strategy must include a method of evaluation as well as a target date for completing a given activity. Debriefing sessions often ask a student to comment on the movement toward meeting a learning goal; focused discussions generally lead to more insightful reflection. These debriefing sessions expose students to the content of other internships as well as to how the student is making sense of his or her site. As the internship progresses, students will be asked questions that move them from reflection to abstract conceptualization. They think not merely about what is happening at one's site, but about the general patterns of behavior that have been discovered through one's experience and reflection.

As I worked with more interns, I discovered that students were having richer experiences over time. Often, their interpretation of events did not fit comfortably within the confines of integrating political science theory with practice or understanding the content of local public affairs. Their experiences were leading to personal growth, and they also were becoming acutely aware of the normative dimensions of their internships. As a result, more seminar time is set aside for personal growth issues: How can I be more self-confident? How do I gain respect from co-workers? How can I show that I am competent to handle a particular task? These issues are cast not only from the personal growth standpoint, but also from the viewpoint of being an effective participant observer. Establishing rapport and gaining access to a research site are crucial if one is to gather valid data.

Readings have been added that address these issues from the participant observer perspective as well as that of affective development. An article by Edward Cell (1993) has been particularly useful. Cell argues that students participating in internships need to be aware that personal growth often is impinged on by the necessity of accepting orga-nizational norms. Students frequently spend so much time attempting to learn organizational norms (and those who do a good job are re-warded so handsomely) that they rarely question if this is good for the individual. Internship enthusiasts assume that these experiences contribute positively to personal growth, but that may not be the case. Cell's work asks students to reflect on their socialization in the work site and the impact of that process on their individual growth.

Another component of affective development addresses the educa-tion of the emotions. Interns, especially those working in social service agencies, often need time to talk, if for no other purpose than to detach themselves from the wrenching situations to which they are exposed. Students who work with child neglect cases or a murder trial (to name but two) need a supportive environment in which to discuss how this experience has shaped them emotionally. Other students have written opinions for the local newspaper that have received hostile responses from readers, while some have wrestled with the conflict between their values and those of their supervisor. Interns quickly learn that partici-pating in the real world and having to take responsibility for one's actions are very different from living within the confines of an aca-demic institution.

Over time, the seminar has incorporated more information concern-ing learning theory in general and Kolb's learning styles in particular. While some programs administer Kolb's Learning Styles Inventory to determine which style of learning best describes a given intern (Crom-well 1994), I have not done so. I have, however, assigned readings that explain Kolb's theory (Stanton and Ali 1994). Interns discuss the rele-vance of learning theory for understanding how they come to know the world and process that information. We also use Kolb's theory to evaluate the activities selected by interns to fulfill their learning objec-tives and how they comport with a student's preferred learning style.

Of central importance to the essays in this volume is citizenship edu-cation. Like learning theory and affective development, I have come to realize the importance of this aspect of the internship only recently. Students come to the internship with entrenched ideas of what consti-tutes politics. Many view it as a necessary evil and view most people who enter politics as corrupt. The discipline's emphasis on a rational choice model of politicians maximizing their chances for reelection fits well with this popular perspective.

Interns, however, have the chance to gain a much more nuanced un-derstanding of political life, a viewpoint beyond learning content or integrating political science theory with experience. Students often leave public affairs internships with a deep respect for elected officials. Interns who work for elected officials frequently speak of members' dedication to their constituency, desire to make informed policy choices, commitment to public service, and strong work ethic. Interns also begin to understand the complexity of public policy issues. Students often work on similar issues at different internship sites, and the level of sophistication with which they understand a policy debate is remarkable. The time spent in an internship discussing issues and their dimensions greatly increases the intern's reflective and deliberative skills.

Faculty play an important role in developing their interns' attitudes toward citizenship. On one hand, faculty need to encourage students to be critical. American democracy has many flaws, and an intern should recognize them through his or her internship. Equally important, however, is to avoid making students cynical or apathetic.

Reflection is not limited to the internship seminar. Students keep a journal during the internship and make a presentation in the seminar at the term's end. The journal assignment is divided into three components: field notes, critical incident entries, and integration of literature with experience. First, I ask students to keep field notes for two weeks in the tradition of a cultural anthropologist. I want students to provide thick descriptions of the people, norms, and organizational rhythms of their internship sites to draw a portrait of the landscape, noting everything in the picture. During the next two-week segment, I ask students to narrow their focus to critical incidents; events that lead to growth and change (Stanton and Ali 1994, 66–68) and that have been identified as internship goals in their learning agreements. During the third two-week segment, interns turn their attention to integrating theory and experience. Students locate articles in the political science literature related to their internship; they then assess the applicability of these writings to their internship setting and construct generalizations about their experiences. For example, a student might evaluate why a member of Congress engages in so much casework if it bears no relationship to the margin of reelection. The ultimate purpose of this journal is to build generalizations and see how they relate to political science scholarship (Halva-Neubauer 1995).

The seminar presentation represents the most complete integration of knowing and doing. During the presentation, the intern illustrates how one principle derived by the student during the internship is similar or dissimilar to conventional wisdom contained in political science literature. Students use at least two mediums to present their findings, and the presentation cannot last longer than fifteen minutes. All presentations are peer reviewed.

## Resources

The Furman program is built on the standards outlined for high-quality experiential learning programs. To carry out this ambitious program, however, one needs resources. The university has reduced my course load to administer the internship program, and I also am given credit in my course load for teaching the internship seminar. This level of support means that the internship program is not marginalized in the curriculum and that standards for the program are maintained. No additional support staff are assigned to the internship program, and there is no budget line for the program's operation.

Despite lack of staff and money, the program operates in an enviable political environment. It enjoys widespread support from the department and the administration, and has been used as a model in other Furman departments and by other colleges and universities. Support from the community, too, has been strong. Of course, the program has no better ambassadors than the interns themselves. The program has not had to fight for respect in large part because of our successful Washington internship program. Faculty and administrators knew the power of these experiences before the state and local program began (Halva-Neubauer 1991). While support for the program is grounded in a belief that internships are superior learning experiences, what evidence is there to sustain these claims?

## Outcomes: Do Internships Produce Better Citizens?

It is difficult to assess the impact of Furman's state and local public affairs program on learning in general and citizenship education in particular. The data presented here are anecdotal, as a more systematic analysis of the program awaits further investigation. Despite the various forms of experiential education, many theorists doubt the importance of internships to produce better citizens, and some even imply they may produce worse citizens. Richard Couto and Theodore Becker (1996, 75–76) believe that most institutions view internships as training courses, ways to test information learned in public administration and criminal justice courses (to name two) in the real world. Thus, internships promote vocationalism: They may make students better police administrators or business persons, but Couto and Becker doubt whether they will make them better citizens. Fred Newmann (1990) argues that participation in internships does not lead to the development of public citizens (people interested in debating the public good and who conceive of politics as moving a group to make a decision). This stands in contrast to what he calls the dominant view of politics, a perspective characterized by the clash of private interests each seeking to win dominance over the other. Newmann fears that participating in the political process only reinforces an intern's view of "politics as usual," which leads to further diminishment of civic life, rather than enhancement of it.

More systematic analyses of the effects of internships on students have produced mixed results. Alan Balutis (1977) found no significant changes in the political efficacy or political cynicism scores of interns participating in the New York State Assembly program. In contrast, Janet Eyler and Beth Halteman (1981) report that interns in the Tennessee legislature understood the nuances of politics much better than their counterparts who studied it in the classroom or who were not selected for the internship program. Ironically, Eyler and Halteman's findings only add fire to Newmann's fears about internships.

In my view, the Furman program attempts to avoid the pitfalls discussed by Newmann and Couto and Becker as well as draw on what Eyler and Halteman consider to be strengths of the Tennessee legislative program. To wit, the program attempts to educate students not only to the realities of politics, but also to the normative implications of those arrangements. Students participating in the state and local public affairs internship program demonstrate this ability to understand reality and to critique it in four distinct ways, and each contributes to the development of better citizens. First, Furman interns leave the experience more passionate and interested in politics. Second, they are more sophisticated in their understanding of the complexities of public policy and the difficulty of making decisions. Third, former interns also know the difficulty of operating a political system democratically. And, finally, they leave their internships with a deeper respect for the system, both its strengths and flaws.

One of the great strengths of internship programs with strong reflective components is that students become more passionate about politics and public policy issues. Students begin to read the newspaper on a regular basis (they find it impossible to survive in their internships without doing so), which leads to a continuing debate about public policy. If one of the goals of citizenship is constant deliberation and political talk, internships seem to produce this result. The passion has another result: Students are more interested in participating in traditional classroom discussions and feel more confident in speaking. This passion creates more desire to participate in community activities and on-campus activities.

Students also begin to see issues in terms other than black and white; even students who have worked in partisan settings return with a better understanding of the nuances of public policy. This, too, contributes to the development of better citizens, for it indicates that interns are trying to seek the common good. Many of our interns eventually work in public sector settings or with advocacy groups, and the program has contributed to their desire to seek such careers. A commitment to seek a common good seems to be instilled in students through the internship experiences.

Few interns leave the internship without being exposed to inequality and injustice. Legal services interns constantly bring examples of the problems indigent clients face in securing adequate representation. While attempting to understand how the political process operates (and power relationships in general), students do not lose sight of the normative consequences of empirical relationships. While the Furman program may favor making sense of empirical observations, it does not eschew normative analyses.

While criticisms of the system are known, interns also leave with a well-grounded appreciation of representative government. They understand that many elected officials are very concerned about their communities and are attempting to enact better public policy. This deepening respect for elected officials seems necessary to foster greater respect for the system. And this greater respect contributes to better citizens.

While "producing better citizens" is difficult to assess, the Furman program seems to have accomplished this goal. Participants leave the internship with an elevated passion for politics, a more nuanced understanding of public policy issues and the need to seek the common good, an empirically grounded but normatively sensitive view of power relationships, and a healthy respect for the American political system. These characteristics seem to hold for both the long term and the short term, though the program has been in existence for a relatively short period.

## Coming of Age: The Challenge

For many years, public affairs internships occupied a space in the recesses of the political science curriculum. In the past ten years, however, public affairs internships have come of age largely because of their potential to teach students to be better learners and problem solvers, to integrate theory and practice, and to provide citizenship education. To accomplish these lofty goals, administrators and others charged with directing internship programs need to pay careful attention to the literature on experiential education. Merely sending students out into the field will not accomplish the aforementioned goals.

The Furman program appears to have met important goals (among them producing better citizens), and it has done so because of its stalwart commitment to reflection through journal exercises, seminar presentations, and weekly debriefings in the internship seminar. Care also must be taken in selecting agency supervisors and ensuring that students are adequately prepared to enter the field. Internship proponents must seize the current era of goodwill toward experiential learning and use it to promote theoretically informed programs. To do less will ensure that internships once again will be returned to their lowly status, and the moment will have been lost.

*6*

# Enhancing Citizenship through Active Learning: Simulations on the Policy Process

*Joseph Cammarano and Linda L. Fowler*

Americans of all ages are increasingly cynical about government and politics, but their level of dissatisfaction is most pronounced—and disturbing—among the young. For political science professors this trend poses a particular challenge because students mistrust the people and processes we study, and they bring attitudes into the classroom that are often at odds with the facts we teach. If students equate politics with corruption, how do we convey the difference between legitimate compromise and "selling out"? If they see public officials as scoundrels, how do we get them to recognize effective leadership? In our classes, we have turned to policy simulations to help students appreciate why politics produces particular outcomes, in the hopes of supplanting cynicism with understanding.

There has been a general decline in public trust in government among all adults since the 1960s (Lipset and Schneider 1987). The irony of American democracy is that as our political system has become a more open and democratic system, the public's disgust and dissatisfaction with government has increased. Since 1960, the level of trust and faith in our national government has plummeted. Various analysts disagree over the causes and the effects of this negativity, but one thing seems clear: Americans are less than admiring of government and governmental processes. Empirical evidence abounds on this point. For example, results from the 1994 National Election Study reveal a wide-

101

spread belief that government wastes money and does not look after the interests of common citizens.

Just as faith in government is low among adults, a yearly study, *Monitoring the Future*—an ongoing study of the lifestyles and values of high school seniors—verifies that low levels of trust and confidence in government exist as well among young people. In the spring of 1993, over 90 percent of high school seniors believed that government officials did not know what they were doing in their jobs, just 20 percent approved of the performance of the U.S. Congress, and only 13 percent said they were satisfied with the way the government was operating.

Nowhere is this distrust more widespread than the feelings people have toward the Congress. Support for Congress is consistently lower than for the presidency or the Supreme Court (Hibbing and Theiss-Morse 1995). Even those who have served in Congress have joined in the criticism of the institution (see, e.g., Penny and Garrett 1995). There are several explanations for this increased negativism toward legislative democracy. Some place blame on the highly partisan nature of the contemporary Congress at a time when the electorate is less partisan in their political affinities than in previous generations. Others focus on the misdeeds of highly visible individual members. Still others point to the rise of individualistic politics, where self-interested careerists seek to maximize their own political fortunes by criticizing the very institution in which they serve. Perhaps the most provocative explanation, however, comes from John Hibbing and Elizabeth Theiss-Morse (1995) who argue that the public distrust of Congress is caused in part by the nature of the institution itself and in part by the distaste of the American people for the natural process of legislative decision making. In a comprehensive study of the rising distrust of Congress among the public, Hibbing and Theiss-Morse contend that along with our love for democracy is a general disdain for democratic processes that are by definition slow, full of compromises, and unable to definitively solve perceived social problems. Thus, the democratic process itself, replete with vacillation and deal making, has turned off the public. They conclude, "A surprising number of people dislike being exposed to processes endemic to democratic government. People do not wish to see uncertainty, conflicting opinions, long debate, competing interests, confusion, bargaining, and compromised, imperfect solutions" (1995, 147). In short, people do not like democracy as it is practiced in Congress.

To be fair, some of this skepticism expressed by the public is based on an accurate reading of the policy process. Those individuals and groups with substantial political resources *do* tend to win out over those with fewer political resources. The policy process *is* extremely messy, complex, and elongated. Public problems are almost never fully solved by new laws. And there is a tremendous amount of conflict—something many people spend much of their lives avoiding—in the policy process. Politicians and political analysts are to some degree out of touch with the concerns of much of the public. On the other hand, many of the criticisms of Congress are exaggerated, and stem from a basic misunderstanding about political structure and process, the lack of attention many people give to the policy process, and a distorted view on the part of citizens about how and why political elites behave as they do. Also, there is a substantial misreading of the policy process itself. What is often interpreted as partisan bickering, gridlock, and political grandstanding is, in reality, democracy at work. Rather than understanding the pluralistic forces at work in the formulation of public policy, Americans tend to turn away in horror and disgust. We seem to have accepted the admonition of Otto von Bismarck that laws, like sausages, should only be viewed in their completed form.

The level of distrust and dislike of government is related to the drop in participation over the past twenty-five years. The overall percentage of eligible voters who decide to vote has declined since 1960, with the exception of the 1992 and 1994 elections (Conway 1988; Teixera 1987; Burnham 1987; Gant and Luttbeg 1993). This drop in voting rates is most pronounced among young Americans. Although the rates of participation among young voters have never approached the rates of older segments of the population (Wolfinger and Rosenstone 1980), the magnitude of the decline since 1972 is greater than the decline among those of other ages. So, alongside a general decline in political activity among the American people—a troubling pattern itself—our youngest citizens aren't getting involved in politics.

The need for active, optimistic, and engaged citizens is particularly important in contemporary times. The current state of American politics arguably demands more of citizens than at any other time in our history. Although American government has been considered a democracy since the eighteenth century, it was not until the twentieth century that our government evolved into a system with widespread suffrage and mass political participation. The enfranchisement of women, African Americans, and young adults has served to increase the number of people eligible to vote in elections. The Progressive Era reforms of initiative and referendum put policy decisions directly in the hands of voters. Polling and communications technologies make citizen input into government action not only commonplace, but expected. The irony of less participation in a more open, more democratic political system and consistently lower rates of participation among young people presents perhaps the most important puzzle for those who study political participation, and it is an important challenge to political science teachers. How do we instill our students with a sense that their own interest and participation, in politics do matter?

Political science education has always attempted to provide a depth of understanding that is in part an antidote to political mistrust and cynicism. The great challenge for teachers is to present information to students that acknowledges both sides of this equation, solutions that seek to educate students about the workings of Congress while also acknowledging that the process has its problems. Many of us who teach courses on Congress, the legislative process, and public policy do offer potential institutional reforms for fixing the problems of Congress. However, we must also consciously try to use the policy process itself as a tool to reduce political cynicism. Often such efforts are only implicitly included in the curriculum and unconscious in our methods. But by consciously providing a framework for analyzing political institutions and processes, our courses can give students a better understanding of the complexities involved in political decision making and, one hopes, reduce the animosity toward those in the policy process.

In the remainder of this chapter we discuss how simulations can offer students a different view of the policy process. In effect, students learn firsthand how rules, institutions, and political incentives shape the policy process, and they have to deal with the uncomfortable truth that good people can make poor policies for perfectly understandable reasons. We begin with a brief discussion of simulations and their pedagogical benefits. Next we consider how political science is particularly well suited to the use of simulations, as these exercises can convey the complexity and nuances of politics in a way that readings and class discussions can sometimes miss. Although students can read any of a number of excellent books that detail the policy process, by taking the role of a player in the policy game they gain a clearer understanding of *why* members of Congress, the White House, the press, and interest groups behave the way they do. Simulations thus help students understand the difficulty of political decision making and can even give them a better appreciation for public service.

After our discussion of the value of simulations, we turn to a description of a simulation we conducted that simultaneously encompassed two courses, one on the U.S. Congress, the other on the presidency. The simulation required students to pass a federal budget resolution for the upcoming fiscal year. We describe the steps we took in preparing for the simulation, the rules developed for the simulation, and the way the simulations played out. We understand that every instructor who uses simulations conducts them in a unique manner, and we offer this description as but one example of how to operationalize course objectives in a simulation. Finally, we draw conclusions about the advantages and the disadvantages simulations offer for those who are concerned with providing citizenship education. We believe that students gain both intellectually and personally from participating in simulations, and in doing so, they can be nudged by such experiences toward better citizenship.

## Simulations and Active Learning

Simulations are not new. In one form or another, they have been around for thousands of years. They have been used to teach soldiers how to act in times of war since at least the nineteenth century, and many games of strategy have the same purpose as simulations: to incorporate content learning into a fictional competitive environment (van Ments 1989). In education, simulations increased in popularity during the sixties when psychologist Jerome Bruner advocated the use of games to motivate students to be more active in learning about social organizations (Bruner 1963). The advocacy of active learning in education that occurred in the 1960s led to the establishment of several organizations that developed games and simulations for classroom learning (Taylor and Walford 1972). The use of active learning strategies may have waned somewhat in the 1980s, but it never disappeared. The 1990s have seen a resurgence of various forms of simulations, aided in large part by the development of complex computer programs that can closely mimic actual events in the world (Towne, de Jong and Spada 1993). In political science, for example, there are many computer simulations available in foreign policy, political campaigning, and other political processes.

John Taylor and Rex Walford (1972) cite three major attributes of simulations that are important for our concerns. First, they are focused on learning through activity. Second, they are problem-solving exercises that encourage the use of social skills needed for real-world work. Third, a simulation is by nature dynamic, requiring flexibility and adaptation during the exercise.

Chesler and Fox (1966) cite additional advantages to using simulations. By requiring students to take an active role in the exercise, simulations motivate students to be involved in course content. They allow students to see how readings relate to actual circumstances of politics. Simulations can also motivate students who are not active in other areas of the course. Many students claim that they are better at activities than they are at writing papers and answering exam questions, and that by playing a role, they are better able to understand the course materials. Simulations give such students a chance to prove themselves. They can also force students to take responsibility for the success of the exercise, and see to it that the game is played fairly, fully, and successfully. At times, they change the attitudes of students as well.

In our experience, a simulation is an excellent tool for promoting citizenship education. Using the presupposition of citizenship education presented in this volume—that the key to promoting citizenship is making students active—simulations fall comfortably into the category of teaching techniques that promote citizenship. In the effort to find solutions to real issues that are amenable to a majority of individuals in the exercise, students learn to appreciate the inherent difficulties, not only with the exercise at hand, but also with the legislative process employed by Congress. This in turn leads them to be more understanding and empathetic toward political elites. By requiring active participation and encouraging students to take an interest in the project, simulations also promote a shift from teacher-based instruction to student self-instruction. In working through problems on their own, students come to understand the connection between their own behavior and the success (or failure) of political processes (Brandhorst 1990). The end result is that students learn that political processes are as much a product of the interests involved as the process by which policy is made, and that their own activity or inactivity could have significant consequences on the output of the policy process.

## Using Simulations in American Politics Courses

Simulations are a natural fit with courses in political science. The goal of most undergraduate courses is to introduce students to the content of the field, the details of the subject matter, and the complexities of the subjects under study. Since most political science courses address questions of the distribution of power and authority, there is a close connection between traditional course content and the use of simulations. They can, in other words, supplement lectures and readings with the application of concepts to a specific case or cases. By connecting the academic curriculum with a game of the actual processes under study, students are better able to see the connections between the ideas presented in the course and the practice of politics. For example, in a course on the Congress, a simulation reinforces the lesson that it is difficult to operate in a system of decentralized power, atomized interests, and constant political competition. For courses on the presidency, a simulation drives home the problem presidents face in trying to build coalitions in a system focused on individual congressional representatives and their constituency interests, as well as interest groups mobilized for particularized interests. Simulations in courses on parties or interest groups force students to come to terms with trying to seek influence in a system designed to thwart direct influence. Simulations require students to apply their knowledge of politics, and in doing so, help them to integrate information into political practice and develop a richer conception of American politics.

As with any simulation in education, there are some other major advantages to conducting simulations in political science courses. First, they increase student interest and motivation in the course. Our own experience supports this. Students who were marginally interested in course materials became more engaged with the course as a result of the simulation. Second, by putting students in a situation where they have either limited or no direct experience, and by giving them control over the decisions to be made within the simulation, they are forced to develop their own ideas and solutions. By challenging students to solve their own questions, simulations provoke students into thinking about how to apply course information to the context in which they find themselves. Third, students get a clear indication that their actions have consequences. Decisions they make can often be directly linked to actual outcomes. Actions they take or fail to take have an impact on the final result, which makes clear to them the importance of personal initiative for political processes.

In addition to providing students with the motivation to learn about the subject of the simulation, these exercises offer benefits that go beyond those obtained by traditional teaching methods. One such benefit comes from the human interaction that occurs. From working with others in a cooperative game, students come in contact with individuals who have different personalities and worldviews. They learn firsthand that political decisions must be reached through working with others who may not share the same ideas or interests. They also learn to deal with different personalities, and come to realize that the process of making decisions is more than simply taking a vote or imposing one's view on others. Finally, students see how others behave in simulations, which in turn helps them to make generalizations about human behavior. Learning about personalities and human behavior in social contexts is an important addition that simulations offer to classroom learning (Taylor and Walford 1972).

Although there are many positive benefits to using simulations in courses, there are also some pitfalls, the most significant being time. Too much time taken in a simulation can distract the students from learning an adequate amount of course content. Because simulations involve complex processes, they are usually very time-consuming, both for those taking part and for those who coordinate the game. There are significant operational concerns. Securing proper rooms, setting up the rules of the game, monitoring the participants, and consistently enforcing policies can all be problematic, and such tasks present demands on time above and beyond that normally spent on class preparation. There is also a question of equity. Some students take an active role in simulations while others do not. This can occur by choice, and sometimes it is the effect of the unequal balance of power and authority in the real world. Additionally, there is the difficulty that occurs in grading students on their work in simulations. Although written assignments can and should be required parts of simulations, it is not easy to capture the quality of students' performances in a fair and consistent manner. A final pitfall concerns the perceptions that students may have about simulations. Since they are enjoyable and do not always require students to work in the traditional sense of course requirements, there is always a danger that students will not take simulations seriously. Given these various problems related to conducting simulations, teachers must weigh the relative costs and benefits before deciding to conduct them. Although there are some dangers, our own experience leads us to be strong advocates for simulations of the policy process. The academic benefits coupled with the empowering effects they have had on our students make simulations worth the extra work and risk.


## Conducting Simulations

Simulations are demanding of instructors. There are many considerations that must be addressed; among them: having a clear purpose for running a simulation, putting into place the necessary plans for the game, knowing what it is the students are to experience, clearly communicating to students the purpose of the simulation, coming as close to reality as possible without getting bogged down in trivial replication of unimportant details, and properly integrating the simulation experience into the broader course materials. In this section, we describe in detail a simulation we conducted in two political science courses, one on the presidency, the other on the Congress and the legislative process. We have used simulations in different ways than those summarized below, and our experience is certainly not unique (see e.g., Endersby and Webber 1995), but we believe that a discussion of our own experience using simulations will illustrate their value for teaching course materials and for developing a more active sense of citizenship in our students.

Our simulation exercises were unique in several respects. First, we joined two large lecture classes, one on the Congress and the other on the presidency, that met separately during the term. Our joint effort created logistical problems, but it also enabled us to prepare students for specialized roles, with the members of the Congress class assuming the part of senators and lobbyists and those in the presidency class assuming responsibilities of administration officials and the media. It also meant that we were able to field a sizable legislative body, making the simulation more complex and more realistic.

Second, we set the game up to require transactions and bargains among the participants. Players received various types of currency—vote cards, PAC contributions cards, presidential access cards, and so forth—which they used to negotiate desired provisions in the budget resolution. This feature of the game helped to break the ice among students and gave them a stake in the outcome that truly sparked their competitive spirits. To drive home the point that politics depends upon people keeping their word, we required the students to keep a record of their transactions, which we then used as a means of evaluating their performance during the game. In addition, we instituted an ethics violation procedure to inhibit participants from breaking the campaign finance regulations and to deal with egregious betrayals of constituents that no real-life senator would have made.

Third, we used journalists to provide a record of each day's proceedings and to serve as an outlet for players' press releases and public statements. We also used the journalists to ferret out scandals that we planned during the game regarding various players.

Finally, we developed an abbreviated set of parliamentary rules and a concise version of the budget procedures to facilitate floor debate. We had the vice president preside over the Senate, assisted in making rulings on points of order and amendments by one of us.

## Planning

The most important aspect of planning simulations concerns the overall design of the course. The course outline must effectively allocate time for a simulation while not taking too much time from important class materials. In addition, students need to be given adequate background information on the process they will mimic before engaging in the simulations. This means our simulations were generally conducted late in the semester. This enabled us to prepare the students by teaching them the core concepts of the presidency and Congress. When students began the simulation they had already completed most of the course materials. This gave them the content they needed for understanding the mechanics of the legislative process, the motives of the various political actors, and the details of current political debate. Of course, simulations may also be conducted throughout the semester. The advantage to the latter approach is that it mimics the actual legislative process, which is often drawn out and only a part of the daily workload of those involved in the process. In either case, however, students must have a base of knowledge about the process before a simulation can begin.

Course readings naturally complemented the simulation. Students in the presidency course read books that examined some of the recent developments in the institution as well as the processes and politics of the presidency. The readings focused on important trends related to the ability of presidents to lead in an increasingly complex and individualistic political system. Assigned books dealt with the evolution of the presidency from a party-based institution to one dependent upon individual presidents and their loyalists residing within the White House staff. Other readings focused on presidential leadership of Congress under such a system, and the budgetary process. The course on the Congress also used traditional course materials to prepare students, assigning readings on the evolution of the contemporary congressional leadership system, the behavior of individual members of Congress, and the legislative process itself.

Additional preparation for the simulation was given in supplemental assignments. In both courses, students were assigned specific roles, and were then required to research their roles. We decided to assign students to be actual members of the political system rather than creating fictional characters. This made role-playing more concrete, as students could research their character and develop a clear outline of what their role entailed in the simulation. Students in the Congress course were required to submit a brief paper outlining how their particular character should act in the budget simulation. Students in the presidency course were required to meet as groups to plan the overall strategy and to make decisions about lines of authority and communication.

Perhaps the most important planning decision is the topic of the simulation. Policy simulations can take the form of a specific piece or pieces of legislation. The benefit to this approach is that it limits the scope of the simulation to a relatively manageable issue. For example, in past years when we had students develop specific public policies, students reformed the welfare system, created a national service corps, debated the flat income tax, outlawed the use of tobacco, and considered creating a death penalty for those convicted of rape. The downside to this approach is that students can make decisions about the legislation and amendments without any concern for the fiscal realities of lawmaking. Given the current era of contraction in federal discretionary spending, a lack of adequate attention to fiscal matters makes for a less realistic simulation.

We prefer to use the budget resolution as the focus of our simulations for several reasons. First, it involves a process that includes the entire scope of federal government activity. By setting spending targets, students are forced to make difficult decisions about the priorities of government. In addition, the budget resolution permits the use of a wide range of interest group representatives, and it also requires those who play members of the Senate to face up to the competing interests to which they must attend. Third, the resolution is a good balance between giving students a complete picture of the budgetary process and the impracticality of students understanding the daunting task of congressional authorization and appropriations processes. The budget resolution requires students to make overall decisions about government priorities and to use realistic numbers without getting bogged down in specific line items, a task that is surely too great for a simulation only one or two weeks long. Finally, the role of the president is great at the start of the budgetary process, and so we were able to have many roles for students in the presidency course. By using a separate course for the White House, we were also better able to replicate the separation of powers. Although there was much informal talk between students in the two courses, the two classes were generally isolated from each other, and the simulations naturally developed into a competition for power between the different institutions.

One final aspect to planning is logistical. Great care must be taken to ensure that the proper facilities are reserved for the simulation. This includes rooms suitable for legislative hearings, open areas fit for lobbying and press interviews, conference rooms for negotiations or strategy sessions, and a room that is an adequate stand-in for a legislative chamber. In our experience, physical surroundings play an important role in the simulation, particularly in the way they encourage or discourage informal communication between students.


**Running a Simulation**

Since the simulations were applications of much of what the students studied in the course, students were well prepared before the start of the game. Prior to beginning the simulation, we outlined to our classes the process by which the federal budget resolution is approved. We emphasized how the resolution is a blueprint for the actual federal budget approved later in the year. Students were assigned roles for the simulation earlier in the semester and were required to write profiles of their characters. A schedule of the simulation was included within the course syllabus, so students knew when they needed to be ready for the start of the game. Classes were reserved so that students could conduct both formal and informal meetings, and we also instructed students to work outside class time, as the real legislative process is not bound by class schedules. Students were given a minimal amount of structure for conducting the role-play. Again, this was done consciously to convey to students that there is no specific blueprint for those involved in politics, and that individual initiative and planned (or serendipitous) cooperation explains a great deal of the outcome of public policy. Although much of the official simulation occurred during class time or during special hours allotted for meetings, debate, and voting, the results of the simulation were affected more by the informal communication that took place between participants, the deals that were arranged among players in the game, and the organizing that was done by the leaders in the game. Students noted after the completion of the simulation that the vast majority of the time they spent on the project was outside the scheduled events.

In running a simulation an important decision needs to be made regarding the amount of structure to be imposed upon the students. Some of our students have commented that they felt that we gave them too little direction about the specific duties. This is a perennial concern for some, but our overall preference was to give as little direction as possible. Loose structure required students to be more active in making judgments about the extent of their role in the simulation. It also gave creative students the opportunity to inject enormous energy and effort into their role. It drove home the point (with some friendly prodding by the instructor) that the political system has structure and rules but no exact plan or outline for political activism, and that political success often comes from the organization, creativity, grit, and determination of individuals and groups. The downside to loosely structured and defined roles is that some students will not perform their duties. This is a serious problem, one that can be mitigated somewhat by making it clear to students that they will be graded for their work and that any failure on their part to at least attempt to achieve the goals set out for their role will adversely affect their simulation grade. By having students spell out the goals of their character prior to the start of the simulation, we avoided many of these potential problems.

In our experience, simulations, once planned and explained, generally run themselves. Still, there are some important ways for instructors to ensure that the simulation is an effective learning experience. Those students who are assigned to be legislators, congressional staffers, or members of the presidential administration have official roles in the process. However, lobbyists and members of the press have no direct role. To integrate peripheral characters into the simulation we created a system in which interest groups and members of the press have resources attractive to governmental officials. For interest groups, the main resources are money and votes. To simulate this we distributed cards to lobbyists based upon their real-world influence. For example, we gave large amounts of money (in the form of PAC contributions) to representatives of the defense, communications, and agricultural sectors, and many votes to those who represented the American Association of Retired Persons and the National Rifle Association. Those assigned to represent politically weak interests were given few resources to distribute. Members of the press were assigned to file stories and gain access to important officials. The presence of positive stories or the absence of negative stories was used as evidence for or against the performance of senators and members of the executive branch. We also required members of the Senate to accumulate the resources that would best help them achieve their goals. Members of the executive branch were given various resources, including money and access, to distribute to other players in ways consistent with White House strategy.

Keeping a record of all these transactions was the most difficult part of running the simulation. Each person in the game had to keep a tally of any transaction made with another individual and the terms of the agreement reached between parties. Each transaction required the signature of the parties involved, and each side was bound to live by the terms of the agreement; failure to do so resulted in a reduction in the grade the violator received for the simulation. Despite the administrative difficulty of monitoring the hundreds of transactions that occurred in the simulation, such effort was worth the energy. A written agreement provided a paper trail for judging students' performance in the simulation. In deciding whether a senator achieved her goals of reelection, institutional power, or promoting good policy, we were able to evaluate the various agreements reached and determine whether this goal was reached. Without a detailed record of transactions for each student it would have been unlikely that we could have systematically evaluated student performance in the simulation.

Another consideration in running the simulation is the degree of involvement by the instructors. Some involvement was direct. In one year, one of us played the role of the president, delivering the State of the Union address, participating in White House planning, meeting with friendly interests, and negotiating directly with senators when deemed necessary. This had a significant impact on the simulation, as it created a strong and dominant president. This impact, however, was more a function of the authority and personality of the instructor than it was an accurate illustration of presidential leadership. The more realistic and beneficial involvement of instructors is in the form of indirect influence; cosmic interventions were made periodically to right wrongs or to settle intractable conflicts. For example, at various times we created scandals, leaked information to the press, and spread rumors about pending agreements between various players in the game. We also found it necessary in a few instances to stop the simulation briefly and settle personal conflicts or disputes over the implementation of rules.

Our budget simulation began with the State of the Union address, and the concurrent submission by the White House of a proposed budget resolution. From there, time was scheduled for budget committee hearings of expert testimony and for marking up the resolution; for informal gatherings of all students to lobby, interview, and strike bargains with others; and for final floor consideration of the budget resolution. As noted above, this was only a portion of the time students spent in the simulation. Those who had central roles in the simulation conducted many private conversations and meetings to hammer out the resolution and to orchestrate partisan or group activity. When the resolution was scheduled for final consideration, students were warned that they were required to attend this session, and that nobody would be excused until a final resolution was passed. This final session often turned into a meeting of several hours, and the end result was often a document that was dramatically different from what most players in the game wanted. By the final hour of the simulation the pace of compromising and deal making was staggering as students rushed to finish the session and to get at least something they desired in the final resolution.

## Evaluating the Simulation

Students picked up an enormous wealth of information about process, politics, and human relations from simulations. Many of these lessons concerned the interactions they had in the simulation and were self-evident to most students. Still, it was important to have students reflect systematically on their experience. We chose two basic methods to do so. First, we spent a class period debriefing students about their experiences. Each simulation brought a slightly different lesson, but some patterns emerged in virtually every one. First, students were amazed at the unequal balance of influence. Those assigned to represent interests with few or no political resources were frustrated that they had a hard time getting senators to listen to them. Junior senators, those from relatively small states, and those in the minority felt left out of key meetings and discussions. Senators felt a bit flustered by lobbyists throwing cash at them and expecting some tangible benefits in return, and members of the press felt that they were both using members and were being used by them. By discussing the simulation after its completion, students were able to broaden the lessons beyond their own personal experiences. This was also an excellent opportunity to return to course readings and make the connections between the research in the field and the simulation.

The second evaluative tool used was an essay students wrote about their experiences. In this essay, they assessed whether they had set realistic goals for themselves, the degree to which they achieved the goals, the barriers they faced, and whether the simulation was a net win or loss for their character. Students were also asked to take a step back from the simulation, to reflect more broadly on the process of public policy and make conclusions about the policy process in general. These essays often expressed an impressive depth of understanding of contemporary legislative politics. Although it is difficult to generalize from all students, the essays displayed a considerable understanding of the complexities of our pluralistic political system and the challenges presented by modern democracy. Most students commented that they gained a deeper understanding of the policy process and a greater appreciation for members of Congress.

Overall, students learned three general things from the simulations. First, and most important for citizenship education, they felt empowered toward political activity. Some students went into the simulation with career goals related to politics. At the conclusion of the exercise, most of these students had an even greater desire to find jobs in politics. For these students the simulation reinforced preexisting attitudes and served to heighten their interest in politics. A second group of students could be classified as either ambivalent or uninterested in political activity. In many ways, this is the group to which simulations are targeted, as they are like the citizens who are moderately interested in politics, but not predisposed toward political involvement. The simulations did not change all of these students, but many did develop a greater appreciation for the process, and a few of these students became activated through the simulation. Two years after the simulation, a student commented:

> *I wasn't very much interested in this stuff before the simulation, but that experience helped me to see how important it is for those of us who care about others to be involved. If we aren't, only the politically powerful will win. I now pay attention to what goes on and I may even get involved someday.*

A second student who expressed ambivalence about politics wrote in a course evaluation: "I never understood the big deal in Washington. Now at least I know that fights are often over real ideas and that what they do there does make a difference in my life."

Of course, the simulation also had the opposite effect. A third, relatively small group of students commented that they had an interest in politics prior to the simulation, but their experience led them to turn their attention elsewhere. Of the few students who noted this effect, most cited the constant arguing and the petty games they felt they had to play as the source of their disgust.

The second important effect simulations had was that they created empathy among students for those who are involved in real policy debates. One student noted in reflecting on his experience: "I didn't realize how hard this was. I have a lot of admiration for those who have to do this in the real world." This sentiment was common among our students, and verifies that one of the purposes to using simulations—to convey to students that legislators, lobbyists, and presidential appointees engage in a difficult balancing act—was successfully transmitted. Although we did not advocate hero worship toward politicians, we did try to get students to think about them as being subject to complex pressures. The simulations helped us to achieve this goal.

The third important effect that simulations had on students was the demystification of the policy process. Students were often amazed at their own abilities to understand rather complex issues and staggering fiscal details about the federal budget. This helped them to see that public policy, even fiscal policy, was something they could understand. Many students were fearful of the simulation, as they felt they had neither the ability nor the expertise to debate the federal budget. By the end of the simulation, students understood the overall importance of the budget as well as those portions of the budget that mattered most to their own interests. This demystification is important, as it led students to conclude that members of Congress, lobbyists, presidential aides, and the media were no more or less capable than any other group of similarly educated individuals. This humanizing effect was important, as students understood politicians for what they are, a subset of the American people, subject to the enormous demands of a fragmented political system and a pluralistic polity. This, we believe, is an important step in both political science education and education for citizenship.

## Conclusion: The Effectiveness of Simulations

In assessing the usefulness of course simulations, there are two important considerations. The first relates to whether simulations are effective for teaching about American politics. We are confident they are. Our own experience leads us to conclude that students have a much better understanding of the legislative process, particularly the budget. They develop a more complete awareness about the complexity of political decision making. They also tend to become more sophisticated in their assessment of congressional behavior. The sheer intricacy of budgetary politics is made clear, and students begin to see political officials as having a much more difficult job than most people imagine.

We have anecdotal evidence that in addition to learning within the confines of the course, students learn useful things in the simulation. We have had several students over the years who have gone to Washington to work as interns or in full-time positions in and out of government. These students have frequently commented that the simulations were excellent preparations for their Washington work. Some have commented that the hands-on nature of the simulations made the connections between academic learning and real-world experience easier to see and to apply. In addition to the comments of these students are comments we received from students in their evaluations of the courses. Positive comments about the simulation were frequent, with students citing the fun they had in the simulation, the amount of information they gained in the exercise, and the desire to expand the simulation to permit more time for the game.

The second consideration is whether simulations offer students anything in the form of citizenship. Again, we believe that they do help students to become better citizens. As noted above, much of the contemporary distrust of Congress among the American people is the result of a basic misunderstanding of democratic processes. Compromise, argument, protracted debate, and paying attention to the needs of interest groups are all part of our brand of democracy. When students are faced with the realities of the process, they begin to see politics in a different light. The more realistic, demystified understanding of politics that emerged helped to reduce the skepticism that seems all too frequent among our students. The better understanding of the process gave them a new appreciation for the importance of the legislative process in their own lives. By increasing students' consciousness, simulations help to activate them to better citizenship.

7

# Doing the Rights Thing: Tales of Citizenship and Free Speech

*Marc Lendler*

Let this be the distinctive mark of an American, that in cases of commotion he enlists under no man's banner, but repairs to the standard of the law.

—Thomas Jefferson

Like many teachers, including other contributors to this book, I have often found that student involvement in political life enhances the classroom teaching and learning experience. In a course on elections, I required students to choose a campaign to work in; in courses on workplace democracy I have benefited greatly from the contributions of students who had spent time doing blue-collar work. I have had students who interned for legislators, worked as lobbyists, or participated in cause-related organizations. The value that hands-on experience has for the students and the contributions it enables them to make to class discussion is considerable. Concepts come to life; the purposes of compromise become clearer; and above all, the serious stakes behind the public circus of politics become more apparent. Confronting practical situations can be a valuable aid in focusing attention and clarifying underlying principles. The 1960s rallying cry of "relevance" may have been overdone, but it did have some kernels of truth.

This education-through-involvement effect is magnified when the "practical politics" side is one of high stakes and passionate argument. That was the backdrop of the three terms in which I taught a course at Bennington College entitled Free Speech in America. In the four-year span of the course, there was escalating controversy over the very is-

119

sues that we were studying. Twice, campuswide conflict over free expression broke out in the middle of the course. What was evident both in and out of class was the development in student judgment and the way in which a more complex understanding emerged of the relation between different kinds of rights and between the right of free expression and other values.

The campuswide speech rights debates emerged as the college began to move toward the "restructuring" that included mass faculty firings and created a firestorm of controversy and publicity in June 1994.[1] As one part of the "reinvention" of higher education, school officials appeared to be drawn to the argument that there has been an excessive emphasis on individual rights and that students and faculty have lost sight of "the other half of freedom": responsibility (Symposium Report 1994, 12). That problem was seen as endemic: both the college and the country had suffered from a deemphasis on community. Thus the free-speech debates in class and on campus unfolded with an administration increasingly committed to the view that free speech is only one value among several and one that has been prone to abuse.

I should note at the outset that I am not advocating precipitating or taking steps to involve students in campus speech controversies (much less ones with the intensity of Bennington's) for the sake of better classes. Those debates seem to spring up frequently enough anyway. But using campus-based conflict as a microcosm of some otherwise abstract principles can be revelatory.


## Round One


Bennington was (and is) a tiny school that faced sharply declining enrollment and financial pressures during the time these events took place. The student body has always been composed disproportionately of those interested in the visual or performing arts; as a consequence, freedom of artistic expression has been high in the pantheon of student values. One symbol of the importance of art was the tradition of the President's Gallery, a rotating exhibit of student photography, painting, or sculpture in the hallway leading to the offices of the president and the dean of faculty. The hallway was also a throughway for students and teachers going to class, prospective students visiting campus, official visitors, and office staff going to work.

The duration of a student exhibit was between one and three weeks, and the method by which the space was reserved was a simple sign-up list in the Visual Arts Division. As could reasonably be expected, some of the exhibits featured nudity, and there were occasional murmurs of disapproval from those working in nearby offices or from passersby. But those who objected generally did so quietly.

In the 1991 fall term an exhibit appeared that escalated the murmuring to an uproar and posed the question of whether the school should prescribe what appeared in that space. A student hung a photography exhibit in which one of the pictures was a close-in shot of a female torso with a small amount of blood dripping from the vagina. Many passersby found it distasteful. The group that protested most vehemently was the office staff whose only means to and from their workplace was the hallway displaying the exhibit. They complained to the school administration and to the Visual Arts Division that they had no way to avoid seeing the photograph, which some said they found so upsetting that they were unable to perform their jobs. Some of the office workers pointed out that they had put up with a great deal that was offensive to them previously but that this went beyond the limits of what they should be asked to tolerate.

The exhibit was not removed. It stayed up for two weeks, longer than some others. The night before it was scheduled to come down as part of a regular rotation, someone stole the offending photograph. The exhibit was taken down without incident and the episode ended inconclusively. The school had neither ordered it taken down early nor issued any statement defending the student's right to exhibit it.

## Civil Liberties and Poetic License

The issues raised by the exhibit were not simple, but they were also not insoluble. The complexity existed primarily because this was not a traditional gallery, an area people could enter or leave at their own discretion. The traffic in the hallway was not voluntary in that sense. Those walls were also the most visible face of the college apart from the front gates and that would seem to argue that the school should have control over the decor. But the use of the term "President's Gallery" and the use of the space by signing and rotation implied to most students that the school had no right to review the contents of any exhibit before or after it was displayed.

There was an additional complicating factor. The fact that this hallway led directly to work space posed the problem of a captive audience

(Emerson 1970; Haiman 1981). Expression has always been subject to regulation of place, as well as time and manner (Cox 1981). And it was precisely the office workers who were raising the most vociferous objections.

The Supreme Court has reasoned that nonconsenting viewers may be protected from offensive material[2] but has placed a heavy burden on those who ask for protection to establish that they have no other means of avoiding the offending words or images.[3] The Court has also insisted that regulation on the grounds of time, place, or manner be content-neutral (Tribe 1988).[4] Applying these general principles to artistic expression, Carol Simpson Stern (1994) concluded that faculty and student artists should expect displays to be subject to refereeing to set qualitative standards and generally applied rules about placement. But ("above all") there should be no selective tests of propriety or ideology.

The exhibit debate occurred just as my class was discussing recent speech code and hate speech controversies on college campuses. At the beginning of the term I had told students there were two rules for the class. One was that in discussing offensive expression we had to use the words that were actually at issue. The other was that the class would not duck any relevant issue arising on campus, no matter how controversial (something of a risk in a school with no written statement on academic freedom). So I threw this one open to the class, hoping both to use it to ground our discussions and (for myself) to learn more about how students reacted to the situation. I caught the drift fairly quickly when the first comment was "Why are we even discussing this?" from a student who felt that this was such a clear-cut case of censorship that it was not worth debating. Prevailing sentiment in the class was the same, although a handful of students found the photograph and particularly its placement disturbing. Most students saw this as the ancient battle of avant-garde artist against narrow-minded and confining philistinism. The office workers were demanding censorship and the school administration, while it had taken no action, had a barely suppressed inclination to comply.

My own views on the exhibit were somewhat different and I outlined them to the class this way: the school had a right to decorate that area in any way it saw fit and had erred primarily in allowing those walls to be used for student-selected exhibits. In addition, the school had an obligation to pay attention to the complaints of the office workers since the hallway could be considered part of their work space and they were at least arguably a captive audience. I added that these principles should guide future policy. Up to that point this had functioned as a normal gallery and the school would have been wrong had it acted in an ad hoc way against this particular exhibit. That last point did not help; I had lost my audience. Before their eyes I had become Jerry Falwell railing against the Mapplethorpe exhibit.

Those who spoke in class seemed to be representative of student thinking in the school as a whole.[5] They accepted the notion that the degree of offense taken should determine what kind of art could be exhibited; the problem (to them) was that the office workers were excessively prudish. The specific conclusions they reached seemed less significant than their framing of the issue: any interference with artistic expression in that hallway was the equivalent of governmental suppression of *Ulysses*. This was simple (and typically youthful) libertarianism: no one can interfere with my rights to do what I want, when and where I want.

The school reacted to this and subsequent incidents with an equally simplistic communitarian rhetoric. There has been a substantial literature arguing that excessive rights talk "independent of any necessary relationship to responsibility" has distorted American political discourse (Glendon 1991, 11). "To take and not to give" (Etzioni 1993, 10)—the attitude said to be typical of rights-wielding lone wolf citizens—is responsible for a perceived decline in civil behavior (Galston 1995).

There is no single communitarian position on speech rights. By the very nature of the critique it makes of the place of rights in American political culture, it tends to draw attention to "indirect harms, cumulative injury, or damages that appear only long after the acts that precipitated them" (Glendon 1991, 110). Those "indirect harms" are what noncommunitarians such as Catharine MacKinnon (1993) point to in proposing legal sanctions for some categories of offensive expression. On the other hand, some prominent communitarian writers such as Amitai Etzioni (1993, 41) have specifically argued against suppressing "uncivil" speech: "Nothing should be done . . . to prevent creating or displaying works of which many may disapprove."

Referring to the school administration's arguments as a variant of communitarianism is inescapable shorthand. It does not imply that communitarians would agree with each of the positions taken. But it seems clear that their general analysis of rights and responsibility strongly influenced official rhetoric. Communitarians generally believe that civility and social responsibility are values co-equal to individual rights.

It is nevertheless entirely consistent to advocate achieving them by incentive and persuasion rather than coercion. School officials made no such distinction in the aftermath of this incident. The president argued that the way to resolve the conflict was to bring the student artist together with the office workers to hear personally how real their anger was. Bennington's size could be an advantage, she said, because a community as small as this should be able to discuss these matters within itself, learn more about each other's values, and make decisions based on increased mutual understanding. "Rights" was too fragmenting and depersonalizing a concept to be useful in adjudicating conflicts, and a preoccupation with them corroded a sense of community. The office workers should be heard (in this rendition) not because they were a captive audience, but because they were offended members of the community. It was the degree of offense taken, not the ambiguity of the "President's Gallery" that was the issue. In keeping with this approach, the school would not pledge to permit offending displays in areas more conventionally understood as galleries.

## Round Two

After the exhibit came down, the school organized a discussion group of faculty, staff, and students to examine the controversy and the broader issues of free speech and artistic expression on campus. The group held several discussions and left the issue unresolved, due in part to the normal force of entropy but also in part to the administration's position that collective discussion was more important than establishing policy. The only change made was that the Visual Arts Division would review potential exhibits to determine their appropriateness for the President's Gallery. The new policy was quickly ignored in practice, and the situation returned to the status quo ante: students displaying their work simply by signing for the space. This made it almost certain that there would be a next round of debate, and there was, coinciding with my second free speech course.

What caused the controversy this time was not offensiveness but content and timing. After having signed for space in the normal manner, a student hung an exhibit of photographs and writings that contained criticism of an administration decision from the previous summer about student housing. This display was crude, even chaotic, and included writing on the walls in violation of a "place" regulation that was well known. But much the same could be said about other exhibits in that area. The real problem was that it was hung on the day prospective students were visiting campus.

Bennington has been underenrolled for several years, and recruiting freshmen was seen as critically important. Some school officials, apparently concerned that this exhibit might have an adverse affect on recruitment, called the chairman of the Visual Arts Division and asked whether the exhibit met the unwritten guidelines for the President's Gallery. The chairman came to the hallway, looked at it, and concluded it did not. He asked the student to move it to another viewing area; when the student declined, a security guard removed it and put it in a less visible area.

As an example of conflict management, the decision was an immediate and predictable disaster. Rather than walking by an exhibit that was largely incomprehensible to outsiders, prospective students were treated to two days of sometimes vituperative debate and accusations of censorship. The scope and intensity of the controversy dwarfed the first incident. When the exhibit was taken down, some students responded by putting up an even cruder display in protest, including a poster of the school president as a Nazi. Ironically, this poster stayed up for several days and was seen by more prospective students than the one it replaced.[6]

This round culminated in a heavily attended community meeting. Several faculty members defended the removal by alluding to some aspects of Supreme Court reasoning in speech rights cases. One argument drew on the *Tinker* decision, which in part held that an institution has the right to prohibit forms of expression that substantially interfered with its work. In this case the dwindling enrollment posed an immediate danger and the critical exhibit might hinder recruitment.[7] There was also the often-cited bowdlerized version of Robert Jackson's dissent in *Terminiello*, "The Bill of Rights is not a suicide pact."[8] The school's public relations director said that this was not a case of viewpoint discrimination but of process; there was a way to determine what could be shown on the walls and the school went through the proper steps to obtain that determination. The president also made an emotional protest against the Nazi poster, asking "What are we about as a community?" when criticism took this strident form.[9] Students who spoke all opposed the removal of the exhibit, generally calling for clear written guidelines on acceptable displays. Late in the meeting, an especially courageous student argued that guidelines were not an answer to the real problem—viewpoint discrimination—and added that censors often had guidelines.

From the meeting, from class debate, and from informal discussion with students, it appeared that there was near-unanimity this time on the central issue: whether taking down an exhibit because of its potential bad effect was justifiable. The circumstances were more stark. It was clearly the content that was the problem, and those who had taken offense were not office workers or passersby, but school administrators. Also, there was a physical act of removal, while in the previous incident it was considered and discussed, but not enacted. What was surprising was the subsequent growth in understanding among students about the place and purpose of civil liberties.

## Rights Reasoning

Some students still took the "simple libertarian" position: Bennington was an art-oriented school that placed a premium on creativity, and unrestricted art belonged in any space the creative impulse led the artist. But what marked student discourse as a whole, in class and out, was a decidedly greater willingness to entertain more complex arguments. Herbert McClosky and Alida Brill (1983) describe the essence of civil libertarian thinking as internalizing the principle of reciprocity: that the claims made for one's own rights are no more worthy than the claims made by others. In the debate over the first incident, little thought was given to competing rights or other claimants.

The second round forced many students—especially those most passionately opposed to the removal of the exhibit—to present a more integrated map of mutual rights. There was a growing recognition that the school had a right to regulate the place of artistic expression but not the content. The specific reciprocal arrangement that now seemed fair to students was that this space should not be considered gallery space in the normal meaning of the term, but that other such space should be provided, and that in those areas, the school would pledge not to remove exhibits based on their offensiveness to anyone.

Why would a sizable number of students adopt a position they had indignantly rejected in the previous debate? Students, no less than the citizenry as a whole, are especially solicitous of their own rights. Public opinion research on tolerance from its earliest days (Stouffer 1955; Sullivan, Piereson, and Markus 1982) has consistently demonstrated that Americans support free speech strongly only when it is posed in the most abstract form. But it is possible that abstract questions are not tapping feelings about civil liberties at all. People may be responding to the notion of a government taking away their rights as it might some other good, and therefore be a measurement not of tolerance (even in the abstract), but of individualism. That appeared to undergird students' reactions to the first incident.

Tolerance is a learned response, not a natural instinct. McClosky and Brill suggest that a crucial variable in the learning process is repeated exposure to civil libertarian norms. That accounts for their counter-intuitive finding that police officers are unusually supportive of due process norms; a great deal more so, for instance, than school administrators. Police confront those norms constantly in their professional lives and have come to appreciate the logic behind them.[10]

When the debate about the President's Gallery recurred, it became clearer to many students that an extended framework that took in the competing claims of others would be necessary to secure their own. The intensity of the conflict forced everyone deeper into arguments over the meaning of civil liberties and "You can't stop me from putting anything I want on those walls" no longer seemed like a compelling argument. Students who felt strongly about the issue were forced to reason further and develop a more complex and consistent scheme of rights. They had a powerful incentive, something to be gained that they valued highly (freedom of artistic expression).

Both class and campus discussion paradoxically benefited from the fact that they took place in a private college, which has some flexibility in determining what rights of free expression to permit. In that context, Supreme Court decisions play a different pedagogical role than in situations where they are binding. It was not a matter of discovering what rules *do* apply, but of considering what rules a community *should adopt* if it were free to do so. That had the salutary effect of steering discussion toward the underlying issue: the role and value of unfettered expression to a community. It also eliminated the temptation to end debate by appeal to holy writ ("Offensive expression? The Court already decided that in *Cohen*. Next question."). Relevant Supreme Court reasoning on these issues became a hot topic, but the focus was on their persuasiveness, not their authority. (My own references to Court reasoning above are in that spirit.) Students had to puzzle through the relation of individual rights, majoritarianism, and the needs of community on their own, with a guide from legal doctrine, but with no troopers to enforce a decision.

## First Two Times Tragedy, Third Time Farce

Official rhetoric was becoming increasingly, if loosely, communitarianism. If anything, the fact that a furor had arisen over free speech seemed to confirm the view that rights claims could be divisive. When the Board of Trustees announced in the 1993 spring term that it would be undertaking a major "restructuring" of the school, it posed this question among others to be studied: "On what kind of order does freedom depend? What responsibilities attend the ideal of self-governance?" The trustees answered their own question a year later in the Symposium Report and codified the communitarian critique of rights into an orthodoxy. The report (p. 10) called for "a robust social ethic" to replace the "protectionist personal ethic" that was said to have undermined a sense of community in recent years, and for "covenants that could be binding on all members of this voluntary community." There were seven references to the negative effect of rights claims in this thirty-six-page document.

What those general principles meant became clear the term after the report was issued. When the remaining faculty (one-third of the old faculty having been fired after the Symposium Report) began to consider drafting a statement on academic freedom, a faculty member also in the administration wrote that "the very definition of academic freedom" must "co-evolve with, and be inseparable from, a definition of academic responsibility." He also advocated "reasonable bounds for speech protected by academic freedom." The president told an inquiring student that in her vision of community, "the right of community members not to have their feelings hurt" would be as enforceable as the right to free speech. The school would now supply the "missing language of responsibility" by mandate.

With these conclusions now enshrined, it is not surprising that another speech controversy developed. This one involved an application of Bennington's speech code, which prohibits "verbal abuse or intimidating behavior of any sort, including not only direct threats of any kind but also psychological and sexual harassment." As with many other schools, these prohibitions are called a Behavior Code, not a speech code, although it mixes words and conduct without distinction.

Round three did not center on the President's Gallery and grew from an exchange that in less heated circumstances would probably have gone unnoticed. But here it led to an incident that found its way into *USA Today* and the Providence *Journal-Bulletin*. A student received a notice from the head of housekeeping telling him to remove garbage outside his dorm room or face a $50 fine. The student looked in the hallway and saw only his bicycle. Thinking that might be the "garbage," he wrote "Go to hell, it's my bike—I park it where I want" on the notice and sent it back to housekeeping. In other times, the response might simply have been a letter back to the student or an informal reprimand about manners.

But having decided that civility was enforceable, the school charged the student with "verbal abuse." The case was taken out of the hands of the Student Judiciary, which normally handled minor violations (which by any standard this was), and given to a committee of faculty and administrators that existed to handle major disciplinary problems. The committee convicted the student, citing the speech code, and put him on probation for the rest of the academic year. Over a hundred students—roughly one-third of the student body—sent a petition of protest to the committee. The argument of the petitioners was not so much that these words were protected speech[11] but that the method and severity of the punishment seemed designed to send a "community values" message.

A statement given wide circulation by a faculty member supporting the decision made that message explicit: "When my right to free speech assaults your right to self-respect, dignity, freedom from fear, then I have overstepped my boundary, and invaded yours." Examples of punishable words included "*ad hominem* invective, derisive talk, assault, cursing, verbal abuse." Another faculty member provided the "communitarian" underpinnings in the *Journal-Bulletin* story: "We have this culture on campuses in America where it's cool to be cynical and to be angry and to be negative and to be disrespectful and you don't get a good society out of that." The executive director of the Vermont ACLU responded (in the same story) that it appeared the school wanted "a campus of unthinking robots who simply say what's nice."

Benjamin Barber (1992, 4) speaks of the fundamental task of education as "the apprenticeship of liberty: learning to be free." If so, this cycle of experiences was a powerful teacher. The reaction of many students to the events outlined here took on a distinctly civil libertarian hue. One student entered the academic freedom exchange, an act notable on its face since the other participants were faculty and administrators. He wrote a public reply to the author of the call for setting reasonable bounds for academic freedom, drawing largely from John Stuart Mill.[12] Another student who had previously been a lobbyist in the state convinced six legislators to introduce a bill that would extend

First Amendment guarantees to postsecondary institutions. If passed, it would provide a legal basis for challenging Bennington's speech code.[13] A student statement protesting the Trustees' "restructuring" decision began by explaining the ethical and practical value of due process. That statement was signed by over two-thirds of the student body. In this time of great commotion, many students were acting exactly as Thomas Jefferson hoped Americans would—repairing to the standard of the law.

## Risk, Rights, and Community

The lessons in this experience come in different sizes and shapes. On the most mundane level, it suggests that students can learn a great deal about governance by discussing relevant campus issues in class. There is a tendency to think that we have to send students out beyond campus to get their hands dirty in the realities of democratic citizenship. Certainly there is an important distinction between an academic institution and a polity, but students can learn a great deal by discussing and debating how their immediate community grapples with contested issues. Such discussions are likely to be very different from the normal teacher-imparts-knowledge format, but that is to the good for both sides of the aisle. The second incident—the removal of the exhibit critical of the administration—occurred during and immediately downstairs from my class. To have ignored the obvious intense student interest would have been worse than missing an opportunity; it would have created diminished respect for the principles we were studying. Class discussion of controversial issues carries risks—it certainly did in this case—but that is instructive in itself. Teaching about liberty, tolerance, and citizenship cannot remain risk free.

Second, the charged atmosphere in which these ideas were being battled out contributed to the learning curve. Research has suggested that periods of intense conflict have an important impact on political thinking and rethinking (Pierce and Converse 1990). Participants develop an increased sense of political efficacy and reach for a broader framework to explain the rapidly unfolding events. It is hard to imagine class discussion alone or even skillful simulation producing the same reaction. The last two of these controversies took place with the backdrop of the Trustees' restructuring decision that included the replacement of a large part of the faculty and the suspension of faculty and student government. It was accompanied by rhetoric about a "revolutionary" reconstitution of education (the Drama Division temporarily renamed itself the Drama Collective). Faced with the necessity of rethinking fundamental principles of governance from the ground up in the midst of heated conflict, many students worked out a more finely tuned and consistent civil libertarian approach. In these foxholes, there were Bennington-style communitarians and civil libertarians; there were very few agnostics.

Third, the whole experience revealed a great deal about the relationship between speech rights and citizenship. School officials claimed throughout the period that the two were at odds, that rights claims were a form of selfishness which could not sustain community. But is there any principle more fundamental to citizenship than reciprocity: the understanding that one's own rights depend on the willingness to treat equally the rights claims of others? It certainly appeared that many students understood the value of reciprocity more clearly by virtue of having gone through these debates. Is there any more challenging and demanding path to learning and truth-seeking than that described by Mill in *On Liberty*? Mill describes the hollow complacency masquerading as settled knowledge that results when a community or (even worse) authority is permitted to define what words and ideas to prohibit as unacceptable. Finally, are there any more compelling—if disquieting—prescriptions of democratic citizenship than those in the First Amendment opinions of Oliver Wendell Holmes, Louis Brandeis, John Marshall Harlan, and William O. Douglas? Some students concluded that the turbulence and demands of tolerating free expression were worth the risk. That conclusion strikes me as a long step toward, rather than away from, responsible democratic citizenship and provides the only workable basis for coexistence in a heterogeneous community.

## Notes

1. For a description, see Edmondson (1994) and "Academic Freedom and Tenure: Bennington College," a report by the American Association of University Professors that led to that organization's censure of the school.

2. *Rowan v. U.S. Post Office*, 1970. The Court ruled that a person getting obscene advertisements in the mail has the right to get an order for the sender to stop. "A mailer's right to communicate must stop at the mailbox of an unreceptive addressee."

3. *Cohen v. California*, 1971. The Court overturned the conviction of a man

in a mall wearing a jacket with "Fuck the Draft" on the back. "One man's vulgarity is another man's lyric."

4. In *Erznoznick v. Jacksonville* (1975), the Court invalidated a municipal public nuisance ordinance prohibiting nudity in drive-in theaters visible to noncustomers. But it left open a ban on visible drive-ins in toto that was not content-specific. "Much that we encounter offends our esthetic, if not our political and moral sensibilities. . . . [T]he burden falls upon the viewer to avoid further bombardment of [his] sensibilities by averting [his] eyes."

5. I have no way of substantiating this or other remarks in the article about student sentiment outside the classroom, but in a school as small as this (500 students at the time of the first incident, about 300 at the time of the last), it is not difficult to get a good read on student views of hotly debated topics.

6. A freshman advisee of mine suggested a much more sensible approach in terms of conflict resolution. Student guides could have pointed out the exhibit, mentioned that it was critical of the administration (it was that hard to understand), and explained that Bennington was so supportive of artistic freedom that it permitted the display on the walls leading to the president's office.

7. The irony is that *Tinker v. Des Moines School District* (1969) is best known for the fact that the Court overturned the suspension of high school students for wearing black armbands protesting the Vietnam War.

8. The circulation given to this paraphrase of Jackson is somewhat puzzling, since he was dissenting in one of the landmark free speech cases, *Terminiello v. Chicago*. Far fewer people seem to remember Justice Douglas's majority opinion, which came to be (and remains) mainstream Court doctrine: "[F]reedom of speech, while not absolute . . . is nevertheless protected against censorship or punishment unless shown likely to produce a clear and present danger of a serious and substantive evil that rises far above public inconvenience, annoyance, or unrest."

9. The "Nazi poster" became an interesting sidebar issue. The president added in her speech to the meeting that she was especially offended because she was Jewish and her relatives had fled Europe. Some faculty members called it hate speech and criticized the anonymity of the author. It *was* extravagantly harsh, but to call it hate speech makes a point speech code critics have long argued: that those codes would eventually be used to suppress political criticism. The implication was obviously that she was repressive, not that she was Jewish. Protection of even rough "public examination of public characters" was the central purpose of free speech in a democratic society to James Madison, whose contributions to *The Federalist Papers* and authorship of the Virginia Resolution were anonymous.

10. McCloskey and Brill 1983, 267–68. The results are controlled for education.

11. It does seem, though, that the Court doctrine of "overbreadth" makes good sense here. "Overbreadth" means essentially that a conviction that might be upheld if based on a narrowly written law can be overturned if the law is

too vague. The Bennington speech code is so broad that it is hard to imagine any emphatically argued opinion that could not be said to violate it.

12. The student was Douglas Faneuil. Academic authors often thank undergraduates for their general input without naming them. This contribution was important enough to deserve more.

13. It was based on a similar law enacted by California. The student who suggested and helped draft it was Emmett Finocche. To date there has been no action on the proposed law.

*8*

# Teaching the Art of Public Deliberation: National Issues Forums on Campus

*Daniel W. O'Connell*

The National Issues Forums (NIF) on Campus, a public deliberation model for training competent citizens, is one of four general approaches to citizen education. These teaching or pedagogical options are not mutually exclusive. Training in public deliberation must, however, be an essential component of any serious effort at engaging students in the practice of democracy. First, let us review why we teach citizenship and examine the four general options for teaching democratic citizenship.

Citizenship education has been a major objective at all levels of schooling in the United States. State and national reform efforts have recently led to the publication of guidelines for teaching civics and government, including *Civitas, A Framework for Civic Education* (Bahmueller 1991). Most colleges and universities include in their mission the goal of preparing students for citizenship. The mission statement of Palm Beach Community College gives its highest priority to providing "an academic environment . . . where individuals can attain knowledge and develop the skills and attributes necessary to become effective citizens who meet the challenges of a dynamic, multicultural world" (Eissey 1996, 1).

Four options or approaches on how to prepare students for life as good citizens were presented for deliberation in an NIF issue book

135

entitled *Politics for the Twenty-First Century: What Should Be Done on Campus?* (Morse 1992).

The first option is titled "Learning by Doing—The Public Service Component." It involves students in off-campus communities. Its main rationale is that service programs teach the values of compassion and personal responsibility, which are at the heart of true citizenship. The second option is called "Learning by Talking—Acquiring Deliberative Skills." Politics is about solving problems in common. This means that colleges should teach deliberation by encouraging students to engage in political talk with others. The third option is titled "Learning by Practicing—Democratizing the Campus." Citizenship is about the exercise of political power. Thus, students must learn citizenship through participation in their own campus communities. The final option is called "Learning by Learning—A Classical Academic Model." Colleges train citizens by stressing intellectual rigor and academic excellence in all fields and courses. No special or separate emphasis or program on citizenship is needed.

In practice, most institutions or teachers combine these approaches and options in their courses or as a part of their campus or community activities. This chapter will focus on institutions and teachers who give a dominant role to the second option: learning by talking. It will highlight the pedagogy and texts that support the public deliberation model.


## Education and Deliberative Democracy

The deliberative-skills model can be traced back to Aristotle, who stresses the importance of practical wisdom and the role of deliberation in achieving it. In the *Nicomachean Ethics*, he states that "the art of politics, or practical wisdom, is the best knowledge" (Book VI, Chapter 7) and "the man who is capable of deliberating has practical wisdom" (Book VI, Chapter 5). Two of the most articulate current advocates of deliberation are David Mathews and Charles Anderson. In *Politics for People* (1994b), Mathews writes about education for a different type of politics. He contrasts traditional citizen education with education for citizen politics. Traditional citizen education focuses on expert information, critical evaluation, instruction in voting, knowledge about government structure, and instilling a sense of duty. Education for citizen politics sees citizens as the primary producers, not just as clients, consumers, or constituents:

> Citizens are the primary producers because they have to make the choices
> that give direction to governments and define the common purposes of
> community. Their education has to prepare them for making choices to-
> gether, for creating power, for building relationships, and for generating
> political will. (Matthews 1994b, 154)

At the center of citizen politics is the deliberative dialogue. Mathews highlights the special ingredients of public talk or deliberation in the *Kettering Review* (1994a). It promotes the type of reasoning required for making choices. It requires that we weigh carefully the costs and consequences of possible actions as well as the views of others. It is a serious and intense interaction among people, not a casual conversation or debate. The object is not to win but to make sound decisions. Finally, it is an exploratory dialogue, open to all options, and reflective.

These components and this perspective of citizen education underlie the pedagogy and curriculum of the NIF on Campus program and its national network of practitioners. Anderson, another deliberation scholar, has written about the aims of political education and the skills of civic competence. He concluded in *Pragmatic Liberalism* that political deliberation is the critical skill. For him, "the appraisal of, and decision among, competing claims and cases is in fact the basic task of citizenship" (1990, 166). For Anderson, the ability to make sound political judgments requires effective political deliberation. This involves the practice of four types of reasoning. He calls them the four themes of reasoning: reasons of trusteeship, critical reasoning, entrepreneurial reasoning, and meliorative reasoning (168).

The theme called "reasons of trusteeship" involves making the case for the prevailing practice. The rationale for the current policy or practice must be fully appreciated before reform is attempted. "Critical reasoning" involves pointing out the values or principles that the current policy is violating, the disparity between theory and practice. Invoking principle against practice triggers the process of political deliberation. "Entrepreneurial reasoning" proposes a new undertaking, a project or policy, a better way of doing things. The burden here is to find an improvement that wins the support of voters and power brokers, fashions a coalition, and develops the mechanisms to implement the new policy. "Meliorative reasoning" goes beyond the incremental or trade-off approach and tries to accommodate the concerns of the silent, the awkward, and the oppressed as well as those of the vocal, the active, and the intense.

Anderson insists that we go through these four modes of reasoning as a part of political deliberation. This is because the overall object of deliberation is to broaden our sense of the considerations that bear on a government policy. He explains:

> The aim is that each *assimilate* the point of view of the others and in this way come to a more complete understanding of the desiderata of public action. And ultimately, the goal is that each might be moved, potentially, to a change of mind, that the protagonists might come to adopt a different orientation than that from which they started. . . . It is this possibility of "changing one's mind"—the mysterious capacity of people speculating in the company of others, our ability to end up in a position we could not have anticipated before we explored the views of others—that makes reasoned deliberation so different from any system of formal logic consciously insulated from other modes of thought. (Anderson 1990, 177–78)

To follow Anderson, the teacher of deliberation must design a curriculum, give classroom assignments, and conduct study circles or forums, all of which touch on these multiple perspectives and modes of thinking. To help the teacher, Anderson has developed a comprehensive and sequential scheme for building the skills of civic competence.

> The scheme represents a movement from a passive "consumer" orientation to public life to an active "participatory" engagement with public issues, a movement from the view that the best one can do is to understand the political forces that act on one's life to the view that one can assume responsibility for deliberating and trying to resolve public issues. (196)

Level one is the ability to understand how institutions work. This is a consumer skill and involves the ability to understand the prevailing practice. Level two involves the critical ability to understand the rationale behind the system, e.g., traditional, liberal, Marxist, or fascist. Level three is the active skill of supporting a judgment. The student must give reasons why this interpretation is the most adequate public approach for addressing the problem. This level three skill of reasoned argument is the first stage of reasoned deliberation and the beginning of civic competence. Level four requires the student to interpret public issues from diverse points of view. This involves a sympathetic understanding of how policies will affect people situated differently. Level five involves the skill of adjudication or the ability to develop alternative compelling cases and decide among them. The student must present good reasons for what is a tough choice or hard case. This requires the student to find a principle or common basis for collaborative action. Level six, the final level, is called "theoretical self-consciousness," or the ability to dispassionately critique the prevailing model, i.e., the liberal democratic model.

The objective for civic educators who follow Anderson is to lead students up this ladder and toward progressive levels of civic competence. Several different models and sets of material are available for teachers who want to help students learn by talking, thus acquiring deliberative skills. The NIF teaching model is presented in this chapter. Its goal is to bring the student up through at least the fifth level of citizenship. The NIF model of public deliberation addresses the pedagogy and proposals of Aristotle, David Mathews, Charles Anderson, and the other proponents of the public deliberation model of civic education. The first challenge to implementing these ideas comes from students.

## Do College Students Desire Citizenship?

The preceding description of citizenship education concentrated on skill development. Other important aspects of citizenship are desire and motivation. In *Generation at the Crossroads: Apathy and Action on the American Campus* (1994), Paul Loeb describes a culture of withdrawal on college campuses, some of the reasons being historical ignorance, relentless individualism, mistrust of social movements, and a general isolation from urgent realities. Another perspective on why students avoid politics is presented in *College Students Talk Politics* (Harwood Group 1993). Focus groups of students were convened on ten college campuses to discuss these questions: What do college students believe it means to be a citizen? How do college students view politics today? How have college students come to learn what they know about politics and citizenship? How would college students like to see politics practiced? What opportunities do college students see for learning politics at the university?

The student answers contain useful messages for teachers who want to motivate students to learn the critical skills of active citizenship. The Harwood study concluded that

> most everything they see and hear involving politics, makes them believe
> that it is not about solving problems; instead, it is individualistic, divisive,
> negative, and often counterproductive to acting on the ills of society. Stu-

dents can, however, imagine a different kind of politics, based on different political practices. This study suggests that with some fundamental changes in the way that politics is practiced today, students will seek opportunities to become involved in the political process. (1993, 5)

Students reject the current politics of pessimism. They would replace it with a politics based on understanding issues, seeing different perspectives, making decisions with others, emphasizing listening, and sensing that participation matters (Harwood Group 1993, 8–9). This is consistent with the deliberation model of citizenship and should be good news for teachers who are looking for ways to motivate and encourage students to participate in politics and other aspects of civic life. The report ends with suggestions on political education. It must be different from the education most of them now receive, which only reinforces everything they think is wrong with politics. The recommendations are to:

1. *Teach politics differently and enable students to practice this politics.* Education must make politics relevant to their lives and help them understand how to hold political discussions and make decisions with others.
2. *Help students discover that politics can create change.* They need to have examples of citizens working together to make a difference and understand that people care what they think.
3. *Educate students about the roots of democracy.* They need to know that the core of democratic politics lies in political choices and social compacts, which demand ongoing consideration and participation through politics.
4. *Watch what we "say" about politics.* Messages that are irrelevant or other cynical comments about politics undermine any effort to get students to participate in the process.
5. *Challenge students to take up politics.* They care about their community and world, but are reluctant to take change into their own hands. They must be encouraged and supported to take an active role. (Harwood Group 1993, 10–11)

This report provides additional considerations for civic educators as they prepare to implement the deliberation pedagogy for today's students. The deliberation pedagogy practiced by the NIF network is designed to engage students in this different type of politics: citizen politics.

## The Role of NIF in Civic Education

In order to further the skill of public deliberation, the Kettering Foundation and the Public Agenda Foundation, both nonpartisan research foundations, created the National Issues Forums (NIF) program. Each year since 1981, Kettering and Public Agenda have prepared issue books on several major issues of national concern. In 1987 the National Issues Forums Institute (NIFI) was created to promote NIF. The primary tasks of NIFI are to ensure the ongoing preparation of issue books and other materials that will stimulate serious public deliberation on major issues that Americans face nationally and locally, to encourage collaboration in the NIF network and to provide a legal home for consortia that grow out of this collaboration, to collect and share information about what is going on throughout the NIF network, and to solicit and administer grants for the network. NIFI has explained the underlying premise of the NIF network:

> . . . in a democracy people have to take responsibility for what happens in their community and in the country, and they have to act on that responsibility. In order for citizens to act wisely, they have to make sound choices about how to act. To do that they have to deliberate as carefully as possible. Deliberation is a necessary part of politics at every level. It is the DNA of democracy, the means by which a responsible public forms and informs itself. (NIFI Brochure)

The Kettering Foundation was established in 1927 by Charles F. Kettering. Its current president, David Mathews, is one of the nation's leading advocates of public deliberation and citizen politics. Kettering's research today is devoted to understanding the way bodies politic function or fail to function. Kettering treats politics in its broadest sense, as a dimension of everyday life rather than just what officeholders and governments do. The research is done for practical purposes—crafting tools, e.g., study guides, community workbooks, and exercises, for helping the public act responsibly and effectively on its problems. One of its many missions is to help develop study guides and exercises for use in schools, colleges, and universities that are attempting to improve the civic education of their students.

Kettering also publishes a journal on education, the *Higher Education Exchange*. The 1996 issue focuses on the theme of public scholarship with articles on the disconnected/divided life of the scholar-citizen; the consequences of specialization and professionalization on our campuses; and the need for communication and dialogue, especially deliberative dialogue, between scholars and the public (Brown 1996, 1).

NIF is carried out by a network of more that six thousand civic and educational institutions. The NIF network is not a project of any foundation or single organization. All forum activity is' locally organized, moderated, and financed. The network has been further expanded and strengthened through an NIFI Networking Project. This project involves volunteer network coordinators who are responsible for the following areas: Humanities, NIF on Campus, Cooperative Extension, Corrections, High Schools, Libraries, Literacy Network, Religious Institutions, City and State Communitywide Groups, Leadership, Local Issue Forums, Professional Associations, Seniors, Spanish Speaking, Study Circles, and Women's Organizations.

The NIF on Campus network has approximately six hundred members with three coordinators, one for social science and law faculty, one for humanities faculty, and one for administrative leaders (NIF on Campus network). They publish an NIF on Campus newsletter (*Newsletter*) and deliberate through Internet on an NIF Listserv (NIFORUMS). Members of the campus network use NIF in their classrooms, student organizations, residence halls, community forums, developmental/literacy programs, faculty development, campuswide forums, continuing/adult education, honors, and orientation programs. They also write articles on NIF and deliberative democracy for professional journals (McKenzie and O'Connell 1995, 230), convene or facilitate forums, recruit for or attend NIF Summer Public Policy Institutes, host faculty/administrative workshops, mentor faculty, including adjuncts, write articles for the NIF newsletter, share course syllabi and class exercises, and otherwise promote the deliberative model of civic education.

In order to train people for NIF, a consortium of Public Policy Institutes was created. Most of these twenty-one institutes are conducted during the summer on community college or university campuses. Kettering also holds a Public Policy Workshop each summer to train institute leaders, coordinate networks, and reflect on current research and practice in deliberative democracy. This reflection takes place in the Deliberative Democracy Seminar at the workshop. The 1996 summer seminar was designed to focus on the pedagogy of deliberative democracy and current practices in the college classroom.

Thus, Kettering, Public Agenda, NIFI, and its thousands of NIF practitioners are part of a diverse network of civic educators and practitioners committed to teaching and practicing the art of public deliberation. The NIF on Campus network specifically concentrates its deliberation practices in the classroom and on campuses.

## NIF in the Classroom

The NIF approach is one way of teaching the art of public deliberation. There is no exact model, approach, technique, or formula that can capture once and for all time how best to teach and practice deliberation. Each year, improvements and updates are made to the current NIF practitioner's guide. Furthermore, teachers in the NIF on Campus network use many different approaches and techniques for teaching and practicing deliberation. This does not mean there are no NIF fundamentals or best practices. There are distinctive characteristics to the NIF model of public deliberation and essential components for successful forums. Research, however, continues to improve and strengthen its pedagogy and practices. At this point the most comprehensive approach to teaching NIF in the classroom has been documented in *Public Politics* by Robert McKenzie (1994). This textbook is the result of more than ten years of his experience in teaching civic effectiveness and public leadership at the University of Alabama and at the annual Public Policy Institutes for NIF.

The ideas of Anderson, Aristotle, and Mathews are recognizable in McKenzie's chapter titles. The concern for motivating and engaging students in public/citizen politics is also addressed in the appendix exercises.

*Doing Politics*: McKenzie's title, *Public Politics*, and this chapter reinforce Mathews's educational model in *Politics for People*, i.e., education for citizen politics versus the classic academic or politics-as-usual model; public politics in addition to governmental politics. It also addresses the issues in *College Students Talk Politics* (Harwood Group 1993).

*Learning to Make Choices*: This chapter addresses the importance of Aristotle's practical wisdom and the special ingredients of public deliberation as described by Anderson and Mathews.

*Making Choices in the Face of Conflict*: This chapter starts students up the ladder of skills described in Anderson, from passive consumer to active participant.

*Analyzing Public Talk About Issues*: This and the remaining chapters continue to take students up the ladder of citizen skills and types of reasoning described by Anderson and Mathews.

*Understanding Values as Deepest Motivations*: This chapter adds the insight on values underlying our choices, i.e., choice work requires us to resolve the conflict within us as well as among us.

*Working Through Choices*: This chapter delves into the need for and principles of deliberation.

*Hearing a Public Voice*: This special characteristic and goal of NIF public talk or deliberation is highlighted in this chapter, in particular the distinctions among compromise, consensus, and common ground.

*Connecting Choice Work to Communities and Organizations*: This chapter adds the reality and connection of the public to governmental politics. Reality testing is an essential component of the four reasoning themes in Anderson, in particular the entrepreneurial reasoning that requires us to fashion a coalition to implement a new public policy.

The content and the appendix exercises demonstrate that NIF is a practice-oriented pedagogy. It is learning by doing, and doing things in common with others both inside and outside the classroom. The author has described his courses in a journal article (McKenzie and O'Connell 1995, 230), and many other examples are featured in the NIF on Campus newsletters. Furthermore, an honors course has been designed to use this book as well as other current deliberative democracy texts, including *Coming to Public Judgment: Making Democracy Work in a Complex World* by Daniel Yankelovich (1991). Yankelovich explains how public issues progress through seven predictable stages, from public opinion to public judgment. The syllabus for *The Art of Public Deliberation and Community Building* is available through the NIF listserv.

Most teachers, however, will not be giving a full-semester course in public politics or deliberation. They will be using an NIF issue book, framing their own issue for deliberation, or using the NIF process for a particular portion of a class or for a campus forum. NIF issue books, moderator guides, and starter videotapes are available on many topics: affirmative action, drugs, economy, education, family, foreign policy, freedom of speech, health care, immigration, natural resources, politics, poverty, racial inequality, and violence. Guides are also available from the Kettering Foundation; among others: *Framing Issues, Organizing Your First Forum/Study Circle, Making Choices Together: The Power of Public Deliberation, A Workbook for Teaching Public Deliberation and Public Action*, and *Community Change Through Public Action*.

NIF issue books and the use of the NIF process have proven successful in stimulating student participation and discussion. If the goal is, however, to deepen and strengthen citizen reasoning and deliberation skills, as described by Anderson, one should review the complete NIF process, from the definition of public politics through public action after the forums.

The July 1996 edition of *A Workbook for Teaching Public Deliberation and Public Action* describes the newest ways to explain and practice these fundamental NIF concepts, including public choice, deliberation, and action. This thirty-two-page publication describes the following seven sessions for preparing to teach or practice the deliberation process: The Public's Role in Politics; Becoming Involved: The Importance of Naming Issues in Public Terms; Choice, Deliberation, and the Products of Forums; Moderating for Deliberation; Ending Forums; Applications: Using the Results of Forums to Restructure Relations with Officeholders; and Applications: Using the Results of Forums to Stimulate Public Action.

To show how these NIF principles and practices have been applied in classrooms and on campus, the final section of this chapter will focus on current NIF practitioners. Many of them have been featured in the *NIF on Campus Newsletter*. This description will also include the practice of NIF on Campus at Palm Beach Community College.

## Examples of NIF in Class and on Campus

NIF activity on college campuses is not confined to academic courses. Faculty, students, and administrators are using NIF on their campuses in residence halls, honors programs, faculty development workshops, freshman orientation programs, public forums on local community and campus issues, and in alumni, adult, and continuing education programs. NIF classroom use is not limited to government and political science classes. NIF is used to teach other social sciences, the humanities, journalism, law, and economics, for teacher education, and by many other disciplines and departments. Some use the NIF issue books for the content, e.g., health care issues by nursing and medical faculty and economic issues by economics professors. Others will use the NIF issue books and process for teaching critical-thinking skills, promoting constructive discussions, encouraging collaboration, and other related components of deliberation. Others, like McKenzie, will design courses around the theme of public politics and include numerous issue books and class forums. Others will use the NIF, Kettering, Public Agenda, and other deliberative democracy texts for research and seminar discussion purposes. The latest innovation is to join several campuses for NIF forums over the Internet. The NIF listserv is also being used to help frame new issues, including one on the future of higher education. Some specific examples from the *NIF on Campus Newsletter* will show the diversity of NIF uses:

- An English instructor uses NIF in her freshman composition course, which emphasizes oral communication and writing effectiveness. She has students write a paper in response to their participation in an NIF forum. This requires them to engage in active reflection and synthesis of a variety of viewpoints.
- The coordinator of a university honors program uses NIF to nurture the students' sense of civic responsibility. She uses the process to make students more aware of the greater community by involving them in important local and national issues. With large numbers of foreign students on her campus, she also uses NIF to help bring together diverse peoples and ideas.
- A professor of philosophy uses the NIF process to help students find common ground in what they can tolerate in others' beliefs and values. This professor holds workshops for communications and other college departments for the purpose of using NIF to encourage students to be more civic-minded and citizenship-oriented.
- A community college president uses NIF to lead local citizens in the process of community building. NIF is a program his college is using to build common ground around key issues in his college district.
- The NIF network coordinated forums on campuses to coincide with the National Issues Convention, which was held on the eve of the presidential primary season, January 18–19, 1996. Class NIF forums compared their views on family, economic, and foreign policy issues with the national representative random sample.
- Courses like Contemporary American Issues are especially suited to use the NIF process and issues books. Instructors on one campus report an increased enthusiasm for courses that use these timely topics.
- Another college hosts at least ten NIF forums each year at a variety of sites, from a large-scale community forum to neighborhood forums. This helps build the presence of the college and also demonstrates a model for deliberative decision making in the community. It also helps promote education in citizenship.
- Undergraduate media students and graduate students in adult ed-

ucation participated in an electronic NIF on People and Politics. Another forum was held in October 1996 on the NIF issue book *How Do We Want to Govern America?*

- A professor who teaches introductory sociology as well as sex, family, and marriage courses devotes the last three weeks of the semester to a series of forums arranged and conducted by current and former class members.
- NIF is used in a freshman colloquium on How to Save American Democratic Institutions. NIF is used as a basis for students to examine seven major topics: education, economics, government, values, social organizations, politics, and democracy.
- Another college teamed up with the local newspaper to advertise and promote the NIF issue book *The Troubled American Family*. The newspaper ran the pre-forum family questionnaire for several days. Following this, a community forum convened with college students, residents of public housing, foster parents, county legislators, teachers, and all of the local family court judges. The NIF materials were used as a framework for the discussion.
- An experimental course entitled 1996: Issues for the Next President, using NIF materials, was used for the 1996 presidential election.

The examples above provide an illustration of the diversity of NIF uses and users on college campuses. To provide additional detail and help the reader understand how one teacher has been affected by NIF, I will conclude with my personal story. I came to community college teaching from a political science, law, and public administration background. I was active in politics and committed to the citizenship model of education. When I went from government work to teaching in the late 1980s, I was looking for ways to engage my students in politics and government. I found that many of my students were not interested in politics and were taking the Introduction to Political Science or American National Government courses only for the purpose of graduating from the community college.

I experimented with numerous approaches and strategies to engage students in these courses. I had the most success with the NIF program. In the beginning, I would concentrate more on the subject matter of the issue book than the deliberative process itself. The forum and issue book would be used to supplement the chapter in the textbooks and my lectures on public policy. Students would research their positions, and we would invite guest speakers with expertise on the subject. I would test on the content of the issue book, and each student would write a letter to the president or other appropriate government official documenting his or her solution to the forum issue. This worked well, and students enjoyed the forum discussion. Upon reflection, I realized that I was getting students only up to Anderson's level three: they could support their personal opinion. This, however, is only the first stage of reasoned deliberation.

I now take more time to explain the logic of deliberative democracy, the NIF process, and the purpose of deliberation, and to define the characteristics of effective forums. I also compare different models of political education, dialogue, and debate, and introduce the importance of "blending" ideas and creating alternatives. I have added the idea of "blending" because most of my students have not experienced a deliberative forum. Blending is defined as "any behavior by which you reduce the differences between yourself and another person in order to move to common ground" (Fox 1995, 11). I ask students to do three things: express their opinions, listen to other viewpoints, and focus on shared goals and win/win possibilities (blending). I show a video of a forum in order to model deliberation and contrast it with the *Crossfire* style of debate.

Students easily understand the First Amendment, and most willingly practice their freedom of expression. We have no trouble going through a forum, from the welcome to the pre-forum ballots, the ground rules, the starter video, the personal stake, and the forum deliberation. Problems start when we begin to close the forum. Students in a closing are asked to reflect on their own thinking and how it has changed, as well as to reflect on themselves as a group. The problem comes when they are asked to describe their group result or reflection: What did they hear the group saying about the common ground in the issue or the tension in the issue? Can they detect any shared sense of purpose or direction? What trade-offs are they, or are they not, willing to make to move in a shared direction? You will notice I am moving students up Anderson's ladder; step four requires one to recognize divergent points of view, and step five involves developing alternative compelling cases and deciding among them with good reasons. Level five requires a principle or common basis for collaborative action. I am still developing strategies and techniques to accomplish this.

I still hold students accountable for the content of the issue book. I now require that students' letters or reports to a public official clearly demonstrate the essence of blending. The report now starts with a description and defense of the group's direction and common ground. I require the students to analyze the pre- and post-forum ballots and include the post-forum ballot as evidence of the class or group conclusion. Knowing in advance that they must document what they decide together seems to focus them more on the discussion and push them to get more clarity during the closing. Clarity may not be agreement, but an understanding of the tensions, trade-off problems, or why they are not willing to move in a shared direction. After they account for the group reflection, they can end their paper with their own individual reflection and direction on the issue. To accomplish this, I take at least two weeks of class time and make this the only paper for the course.

Last year, my classes compared themselves to the representative random sample at the National Issues Convention. We used two issues: *The American Family* and *Pocketbook Pressures*. My classes merged in forums with sociology and economics classes. I continue to welcome my colleagues in other disciplines to join in forums with my classes. I begin by reviewing the current schedule for courses that meet at the same time as my classes. I then review the subjects to see which ones would have an interest in the issue books I am considering. As mentioned above, I describe to my students the four conditions of effective forums. John Gastil (1994) has identified four key features of effective forums: participants have read the NIF issue book, written and spoken "Instructions" (Ground Rules) are followed, high-quality deliberation takes place, and participants attend multiple forums.

By "multiple forums," Gastil means that the more you go, the more you learn. People who spend more total hours in forums experience greater positive changes in attitudes, conversation network diversity, and group and personal political action. It is difficult to plan multiple forums in a single course unless you are teaching a course dedicated to public politics or deliberation, like McKenzie or the honors course I designed on the Art of Public Deliberation and Community Building. To address this problem, I have started to involve other faculty members and students in my forums, encourage them to use forums in their classes, help student organizations hold forums, and send faculty and students to NIF training sessions.

I plan to hold a training workshop on our campus next year and involve faculty, students, administrators, adult noncredit students, and other interested members of our local communities. I will also hold forums on other campuses and expand NIF in the classroom to the adult noncredit courses. I will open forums to anyone interested so that we produce multiple opportunities for practice in deliberation. One forum in one course is unlikely to make a permanent or long-term major intellectual or behavioral change in a student. Thus I find myself looking for opportunities on campus and in the community for my students, faculty, and other interested people to convene and participate in forums in order to improve deliberative skills.

It is important to note, however, that NIF can produce immediate effects on the classroom environment and student behavior. Norman Dolch, a sociologist and active member of the NIF campus network, has described to me his experience in a recent letter endorsing NIF booklets for classroom use:

> My students come into classes with very strong ideological positions. The National Issues Forum booklets are well reasoned, balanced presentations which help students to listen to the voices of others. This challenges the common, everyday approach of the students and makes them more receptive to considering social science research on topics such as poverty, affirmative action, and interventions for crime. As the students participate in deliberation, sharing their views and reacting to the expressions of other students, a change occurs which makes them more accepting of others' viewpoints. National Issues Forum booklets help me get past the initial mind set which most students seem to bring into the classroom on very controversial subjects. It actually helps students learn by assisting them to move beyond their preconceived ideas on topics.

I am considering an opportunity for my American National Government class to join in an experiment in on-line deliberative democracy. We might participate in a forum over the Internet with two other colleges. My International Relations class is now preparing to hold a joint forum with an International Relations class at Barry University in Miami. We will deliberate on the NIF issue book *Mission Uncertain: Reassessing America's Global Role*. As a member of the NIF on Campus network, I am also actively discussing curriculum and pedagogy issues with other NIF users. The listserv now includes a draft of an issue book on the future of higher education. Another issue that will soon be discussed on the listserv is the grading and evaluation of deliberation.

Another question is, Who should select issues for deliberation? In the past, I have assigned the most current issue books available from Kettering and Public Agenda. I am now becoming more flexible and going back to prior issue books, e.g., immigration and poverty. This requires updating the issue book with new information. Another option involves having the class frame its own issue. My current thinking is to leave the framing to the honors class as a final project after participating in one forum and moderating a second one. I will probably move toward allowing the class to choose its issue. If one of the current issue books is not selected, I will add an assignment and work with the students to update the issue book, e.g., *The $4 Trillion Debt* will require additions, and *Boundaries of Free Speech* must add current expression issues, such as Internet censorship. The adult noncredit students requested a forum on the 1994 immigration issue book. Our first task will be to update the book, particularly as it relates to Florida. In most cases this will not affect the issue book as it relates to the fundamental alternatives/choices and their underlying values and tensions.

This description of NIF practice provides another example of how NIF is used to teach the art of public deliberation. My desire to motivate students and become an effective political science teacher led me to NIF. My experience led me to rethink how I used NIF in the classroom and on my campus. My reflection has led me to expand and strengthen the deliberation portion of the course. I have also created other opportunities on campus for my students and me to practice the art of deliberation. Finally, I have actively participated in the NIF network to exchange ideas and improve my understanding of the pedagogy and practice of deliberation. I welcome the reader to take advantage of the resources listed in this chapter by contacting the sources mentioned in the citations to this text.

Although this chapter focuses on the deliberative-skills approach to civic education, it is important to note that these are not mutually exclusive options. As a teacher of deliberative democracy and an NIF practitioner, I support efforts to provide public service opportunities, improve the practice of deliberative democracy on the campus, and ensure that all courses stress rigor and academic excellence. I share the judgments of Anderson, Aristotle, Mathews, and McKenzie, however, that political education for the competent citizen must in all cases cultivate the skill of deliberation.

**9**

# Democratizing the Classroom: The Individual Learning Contract

*John F. Freie*

> It gave us the opportunity to work as a close knit group that learns
> from each other and loses the stigma of grades and
> competitiveness. The classroom should be a place for teamwork.
> . . . Whether we like it or not cooperation, learning, and politics
> are intertwined.
>
> —an Individual Learning Contract student

Citizenship educators want students to feel a sense of civic responsibility and to become active participants in the political process. Although the professoriate may be undecided about the extent to which professors themselves should be politically active, few would argue that their students (particularly undergraduates) should not be active. With the goal in mind of developing active citizenship among students the question arises: Can we teach democratic citizenship without democratizing our classes?

In practice most professors organize their courses on the basis of the assumption that we do not have to structure the course in a democratic fashion in order to promote the value of democracy. After all, it is not necessary for the teacher to undergo the same experiences that students experience in order for students to learn. We do not have to actually write the same papers we require students to write, or take the same exams students must take in order to be able to teach them how to write or how to take exams. Indeed, students would find it quite unusual if we did such things. In that same sense, we do not have to experience democracy in the classroom in order to teach students the

153

value of it. In fact, many would argue that we must use "legitimate coercion" to force students to learn things that they would otherwise avoid learning (such as the value of citizenship). If we follow this line of reasoning, undemocratic authority should be used to teach students the value of democracy.

But the issue is more complex than that. What goes on in the classroom—how it is physically arranged, how interactions are patterned, how teachers and students envision their roles, how power is structured—is critical for the learning process (Pauly 1991). For everyone—those interested in teaching citizenship and those not caring to do so—the constitution of the classroom represents a fundamental educational issue. Power in the classroom is inherent in teaching, but for those particularly interested in citizenship education the issue is even more salient. Regardless of how persuasive an argument one may construct in favor of active citizenship and democracy, the skeptical students of today are unlikely to believe in its value if they are taught in a passive, authoritarian manner. In the teaching of citizenship, the pedagogy is the message.

Still, the hypocrisy argument by itself is not compelling; it fails to provide us with a persuasive argument in favor of democratizing the classroom. Perhaps more important is the evidence that many of the kinds of skills and attitudes thought to be critical for the sustenance of democracy are most effectively nurtured and developed through participation in democratic organizations themselves. In their examination of four public high schools that, in different ways, moved toward democratic structures Ralph Mosher, Robert Kenny, and Andrew Garrod (1994) found that students were better able to understand the responsibilities and obligations of democracy. Concretely, they found that students in democratic schools were more highly motivated to participate in school activities and more loyal to the school than students in conventional schools. Additionally, there were indications that the students were likely to continue to participate in the larger political process later in life. John Michaelis (1963) has extended classroom democratization to the teaching of social studies at the elementary school level. Sadly, there are few examples of democratized schooling at the college level.

Because of the multiple meanings associated with democracy it may not be clear what is meant by democratizing the classroom. In its ideal it is closely associated with participatory forms of small-group democracy. A democratic classroom should be comprised of a relatively equal distribution of authority (not an abdication of authority), it should be inclusive of all members of the class, class members should internalize democratic values and procedures, the class should acknowledge each person's individuality and affirm their competence, members should relate to each other in a congenial fashion, and there should be a recognition and practice of the rights and responsibilities of deliberation (Gastil 1993). The democratic classroom should not simulate or try to be a microcosm of the larger political system. Instead, it should provide students with a rich, "thick" form of democracy that goes beyond thinner forms of democracy such as majority rule or representation.

Certainly not all aspects of this ideal vision of classroom democracy may be realized. Each college will differ in the extent to which classroom democracy will be supported, each professor varies with respect to his or her desire and comfort with democratization, and the students in each class vary with respect to their willingness to participate and the skills they bring to the class. Nonetheless, the principal catalyst for democratizing the classroom remains the professor. While initiatives to democratize the classroom by the professor will not assure that it will be successful (it is ultimately dependent upon the students), without the commitment and dedication of the professor classroom democracy is impossible.

## Aims of Citizenship Education

Teaching for citizenship is a formidable task, not just because the college curriculum requires that students be exposed to a wide range of subjects (both in the college core as well as in the major) but also because of the large number of skills and attitudes that are associated with democratic citizenship. From a skills perspective citizenship educators identify the "essential components" of citizenship as including knowledge, critical thinking, and participation skills (Wineman and Hammond 1987), the ability to carry on a public dialogue in a respectful fashion (Barber 1989), the necessity of being an active rather than a passive learner (Morse 1993), the knowledge base required to critically understand the various meanings of democracy and citizenship (Stanley 1988), and the ability to be responsible decision makers (Wright 1983a). In addition to those skills, citizenship education also deals with issues of values and attitudes (Morrill 1982; Bellah, et al. 1991) and the formation of moral character (Etzioni 1993). Variously, citizenship educators have attempted to empower students (Benson 1987), get students to appreciate the multicultural nature of society (Hepburn 1993), and improve the capacity of students to deal with moral and ethical concerns (Shaver 1985; Wright 1993b).

Obviously the task of citizenship education is massive and no single course can accomplish all these objectives. Even the most ambitious citizenship educator is affected by the constraints structured into higher education (e.g., the grading system, course scheduling). Still, there are approaches to organizing the course that maximize our ability to accomplish these objectives.

## The Individual Learning Contract (ILC)

The pedagogy described here is the Individual Learning Contract (ILC) approach to organizing a course. It is a nondirective approach to teaching that accomplishes many of the objectives of citizenship education while working within the confines of conventional education. It may be used in virtually any course at the undergraduate or graduate level; others have used contracts in high schools, elementary schools, and nonacademic organizations (Knowles 1986).

The ILC is a pedagogy that provides the student and professor, working together, with the flexibility to identify and address the needs, concerns, and interests of the students while addressing the goals of citizenship education. Instead of working with the assumption that all students must be treated alike—must read the same material, take the same exams, write the same papers—it starts from the assumption that all students are unique and that they enter the class with different talents, skills, interests, and abilities. Based upon that assumption of genuine diversity, it provides a structured approach to designing a course of study that allows students to improve in their areas of weakness or further develop their talents. With the goal of improving skills required of democratic citizens in mind, the ILC makes it possible to maximize the effectiveness of the course by precisely identifying weaknesses and then designing a series of activities unique for each student that allows for improvement.

In addition to being able to effectively identify and improve citizenship skills, the ILC has the further advantage of demonstrating to students the advantages of democracy by using democratic values and practices in the classroom itself. The approach empowers students and gives them an opportunity to take active responsibility for their own education; it goes beyond the toleration of differences and shows, through practice, how genuine differences (not categorical differences) are valuable both for learning and for creating democracy; it raises issues of power, authority, and expertise in a democratic context and it shows students how individual interests and needs may be integrated into a democratic community. The ILC does all this while treating students ethically, as trustworthy individuals who are partners rather than antagonists in the learning process.

## The Contracting Procedure

Contracts are created through discussions with each student in which goals are identified, activities are devised to accomplish the goals, and evaluation criteria are agreed upon to assess the quality of the completed activities. Because each student is unique (and therefore each contract is different), the number of student-professor meetings required to develop each contract may vary. In most cases, however, two or three meetings toward the beginning of the semester will suffice. Since most students are unfamiliar with this approach it is helpful to carefully and clearly describe the procedure at the outset (I provide a five-page written description for the students) and to clearly separate the three major sections of the contract: goals, activities, and evaluation criteria.

### Goals

After students are presented with an overview of the entire ILC approach, they are asked to begin work on the first part of the procedure, the identification of semester-long goals. Students are encouraged to identify goals they wish to accomplish that fall into one or more of the following areas: substantive goals, skill goals, or life goals. They are asked to write down a list of their goals on a sheet of paper and bring it with them to the first student-professor meeting. This meeting focuses only on goals and may be conducted either as a one-on-one meeting or with a small group of students and the professor.

Substantive goals relate to the designated subject matter of the course (e.g., electoral politics, international relations). Students are encouraged to skim the reading materials listed on the course syllabus to get a general idea of the topics covered and asked to identify any particular questions they would like addressed. They are encouraged to think seriously about this since, if they identify particular questions, they will commit themselves to finding answers to them. They are not forced to come up with substantive issues and sometimes need to be reassured that that is acceptable. For many students specific goals related to the content of the course emerge later, after the course has begun to take shape.

Virtually all students identify skill development goals. By separating skill development from the substance of the course it is possible to get students to expand their notions of how knowledge may be obtained and disseminated. To encourage this I provide them with an extensive list of activities (see discussion below) that includes a wide variety of methods and approaches. Students most commonly think of liberal arts skills such as analytical writing and oratory, but the list may be expanded to include creative writing, poetry, forms of artistic expression, organizational abilities, discussion skills, leadership ability, reading comprehension, listening attentiveness, group facilitation talents, and decision-making skills.

The third area of goal setting relates to the personal life of the student. This is an area of critical importance to the student, but it is seldom considered as a legitimate area of concern in the traditional classroom. Democratic classrooms should deal with the totality of students and not view them merely in a cognitive manner. Teaching citizenship is more than merely an intellectual exercise. Usually only a small minority of students identify such goals. Those students who wish to examine some aspect of their personal life are encouraged to remain true to their concern and not feel under any obligation to necessarily force a linkage of these goals to the substance of the course.

When they are asked to think about their goals (i.e., why they are in the class) as separate from how they will be evaluated, students begin a process of self-reflection and self-evaluation that is encouraged throughout the course. Often this initiates a broader process of self-examination as students ask themselves what they wish to accomplish during their college years. Additionally, the ability of students to set their own goals is empowering and gives them a sense of responsibility.

More precisely from the standpoint of citizenship education, allowing students to identify their own goals is a way of using genuine diversity to build an educational community. The type of diversity that is revealed by students' own assessments of their interests, needs, and talents provides building blocks for the formation of a sense of democratic community. It is a diversity that is not assumed by the professor on the basis of social, religious, ethnic, or racial classifications. What emerges comes from each student's life experiences and is a far more complex and multifaceted type of diversity.

In addition, allowing students to identify their own goals immediately raises issues of authority. In conventional classrooms the professor confuses the authority of knowledge of his or her discipline with professional authority, leading to the use of authority to impose goals upon the students. The professor makes judgments about what is important to know and the skills that are important to learn. This inherently sets the professor and the student in opposition to one another. By way of contrast, the ILC approach poses the problem to students, "What do you wish to learn?" and resolves the professor-student contradiction by creating a partnership between the professor and the student as they discuss how to best achieve the objectives the student has identified. The expertise of the professor in the area of knowledge of the discipline and educational methodology is aligned with the student rather than standing in opposition to the student.

In the discussion about goals, both in the class as a whole and in the individual student-professor meetings, it is important to emphasize that the professor also has goals. The professor should not be seen as abdicating his or her responsibilities. Instead, the professor's objectives become aligned with the student's objectives, and both experience a form of liberatory education. Paulo Freire puts the case succinctly:

> The dialogical character of education as the practice of freedom does not begin when the teacher-student meets with students-teachers in a pedagogical situation, but rather when the former first asks himself *what* he will dialogue with the latter *about*. And preoccupation with the content of dialogue is really preoccupation with the program content of education. (1970, 81–82)

## Activities

The second step in developing a contract involves identifying activities students will undertake to accomplish the identified goals. Students are encouraged to think creatively about ways to improve weaknesses and build upon strengths. To assist them I provide a nine-page list of descriptions of projects that have been undertaken by students in previous courses.[1] They are not restricted to this list, but it does give them a point of departure for thinking creatively about activities. It includes conventional activities such as research papers, essay exams, book analyses, and journals as well as activities that less frequently appear in conventional courses such as film reviews, student-led discussions, and student-organized field trips, and even far more unconventional activities such as artistic performances, poetry readings, random knowledge integration activities, or having students act as teaching assistants or democratic process analysts responsible for encouraging class members to think about democratic procedures and values.

In the one-on-one meetings with the students the types of activities they are considering are discussed and an "activity package" is developed. In developing the package it is important to make sure the activities are carefully and logically linked to the goals and to clearly describe each activity in as much detail as possible. Where deadlines or timetables for the completion of projects are requested either by the student or by the professor they should also be included in the description of the activity. In instances where students are extremely ambitious it may be necessary to rank order the goals and to initially focus the activities on the highest-ranked objectives.

The activity statement is a critical aspect of the contracting process because the activities structure the relationship of each student to the operation of the class and to the other students. Still, the professor may, through the use of mandated activities (or types of activities), subtly structure the class to emphasize particular objectives beyond those in each student contract. For example, if one is concerned that students may not read assigned course material, exams may be required of all students; or if a professor wishes to emphasize the communal nature of the class he or she may require all students to complete a specified number of group activities. The proportion of the contract composed of mandated activities should be kept to a minimum, however.

The activity package often includes both graded and nongraded activities. Nongraded activities provide a safety net that gives students the opportunity to work in areas where they need improvement and to experiment with activities that involve risk without experiencing failure. For the graded activities students determine the emphasis to be placed on each activity by assigning percentages to each of them. It should be noted that both graded and nongraded activities are evaluated. The only difference is that for graded activities the evaluation includes a letter grade, whereas nongraded activities receive evaluations but no letter grades.

The syllabus may be dealt with in a number of ways. At the outset of the course it provides a common reading base for the students while they are meeting with the professor and forming their contracts. Once contracts are completed the syllabus is readjusted to accommodate activities found in the individual contracts that require class time. This may be done by the professor alone or with the assistance of a small group of students. As the class proceeds, the syllabus should be regularly assessed to see if it addresses the needs and interests of the class. The extent to which students are involved in creating the syllabus throughout the semester is dependent upon the professor, but the greater the extent of involvement the greater is the sense of shared responsibility.

## Evaluation Criteria

The third and final area of contracting occurs in developing evaluation criteria for each activity. Since there is a considerable variety of activities, and since similar activities might be used to accomplish different goals, the criteria used to evaluate the quality of the student's performance must be explicit. Clear identification of the criteria prior to a student's beginning the project not only affects how the student will approach the project, but it is also simply fair. Identifying evaluation criteria initially falls within the realm of expertise of the professor. Although discussion may occur in this area to assure that the criteria match both the goals and the activities, the best way to facilitate the discussion is for the professor to suggest criteria and for the student to respond to those suggestions. This may be accomplished most efficiently by attaching the criteria to the suggested activity list. For activities not on the list, of course, this process will require a separate step.

In most instances (especially for rather conventional activities) the criteria do not differ much from the criteria used by most professors to assess the quality of a project. For example, if the student's objective is to improve his or her analytical writing the criteria most likely to be used might include organization of the paper, insightfulness of the paper's position, logic, use of evidence, and the like. Where this approach might differ from conventional courses when dealing with such activities is that the criteria are explicitly identified prior to beginning the project. For activities linked to less conventional objectives the criteria must accurately reflect those objectives. For example, if a student wishes to improve his or her ability to organize, more appropriate evaluation criteria might be the ability to involve people in the project, to work cooperatively, or to anticipate and deal with problems. Generally speaking, the more creative activities require more creative assessment techniques.

## Finalization

The contract is complete when the goals, activities, and evaluation criteria are agreed upon and listed on a contract form. This form is signed by both the professor and the student. The original is kept on file, and a copy is returned to the student. It is the student's responsibility to complete the activities listed on the contract and abide by whatever deadlines and timetables are identified.

The entire contracting procedure works best if it can be completed within the first three weeks of the semester, but this is dependent upon the number of students in the class and the complexity of their contracts. It requires a considerable initial investment of time and energy on the part of the professor since student-professor meetings occur outside the regularly scheduled class meeting time. Even though finalization of the contracts occurs early in the semester, many students change their goals and objectives as the course proceeds. This requires a modification of the contracts and should not be discouraged if changes are requested for legitimate reasons. One way of facilitating changes is to meet with all students at midterm to review their progress. At this point students may reexamine their goals and make appropriate changes (if any). The midterm meeting also makes it possible to troubleshoot problems that students may be experiencing (procrastination is common).

It is difficult not to overemphasize the importance of maintaining flexibility in the structuring and operation of the contract throughout the semester. As the students change their views of what the objectives of the course might be and how they wish to relate to them, the contracts should be modified accordingly. John Dewey's discussion of the aims of education are instructive on this point:

> The aim as it first emerges is a mere tentative sketch. The act of striving to realize it tests its worth. If it suffices to direct activity successfully, nothing more is required, since its whole function is to set a mark in advance; and at times a mere hint may suffice. But usually—at least in complicated situations—acting upon it brings to light conditions which had been overlooked. This calls for revision of the original aim; it has to be added to and subtracted from. An aim must, then, be *flexible*; it must be capable of alteration to meet circumstances. (1966, 104)

## Self-Evaluation

Democratic citizenship does not come naturally. It is a learned behavior that evolves out of an awakening of a democratic consciousness.

Teaching for citizenship requires not only that students reflect upon the subject matter, but also that they are provided with opportunities to reflect on their own behavior as it relates to citizenship issues. Citizenship involves more than mastery of a subject matter; it strikes to the heart of how one orients oneself to the political community.

Experience alone is not enough; reflection is necessary. Thus, in adopting the contract approach it is important to make sure that there is sufficient opportunity provided for self-reflection. This may (and should) be accomplished in several ways. One aspect of self-reflection (not the only one) is to build into the contract a final self-evaluation activity. The self-evaluation is required of all students (although they have the option of taking it as a graded or nongraded activity) and is due at the end of the semester. In it students are asked to "make sense" of their involvement in the course. It is not used, as many forms of self-evaluation are, for the student to assign himself or herself a grade for the course, but rather as an activity by which to think about issues such as democratic authority, individual and group responsibility, the meaning of citizenship, how the subject matter of a course is related to the manner in which it is learned, and the like.

The above elements are included, in some fashion, in all contracts. The particular nature of contract learning, however, should remain flexible because of the unique nature of each student and each teacher, as well as the particular subject matter of the course. Variations of this approach can be found in virtually all types of courses at all levels of education and, while it provides an important precondition for democratic classroom management, by itself it does not go far enough. The final component of democratizing the classroom lies in the creation of a sense of community in the classroom itself.

## Classroom as Community

There are many different meanings of democracy. But those interested in citizenship education are in general agreement that the form of democracy to be nurtured (although going by many different names) is participatory and communal. It envisions citizens who not only believe in democratic values but who also practice those values in their everyday lives, taking responsibility for themselves and their community. It encourages citizens to become involved in politics rather than to reject political activity.

In addition to overseeing the implementation of the contracts over the semester, the professor in the democratic classroom must focus on the classroom atmosphere. While the ILC provides the necessary conditions for the development of individualized democratic skills, it does not necessarily provide all students with the opportunity to practice those skills in a democratic organization. It is in the operation and dynamics of the classroom that this takes place.

At the outset of the course, other than the use of the contracts themselves, the classroom atmosphere might appear as a standard seminar or discussion-oriented course. Reading materials are selected by the professor, reading assignments are initially made by the professor, and discussions are directed by the professor. In the first few weeks of the course (while the contracts are being developed) the course is professor-based. Once the contracts have been completed, however, the atmosphere begins to change, as the activities included in each student's contract are accommodated.

Many students will have identified activities that involve the entire class (e.g., leading discussions, taking the class on field trips). The scheduling of these activities may best be accomplished by working with a small group of students outside class time. This group acts as a steering committee and works with the professor throughout the semester to develop and maintain a schedule. At this point students begin to take responsibility not just for their own learning but for the entire class. This encourages students to see how their own particular interests are interdependent with their colleagues. When students successfully complete group-related activities, a sense of camaraderie develops and all students feel a sense of pride in the class. When students fail to perform adequately, real consequences ensue—schedules must be adjusted or additional activities must be included.

The process of facilitating the creation of a political community in the classroom is slow and gradual and, in all honesty, is accomplished in only a minority of classes. The professor's role is to shift the responsibility for the operation of the class from his or her shoulders and allow the students to bear much of the responsibility. This may occur in a dramatic fashion—such as when the students decide, as a class, to restructure the entire class for the remainder of the semester—or in a slower, more gradual manner, as students step forward to lead discussions or give presentations not required in their contracts.

There are many techniques that may be used to try to create community in the classroom: using an undergraduate student as a teaching assistant; using a student as a democratic process analyst; requiring group activities; requiring class participation as a graded activity;

using cooperative learning techniques; taking classes on extended field trips, etc. The ILC allows for the use of any of those techniques. But more important than the particular techniques that may be used is the orientation and commitment of the professor to move the class in the direction of a democratic political community. The professor becomes a facilitator of learning and a manager of democratic procedures (a politician) rather than merely a transmitter of content. To be successful requires the practice of skills more closely associated with a counselor or consultant than those of a didactic teacher. Such a perspective means supporting students as they struggle to accept responsibility for the operation of the class, supporting a learning environment that allows students to practice their political skills of discussion, critical thinking, and organizing, and encouraging reflection about democratic values and discussion and action about the nature of democratic authority. The objective is not to merely get students to work together in groups, but to have them learn to appreciate the political nature of the classroom and to experience the difficulties and successes of actively participating in a democratic fashion with others. In many ways this psychic adjustment is the most difficult adjustment to make for the teacher in a democratic classroom.

The ILC, used in conjunction with a commitment to construct a democratic political community, starts with the particular interests of the students and attempts to transcend each of those self-interests to create a sense of communal interest. It assumes that participatory forms of democracy possess educative qualities, not the least of which are to increase feelings of empowerment, improve skills associated with democratic decision making, and develop new attitudes and beliefs consistent with democracy. Some of these objectives may be met merely with the implementation of the contract, but to fully experience the benefits of the approach it is necessary to move toward political community. It is in political community where the social skills needed for democratic participation may be honed and where one's values and beliefs may be tested.

## Outcomes

Democratic political theorists have long claimed that political participation will encourage the development of democratic attitudes, behavior, and skills. Interestingly, little empirical study has been conducted to test this fundamental assertion. This essay will add only modestly to that speculation by selectively reporting comments from the self-evaluations of students who have participated in ILC courses. The self-evaluations are drawn from a variety of American politics courses (from introductory courses to upper-division courses) over a four-year time span (1992–96). In total, there were 212 self-evaluations with some students writing several because of taking several different ILC courses. Excerpts from some of the more articulate ones are included here to represent the reactions of the students to the ILC approach.

The most frequently appearing theme in the self-evaluations was the notion of responsibility, and, interestingly, that idea, while incorporating individual responsibility, usually was extended to include the entire class. One student put it this way, "When I realized what was going on in this class my participation, attendance and whole attitude changed. It became apparent to me that it was not important to attend class because I was getting a grade but because I have a responsibility to myself and my education as well as to the other students in the class." Another student who had an intense ideological conflict with a fellow student put a slightly different interpretation on responsibility. "His [the student with whom she differed] ideas were so completely off the wall, and in fact sometimes offensive, that it was difficult for me not to become annoyed with him. . . . [However] as a member of our community he has a right to express his opinion and we have a responsibility to listen. By responding, the community learns from one another." For another student the lesson of the class seemed to be to live what you believe. "What I have learned is very simple. I can not begin to change the world until I have changed myself. Unless I am living and trying to encompass the life I desire then all my words and great insights are for naught." In ILC courses in which the communal dimension fails to fully develop, the focus of responsibility tends to be more on the individual student living up to his or her contract, but where a sense of community occurs the concept of responsibility tends to extend to the group and sometimes to the broader society.

While most students were quite similar in terms of race, ethnicity, and social class an appreciation of diversity nevertheless emerged. One older student who had previously felt a sense of alienation by being surrounded by younger colleagues said this:

> *I realized that, not only is it okay to be different, to look, think and act differently, but that it is better for all parties involved and for the quality of life, to have a variety of viewpoints and personalities that add color and stimulate self evaluation/appreciation. . . . I remember my supreme dissatisfaction with high school*

*and subsequent years of employment, because of the utter blandness of association with people who all tried to look, think and act the same. . . . Now I'm finally beginning to openly appreciate differences I may have because of a new-found strength of conviction, a security in my individuality as an asset instead of a liability.*

A Latino student linked participation with the importance of diversity:

*I feel that the significance of participation is to be able to interpret the material into our own words, elaborate on an issue more, see it in a different perspective, and finally one can better understand another person who comes from a different background and ethnicity why that person might see things a bit more differently than others which would help deteriorate ignorance, racism, and hatred.*

In any group experience there are always conflicts. In one class an out-of-town field trip was organized by the students but the behavior of two students created scheduling difficulties for the entire group when they went off on their own without telling others of their plans. This is what one of the principal organizers of the trip said:

*It is true that the best way to learn about something is to actually experience it. The trip was a true learning experience in community participation. Not only did we all experience what it is like to be part of a working group, but we also learned how things can be disrupted when one or two people do not involve themselves in the group and pursue their individual interests to the exclusion of the rest of the group.*

Still, the more common theme is interdependence and an ability to learn from each other. "The paper I distributed to class was not as well received as I had hoped. The criticisms made me realize that it was a poor paper and was not very logical. I think this did more for me (no offense) than getting it back from [the professor]."

Classes of this sort, because of their dialogical character, lend themselves well to democratic norms of deliberation. In these classes it was clear that people appreciated and enjoyed civil dialogue about political issues. Virtually all students mention some variation of this in their self-evaluations. Here is an example: "We all had different opinions, different ideals and different goals, yet in bringing our heads together we found common basic assumptions and values that could be satisfied in a variety of ways not immediately apparent to the single perspective." Students consistently identified the importance of being able to carry on a meaningful dialogue with others. One African American student who became a class leader noted the importance of dialogue: "I fit right in with the community atmosphere of the class. I did not agree with everything that was said but I got my point over in a friendly (brotherly) way. I walked out of the class being able to speak to all my classmates."

It is difficult to determine the success of the ILC at improving particular skills merely from self-evaluations. However, there is little reason to believe that its effectiveness varies much from conventional courses. What it does do that conventional courses do not do is to expand the range of skills that may be developed, and it gives students a sense of self-respect by asking them to assess their own strengths and weaknesses. One senior political science major who had spent three years writing papers and exams saw this as an opportunity to work on his poetry (which he was reluctant to share with others). "One of the most important things I am taking from the class is my poetry. I have learned to express myself comfortably in poetry. I have also learned to feel more comfortable in letting others see my poetry, something that I'm very shy about." Many students like the idea of being able to focus on skill development. "I liked the idea of a learning contract because it allowed me to work on some skills that I think are very important. . . . I know what my weaknesses are and the contract allowed me to work on those areas." While most of the emphasized skills are directly related to those needed to function in a democratic environment, all such activities, regardless of their direct relevance to democracy, occur within a framework that emphasizes respect for others, an important element in a democratic community.

Democratic classrooms are not (contrary to common opinion) chaotic. In all such classes some students assume leadership roles, some formally (e.g., a teaching assistant) and some informally. In one class a student who assumed the role of teaching assistant made this observation: "The way I viewed the class was influenced by my position. I became more aware of class interactions, personality conflicts, and group dynamics. As a teaching assistant I was in the position to influence the workings of the classroom by recognizing the social aspect of education." In a further essay she wrote the following:

*Through questioning the assumptions and placing a stronger emphasis on the consequences of the class, a new structure can be formed. This new structure produces a more active student to actively experience politics. This transformation cannot be forced upon the student. There must be a desire to challenge the assumptions and focus on the consequences and the action must be a group effort.*

Finally, almost all students report feeling a sense of empowerment, both in structuring their learning environment and in feeling that they can effect change in other political arenas. "I learned that I could change problems (along with the public) probably on a local level and then progress to the state and national levels," said one student. Another student went further:

*The most important lesson I took away from this semester is that if I want something changed the change has to start with me. . . . How can I expect anyone to do anything about the environment or anything else they care about when I don't? After I graduate I have decided to volunteer my time at a women's shelter or assistance program. . . . It is time for me to stop talking and start acting.*

## Conclusion

Ultimately the argument in favor of democratizing the classroom rests upon two issues: the aims of education and how those aims may best be achieved. There are, of course, no simple answers to either concern. But the aims of education cannot be divorced from the broader social environment that supports the educational system. It is not enough to merely proclaim that the purpose of education is to enlighten students or to allow them to realize their potentials or to prepare them for the job world. By itself enlightenment offers no guarantee that either social or even individual transformation will occur. Similarly, job preparation, as commonly conceived, fails to recognize the highly changeable nature of business.

The commitment to democracy—its values and procedures—represents a long and rich political tradition in America. But its realization has often been impeded by an education system that has not prepared students adequately for the participatory rigors of citizenship. To serve democratic society well it is necessary to provide its members with an education that allows them not only to understand their society but also to be able to act in a transformative fashion in that society. By doing so citizens also act to transform themselves. Thus, to remain true to our democratic past one of the fundamental purposes of education in America must be citizenship education.

Given this objective, how may we best implement education for citizenship? The argument presented here is that it may be accomplished most effectively through a process of action and reflection in the most concrete arena, the classroom. In the democratic classroom the professor and the students are all engaged in a real, not simulated, practice of small-group democracy that unites theory and practice. Certainly there are many ways of accomplishing this objective, but the Individual Learning Contract offers one effective and relatively easy approach to democratization.

## Notes

1. The entire list of suggested activities may be obtained upon request from the author, at the Department of Political Science, LeMoyne College, LeMoyne Heights, Syracuse, New York, 13214.

*10*

# Wading in the Deep: Supporting Emergent Anarchies

*Naeem Inayatullah*

> I have long been of the opinion that you can't teach anybody anything. It is possible, however, to create opportunities . . . to learn.
>
> —Ralph Pettman, "Teaching World Politics," 140

> Whatever you are is never enough; you must find a way to accept something however small from the other to make you whole and save you from the mortal sin of righteousness.
>
> —Chinua Achebe, *Anthills of the Savannah*, 142

On those rare occasions when we reflect on our past miscalculations we may conclude that we do not always recognize our own best interests. We may even concede that our mistakes occur while others seem to detect our interests with clarity. Such concessions occur infrequently because, in the course of modern life, they feel like betrayals of individual autonomy. Normally, we embrace the more well-versed if implicit notion that no one can know or represent our interests better than we ourselves do. Contrasting the rare and normal in this way creates a rich tension. Can others know, represent, and act on our interests better than we ourselves can? Or, can only we comprehend, authorize, and realize our own interests? It may be worth lingering within this tension. I wish to suggest that engendering in ourselves and others a sense of citizenship requires learning how to appreciate the tension between others' understanding and command of our interests and our desire to claim and represent our interests as our own. The problem is

171

that lingering within this tension may feel less like strolling on firm ground and more like plunging into tricky waters.

Consider the following two seemingly opposite situations. First, students and citizens know exactly their interests while educators and state representatives perfectly reflect those interests both in the classroom and in politics. Here educators and state representatives merely facilitate the unfolding of easily discerned individual interests. Alternatively, students and citizens do *not* know their interests, which must be unearthed, articulated, and promoted by educators and state representatives. These educators and representatives have great confidence that they can speak for, and act on behalf of, students and citizens. Students and citizens respond by fully appreciating and mirroring back this confidence. The apparent difference between these two hypothetical situations hides their similarity. In both, the transparency of interests—in the first case to students and citizens, in the second to educators and representatives—precludes a substantive need for either education or politics. In both, an agreement on the facile and unmistakable nature of interests immediately fuses the two necessary elements of citizenship: the granting of allegiance with and for the entitlement of rights. By starting with this exercise, I hope to suggest that strengthening education and citizenship requires a deeper and richer understanding of interests.

I assume that the immediate activation of the sentiment of allegiance falls short of our ambitions. Instead, we aim to advance a citizenry that deliberates upon, debates, and criticizes the multiple meanings and determinations of interest, the skewed processes through which interests become represented, and the asymmetric relationship between subjects and their representatives. In short, we aim to cultivate a *critical* allegiance. If so, we may wish to hesitate before making commitments to either the idea that students and citizens easily know their interests or the idea that such interests are best acted upon and known only by others.

Such deliberative hesitancy may allow us to consider processes whereby the discovery of our interests occurs neither independently of others nor under their subordination. Instead, we can uncover and constitute our interests through dialogue with others who themselves are engaged in a similar process. The potential benefit of considering and constructing such processes of discovery is easy to imagine. Students and citizens extend their critical allegiance to activities and institutions that express and realize their own work. I take this expression and realization to be the heart of democratic process as well as the key to invigorating both education and meaningful citizenship. Reasonable and well-intentioned people may, nevertheless, balk at the implications of promoting such other involved processes in the discovery of interests. Many, if not most, are likely to determine that this vision is excessively costly. Such processes appear too complex, disorderly, and capricious. They seem to undermine traditions of order, efficiency, and control. They require a perhaps unsubstantiated faith and comfort in what I like to call anarchic forms of participation. Under the pressure of this doubt, rather than hesitate and thereby engage the difficulty over the role of others in the construction of interest, we tend to want to escape this tension. We resolve that our actions promote others' best interests. We rationalize that we must carry out the burden of acting on their behalf, especially when they resist. With such a commitment to order we cut short the pains of deliberation. However, we also alienate the potential profit that comes from the labor of critical participation.

For the purposes of this essay, I wish to label acting on behalf of others without their vigorous participation as the "teaching drive." I have come to accept that in most aspects of life, the teaching drive creates alienation by subordinating and assimilating others. The teaching drive is a source of the contemporary crisis in education and politics. The reason for this is not difficult to see. In contrast to the learning opportunities implied in Pettman's epigraph, the teaching motive conceptualizes learning as a fixed form indifferent to time, space, and the participation of others. Teaching orders space and time while assimilating others to its predetermined blueprint. This commitment bubbles up from two related sources: a mistrust of the diversity represented by external and internal others, and a misplaced fear of anarchic social forms. Rather than appreciating anarchy as a precondition for pluralist democratic processes, political and pedagogical practices misunderstand it as an intrinsically asocial condition. Akin to the "state of nature," anarchy's natural barbarism and savagery must be remade to create both an educated citizen and a "civil" society. Accordingly, advanced segments of society instruct internal and external others on the techniques of citizenship, democracy, and civilizational advance. Likewise we license professors to authoritatively intervene in, adjust, and regulate students' lives. In both the classroom and society the mandatory burden of teaching must be borne in the midst of protest, resistance, and ingratitude offered up by the uncivilized and the uneducated. Under the cover of a civilizing mission, teaching agents violate vital democratic processes for the "higher purpose" of converting anarchy to order.

Despite the usually assumed unidirectional flow of fixed-form teaching, we should not think that it affects only students. The conversionary drive also has import for the teaching agent (Nandy 1984, 32–35). It helps silence and conquer the inner voices that doubt the efficacy and justice of teaching. Thus the internal purging of ambiguity and the external cleansing of the uncivil constitute the same violent purification. Thus it is that teaching violates seeking and seekers.

The reader is perhaps aware that the polemical tone of my prose does not fit well with its message. I admit this contradiction. My introduction so far consists of provocative assertions that themselves seem to be a species of teaching violence. Will this essay, then, vie to provide learning opportunities or will it thrust forward another authoritative intervention? My response to this potentially debilitating question first considers how learning occurs.

Taught otherwise, I experience understanding not linearly, progressively, or cumulatively, but in sudden unpredictable shifts of awareness. I assume this to be typical of how learning occurs.[1] Further, being impressed with the idea that form and content need to cohere, I try to arrange space, time, and instruction in the classroom according to this relatively enigmatic conception of learning. The flow and purpose of the course emerge from the *interaction* of students, materials, and instructor rather than merely from a prior blueprint.[2] This results in seemingly unconnected blocks of ideas appearing, retreating, and reappearing. Participants learn but it is impossible to know when (although students say it often does not occur within the span of a semester). Nor is it possible to target a disciplinary domain. Students claim their learning often has little or nothing to do with the designated subject matter. Admittedly, such a course seems relatively undesigned, undirected, and disorderly. Nevertheless, with the appropriate attitude it is possible to thrive within such an anarchic form. As we move from one theme to another seemingly disconnected theme, I try to remain comfortable with the discomfort of anarchy while reveling in the sometime serendipitous recognition of insightful connections. I hope such a posture suggests to students that we might together create a connective tissue between, or perhaps uncover a holistic pattern among, seemingly haphazard events. They tend to bracket their hesitancy and defer their doubts while playfully accommodating my expectations. I solicit the reader for a similar suspension of judgment and a matching playfulness.

Let me return to the question. Like many academics, the technique of theoretical deduction habituates my style. Still, instead of delivering another authoritative intervention I would like the form and content of this exercise to cohere. I feel compelled in this essay to let the presentation emulate the seemingly capricious drift of discovery.

*     *     *

It is the second week. Forty or so students wait for a course titled Contemporary Issues in International Relations. More than the usual amount of anticipation charges the air. Having heard the syllabus read aloud, they want to know if what they hear is genuine. Will he really present no lectures, no theory, no history, no geography? Will he merely sit on the table and say, "What do you want to talk about?" Will he just listen to empty space if no one speaks? What will he do when everything turns to chaos? Will I learn anything or will this be yet another wasted course? If he is not going to teach, why does the university let him do this? Why did I listen to my friend who could not even say what she learned?

*     *     *

Teachers are those parts of nature that most abhor a vacuum. Usually students cannot imagine that the most anxious person in the room is the teacher. Performance anxiety was the motive force for my first seven or eight courses. It drove me to prepare thoroughly so I would not seem the fool. It spurred me to treat every second of empty classroom space as a potential slide into awkwardness and loss of control. It tricked me into converting every moment of ambiguity into assertions of authority, displays of dominance, and threats of ridicule. Anxiety dominated my classrooms as surely as a low-pressure weather system dominates the moods of those it envelops.

The powerful are anxious because they do not understand their power, do not feel they deserve it, and cannot account for why they have it. This anxiety disciplines their face so how they feel is the inverse of what they show. A simpler and sharper approach motivates students. They wish to satiate their curiosity about the nature of life and their place in it. Beyond this difference, teachers and students are bound together. Each knows the other's rank and role, and their own.

*     *     *

Three essays and three journals are due. I leave the topics wholly to
their design. They must seek out what they feel is important, a responsibility they resist. This resistance reveals their implicit internalization
of the idea that I know better than they what is best for them. It reveals
their participation in their own alienation. The readings on Haiti and
Bosnia are mostly novels. Students dictate the reading pace, usually
reading a novel every two weeks. While the content of novels provides
some information and much needed motivation for theory, geography,
and history the novels serve to provide a common start and spark for
our conversation. We discuss the plot and meaning of the novels intensely but briefly. Art succeeds like nothing else in bringing out politics. We fight over our interpretations. This gives way to concern over
our group dynamics, and then to the class, gender, racial, national, and
political bases of individuals' interpretations. The lack of central control in the classroom, the nature of our conversations, and the possibility or impossibility of learning become later preoccupations of class
discussion. Each new novel becomes the gravitational center for such
dialogues. What, if anything, are we learning?

*     *     *

In the beginning, watching me smile through long and awkward si-
lences convinces them I will not lecture. With much preparation I have
trained myself for these moments.[3] They, on the other hand, cannot
bear the silence. So they begin to speak and to listen. As more voices
emerge so do accusation, confrontation, conflict, and anger. They feel
"amazed" and often "disgusted" by what they hear.
   The thrill of constructing their own conversational patterns and of
discovering each other's voices in the first and second weeks turns into
a disdain for those who challenge and disparage strongly held positions. By the end of the third week the conversational patterns seem
worn; the novel shine of the experiment diminishes. For many, rather
than facilitating self-discovery, others' challenges seem instead to
threaten and undermine precious beliefs. More than grades are at
stake, I can see that. They risk the very stability and cohesion of deeply
felt and sometimes carefully cultivated worldviews. Learning feels
dangerous. I suggest that we do not wish to learn because learning
threatens to rupture our cosmological closure. And yet, we also cannot

resist learning because that danger wraps itself in desire. In the first third of the course they keep up with readings, sustain high attendance, and participate vigorously.

I believe the initial high quality of commitment surges from two sources. First, they begin to accept that they co-construct the course. It embodies and expresses their labor. Second, their candid and often blunt remarks generate a captivating fear. We begin to uncover one of the crucial ingredients of knowing: the inseparability of fear from desire and the necessity of both for learning. We find ourselves creating a process that involves more than the usual trappings of participation. Not just learning but also engagement in democratic processes seems menacing.

*      *      *

Participation occurs in degrees. To avoid class is to participate in a type of critique of the course, the professor, the subject matter, academia, and life. Perhaps avoiding voting is similar. Attending class implies that it might be time worth spending. Participating by doing assignments and dancing to the rhythm provided by the instructor is, perhaps, a step up. Such participation might mean replaying sound bites during those few seconds allotted to the student. It may mean a willingness to play the game of "if you guess what I want you to say now, you will oil the gears of my lecture and perhaps be carried to a better grade."

These are minimal participations. We seem to want a deeper involvement. But I wonder if we can risk its ramifications. Can the students freely comment on the futility of a particular lecture, or the utility of an alternative to the one prepared by the teacher? Can the students take the themes and threads of the course in directions unanticipated by the syllabus? Can students affect the pace, speeding it up here, slowing it down there? Is the flow of "knowledge" reversible? Will the class allow verbal gifts as well as anger, shouting, crying, humor, confusion, ambiguity, and accusations? Will the class honor connections between the inner and outer worlds of students and between the classroom and the culture of global political economy? Or will it serve as a state of nature? Will students participate in the selection of course material? In the determination of their performance and evaluation? How far can it go? What principle speaks to drawing the line of authority here and not there? The parallels to politics proper seem obvious enough here.

In both politics and education, our actions loudly declare that participation is far from a transparent virtue. I suspect that when we sing its praises we do not often realize what we are saying. And when we do, we sour on participation. Springing headlong into concerns over student participation without recognizing that this necessarily carries us to the deep waters of co-constructing the classroom and the world reveals how privileged anxiety limits pedagogical and democratic practice. How can we, who have such little experiential familiarity with swimming and floating in such deep waters, teach participation to others? Instead of noting its capacity to envelop and sustain a diversity of life-forms, we invariably demonstrate our distress about its dangers. We say participation; we mean bathing them in our bath water.

From kindergarten to twelfth grade (and perhaps earlier, and later), we teach them that learning is a matter of assimilating oneself to preconceived, prediscussed, prearranged forms. They learn that rather than the expression and realization of their labor, learning is that labor's alienation. So produced and commodified, our students assemble and package themselves as citizens so that the "teaching drive" may use them as a vehicle to produce a new generation of order.

*   *   *

Discussion of the novels leads to advancing political positions around such questions as the value of U.S. interventions, the nature of the U.S. government, how life in Bosnia or Haiti is similar to or different from life in America, and the kinds of obligations we have toward others. While liberal, conservative, and radical voices contest their visions, only rarely are their arguments remarkable. It is the complexity and intensity of the social dynamics that amaze me. These are striking, unpredictable, continuously shifting and overlapping. Students rearrange their seating and cluster together according to their politics. The uncommitted or confused sit mainly in the middle. Changes in seating positions signal shifting politics. After a few weeks, however, such changes are rare. Everyone settles in for a verbal war. Here are the kinds of things they say:

*Referring to material impoverishment and the extremely politicized nature of Haiti:* "I just did not realize how different their lives are and how lucky I am." Another counters this desire to differentiate and distance with assertions of commonality and continuity: "You know, we too have poverty. You don't realize it but we are also only moments away from revolution." And: "Don't you realize that our lifestyle and our foreign policy have everything to do with their condition?" Self-identified Haitians who perhaps understand the complexity of Haitian society respond to the simplicity of these comments by either lecturing the class or despondently shaking their heads. Another remark produces its own angry response: "They seem just like us. They think about God, and love, and the meaning of life." More shaking of heads, more attempts to envision a horizon beyond simple comparisons projecting mere difference or mere identity.

*In a discussion of U.S. involvement in Bosnia*: "Saving thousands of foreign lives is not worth the loss of one American soldier's life." With this comment the class erupts into multiple loud accusations. They lose consciousness of classroom decorum and of my efforts to enforce it. Some side with the comment, relieved that someone else dares to express their own hidden sentiment. Others do not wish to live on the same planet with those who hold such views. Some press the commentator on how he measures the value of life. Those who have been volunteers in U.N. refugee camps fume in their seats, digging their fingers into their palms.

*The following comment becomes a defining moment for one class*: "I am very proud to be an American, but why does it hurts so much? It shouldn't hurt so much to be proud of your country." Those from the right attack her for feeling shame and for being willing to admit it: "You have nothing to be ashamed of, I don't understand you at all." From the middle, "Why do you *want* to be proud?" And admiring praise from foreigners, "This is an important question." The student who risked the comment stopped attending for two weeks. She claimed to need a break from the intensity. When she returned we were still discussing variations on her theme.

*On the relationship between elections and democracy*: "The United States is not a democracy. Elections are a way of duping us into believing we have a say. All the decisions are made by a handful of capitalist white males. I do not vote because I am not a dupe." This comment provokes everyone. When forms alter, politics cannot be contained by the textbook, the classroom, or the economistic calculus of normal social science.

*After a comparison of women's roles in Haiti and Bosnia with their roles in the United States*: "I do not feel harmed by men or by patriarchy. Does that mean I am oppressed but don't know it?" This comes near the end of the term when some have learned that comments posed as questions invite thoughtful responses. However, most treat this question as beside the point. I note that issues around gender create the greatest anxiety and induce the strongest defenses. I struggle to understand why this is so.

*Not all of it is confrontational. The issue that engendered the most generous climate for discussion concerned interracial dating*: "I am thinking about taking my black Catholic boyfriend home to my Jewish parents over Thanksgiving. Do you think I should do it?" Everyone responds. Much to our surprise at least two-thirds of the forty or so students have experience in interracial dating.

*On the "melting pot" versus the "salad bowl"*: "To me, the melting pot melts away differences. It is assimilation. Assimilation is death. I will never assimilate, never." Like the issue of elections, it is impossible to distinguish between left and right. Many seem to have accepted the efficacy of the "melting pot." Those with a marginalized ethnic heritage or self-identities as foreigners have polar responses. Either they accept a variation of "melting pot," amending that not every difference needs melting away, or they are defiantly communitarian. Women communitarians are the most discriminating in their approach. They wish to retain the identity of their particular culture but not necessarily its strictures on women.

*On Bosnian/Croatian writers' contempt toward the United States*: "Damn it, why are they so angry at us when we are helping them?" A few of the foreign students attempt to explain the inconspicuous but sharp jabs of the aid provider's "charitable condescension." But the explanation works against one of the strongest self-images of U.S. citizens: they see themselves as effective purveyors of good toward others. Here understanding is near impossible, for who will seriously consider that goodness imposed is still worse than the wickedness proposed?

*Using a Marxist analysis Harry explains how the dominant Anglo society marginalizes certain ethnicities, exploits the working class, and imperializes the Third World. Marci's response*: "Why are you unable to apply that kind of analysis to how men dominate women?" It is a precious moment, worth waiting for. For the first time in the semester the immensely articulate Harry hesitates. He is caught. His rhetoric forces him to admit a possible parallel and his possible complicity.

*On the anarchic processes of the course*: "We just talk about the same things. I've learned nothing." Many agree, looking for a defense from me. I do not oblige. Others wait, then counter with "I have learned a lot, but I cannot tell you what." And "I am not sure I am learning anything, but I cannot stop thinking about this class."

*    *    *

As patterns emerge so do predictability and ennui. Everyone assumes that they know where the other sits politically and actually. The discussion does not advance or sustain their interest. Invariably, the next round of confrontation revolves not around *what* individuals believe but *why* they hold their beliefs. The conversation turns to the social determinacy of ideas and ideology. They become social scientists. Thus, Armando is said to believe X because he is a male, or a Hispanic, or a Puerto Rican, or from the working class. Likewise, Jamie believes Y because she is North American, a women, Anglo, and the beneficiary of a trust fund. Sirak's thorough anti-Americanism stems from his investment in a foreign identity. However, sometimes political positions cannot be read from social positions. We devote much energy to puzzling over how social positions produce politics and why they do not. Thus, women who do not feel oppressed by patriarchy are considered gullible; U.S. citizens who demonstrate sympathy to Third World causes are seen as hypocrites who misunderstand the source of their privilege; and marginalized social identities who display conservative colors are deemed brainwashed suck-ups. Innuendo and scorn circulate. The most used opening is "I am outraged at what you just said . . ." or "I cannot believe that in this day and age anyone could believe what I just heard . . ."

Their indignity certainly feels real to me. They read my face to ascertain how far I will let this go. I smile. Increasingly I becoming the target of their anger. Rightfully so; as the representative of the state I do not seem to be doing my job. Where is your teaching drive, they seem to ask. They wonder why I can't see that they need me to stop them from hurting each other. Attendance and preparation decrease. They begin to lose interest in the experiment and faith in the conversational process.

I have been eager to intervene at this point. I have tried to cajole them into recognizing the rich and multiple voices within and alongside their preferred positions, to become comfortable with ambiguity, and to be generous toward recessive parts of themselves and others. These are difficult notions because the teaching drive trains them to argue and converse with a single purified voice. I am up against the lessons of a lifetime. I still avail myself to these cajoling tools but less often and at a later juncture. Instead, I try to use their listlessness as a tool. When they are weary they implore me to do something. We begin to recognize that we are not particularly skilled at conversation. They demand lectures.

I prepare lectures. I have been waiting to have my say. It takes just one to convince them this is not what they want. No matter how insightful or energized my presentation, they cannot go back. They want to sustain the project of conversing with each other. But they are not sure how to go on. Here my intervention has seemed necessary. I do not know whether this is because I create this juncture so that they will need me, or whether they simply do not know what to do. I tread delicately. I ask them to read for each other the assignments they write for me. This decision came easily. Relative to their public utterances, their assigned writings are nuanced by alternatives, counter-voices, shades of doubt and ambiguity. Reading all their papers, I can see how multiple voices within individuals overlap with the multiple voices of others. With their permission class time is now divided between discussing the readings and reading students' work. I do not envision an easy harmony of interests but rather a further engagement in conversation.

Slowly, they begin to recognize that the complexity of their own positions matches that of their adversaries. A spirit of generosity begins to compete with the mood of confrontation and hostility. Clear differences between races, genders, classes, and ethnicities begin to be tempered with a richer complexity constituted by both difference and continuity. Especially in the last few weeks attendance is renewed as the new generosity fuses with a curiosity about how the course will end.

*   *   *

Some despise the course. They lose friends. They feel forced to uncover and defend parts of themselves they would have preferred to leave unexamined. What is most important is that they are no longer sure they want to learn. They start to treat learning with the care and caution deserved by the sharpest tools. Others recognize that what we desire to learn most is what we most conceal from ourselves and, therefore, that learning is finally a commitment to a form of living. Formal and informal course evaluations overwhelmingly suggest that indifference to the format of the course is near impossible. Much like me, they are not often able to clearly specify or assess what happens. Nevertheless, most admit that it is intense and some that it is consequential.

*     *     *

I worry that so far this essay depicts my classroom role as minimalist or noninterventionary, or as promoting laissez-faire. I do not wish to represent my engagement with anarchic pedagogical forms as promoting a libertarianism that suggests only students know what is best for them. Inverting the teaching drive does not interest me. Such a position, I fear, abdicates the critical responsibility of the pedagogue and thereby merely replicates the present and its deficiencies. If along the way I have implied that the state too must be divested of the subordinating assimilationism resulting from the teaching drive, I nevertheless also claim that the state must somehow retain its critical responsibility.

A more critical stance, one with which I sympathize, accepts that students and citizens may not know what is best for them. It accepts that the instructor and state may know their interests better than they themselves. This position, while it embraces responsibility, strikes me as dangerous (despite my sympathy for it) and no less supportive of the status quo. It sustains and promotes epistemological and existential violence.

I want to suggest that a dialectical synthesis of these positions pivots on the following proposition: as an instructor I may often see their interest, better than they, but *only* they can uncover and claim that interest. Only through their own labor do they realize themselves. I like to think that performing that labor and discovering such interests occurs through a conversational process within which each is a potential resource for the other's learning. With this in mind, I aim to use my institutionally sanctioned power to incapacitate my and others' hierarchical teaching and to promote processes of dialogical learning. This personal, pedagogical, and political commitment is nothing if not interventionary. The issue, then, is not the presence or absence of the instructor's institutional power in the classroom or the state's power in politics. Rather, the issue turns on the forms and purposes that power takes.

*     *     *

International relations theory continues to debate whether the United States maintains its global hegemony. I think the more serious issue concerns the response to this potential fall. Some implore revival, fearing not just the loss of U.S. prestige but more ominously the slide from order to anarchy for the whole global political economy. Others, myself included, applaud the loss as a much needed but late lesson on how to live as just another among many.

I hold some rather unwavering beliefs about how the hegemon in international relations oppresses and damages those under its coercive power, especially when it tries to teach. But these beliefs would not stay affixed to the target of my derision nor to the domain of global politics. I had to ask myself if my desire to intervene in the lives of my students differs substantively from the U.S. desire to make the world safe for democracy, freedom, and civilization. In professing what I take to be essential, was I not also destroying the vitality, diversity, and rich complexity that are the prerequisites of democracy, freedom, and civilization? Was I deflecting energy to *their* salvation because doubts about *mine* so fueled my fears? These questions were just a bit too close to home. I had to change either my valuation of the United States on the world stage or my grasp of the teacher's role.

My comprehension of the mentoring role has changed, but I have not given up using my authority in the classroom. I still direct the time when the course meets, the selection of the room, the tone of the syllabus, the selection of the books and videos, the form, content, and number of assignments, grading expectations, and especially the tone and format of discussion. For me, this implies that I cannot call on the United States to either give up its power or adopt an isolationist stance. Giving up mentoring for teachers and isolationism for the United States abdicates responsibility to reconstruct a globe we have done so much to mangle. In any case, as I hinted before, both celebrating and abdicating power are shallow resolutions that avoid assessing alternative uses of authority. I distinguish two analytically separable moments here. One can use authority to recreate relations of dependency employing a double illusion: first, of having mastered time and space, and, second, of tutoring that mastery to others. The full pours into the empty, not recognizing the relative abundance and poverty of each. Alternatively, one commits to using authority in order to undermine power. One attacks all forms of undue advantage including one's own participation in hierarchy (Shor and Friere 1987; Tompkins 1991). Now the other is no longer the barbarian in need of education and civility to be remade in my image. Rather, our mutual differences imply a conversation, leading perhaps to criticism and conflict, but also potentially to mutual enrichment (Blaney and Inayatullah 1994). And one through the other.[4]

*       *       *

The great Sūfī sage Jalāl ad-Dīn ar-Rūmī wrote: "New organs of perception come into being as a result of necessity. Therefore, O man, increase your necessity, so that you may increase your perception" (Shah 1969, 197). Students, like children and "barbarians," can teach us how to create participation. The price of this instruction, though, is that they respond only if we ask them with a needy look. Generating this disposition requires that we first acknowledge a lack within. If this seems a high price to pay, we can remind ourselves that the presence of emptiness motivates our seeking after the other in the first place. All voyages of discovery, including the most celebrated, seek the other in order to expose and fill an emptiness within. I suspect that even the teaching drive can be shown to betray this motive.

*       *       *

> The essential reasoning is simple. Between the modern master and non-modern slave, one must choose the slave not because one should choose voluntary poverty or admit the superiority of suffering, not only because the slave is oppressed, not even because he works (which, Marx said, made him less alienated than the master). One must choose the slave also because he represents a higher-order cognition which perforce includes the master as a human, whereas the master's cognition has to exclude the slave except as a "thing." (Nandy 1984, xv–xvi).

If all students participate, they also all resist. They resist the subordinating assimilationism of the teaching drive sometimes with impetuous defiance but often with a compellingly suggestive inventiveness. Within the confines of their relative powerlessness they respond to hypocrisy and alienation with small but vivid ruptures of illuminating creativity. This resistance, these ruptures, whether in the classroom or the world stage, may be the most potent resource in the hands of the educator who wants to learn about learning. Conceptualized adequately, that is, with generosity and humility, this resistance can lead the anxious, the righteous, and the powerful to comprehend the opportunities learners need in order to learn. If the teaching drive pushes water uphill, then resistance to teaching flows to richer waters.

*    *    *

Even the precise logic of Hegelian deduction cannot make a reader learn what the author intends. Writers present their lessons in alternative forms but the reader reads and takes according to need. Still, because the narrative influences and constitutes the reading, not just any interpretation follows. In this spirit perhaps the reader deserves not much closure but a distillation of the author's hopes.

I do not suppose that many will entirely welcome my claim that teaching obstructs and violates learning when it does not understand that (1) fear and desire of knowledge are both intrinsic to human beings; (2) students implicitly know how to learn; and (3) the primary role of the instructor is to help make this implicit knowing explicit by self-consciously constructing anarchic forms of conversation within which such knowledge emerges "spontaneously" through the labor of the participants. Violent teaching homogenizes space, fixes time, and treats the other's difference as degenerate (Inayatullah 1994). It projects a vision of education and citizenship constructed prior to, and independently of, the participation of students and citizens. Arrogantly indifferent to their potential contribution and transformation of political and educational processes, violent teaching erases their difference and thereby guarantees their alienation.

My essay does not strive to move the reader toward these claims. Rather, it hopes to affirm those who explore open-ended processes, to encourage those who are predisposed toward these moves but who find themselves hesitating ("the water is fine   really "), and to nudge those who overlook the breach between our beliefs and practices. The goal is not to replace the old orthodoxy with a new one, but rather to retain faith in our capacity to go on wading in the deep.


## Discussion

For those whose prime interest remains citizenship I can perhaps tie together a few loose ends. A sympathetic critique of this essay offers the following comment: "Your classes become exercises in democratic conversation. The participants experience all the problems, frustrations, and limits of democratic conversations, but nonetheless, the process infects them. Is there a lesson here for citizenship?" As long as this question separates studentship from citizenship I do not think I can envision much of a lesson for citizenship. To the degree that I see a lesson here, it concerns the overlap between student and citizen. I have claimed that perhaps despite their intentions teachers and state representatives alienate students and citizens through the teaching drive. In resisting the subordinating and assimilating moments of that drive, students and citizens offer rich clues to the meaningful reinvigoration of education and politics.

In part, such reinvigoration necessitates illuminating the inherent diversity of any social context. In reacting to my pedagogy, some students protest that my course format does not so much reflect as create difference and diversity within and beyond the classroom. Perhaps they are correct. However, my experience with most students suggests a different assessment. I read resistance to the assimilationism of the teaching drive as attempts by individuals to protect their particularity. I think that both this resistance and the difference that particularity protects are invaluable to the social whole—so long as we conceive that whole as a *differentiated* unity. In contrast, the protesting students value, and aim to move toward, an undifferentiated unity. From my view, their promotion of assimilationism must be resisted. From their point of view, I create differences, thereby increasing conflict and decreasing harmony. We might imagine that the tension between the two valuations of difference might be fruitful. Perhaps. However, for this tension to be truly productive, I suspect we will first have to undo a half-millennium of the teaching drive, subordinating assimilationism, and the presumptive devotion to the goal of an undifferentiated social whole.

I do not want my appreciation of difference to be misunderstood as promoting the false idea that difference and particularity are given by nature, therefore fixed. On the contrary, I believe that all commonalties and differences are social constructions, therefore mutable. Differences can be, and often should be, transformed. However, everything rests on the *form* of the alteration. Here I identify two pivotal questions. First, does the transformation contain the individual's own labor? Second, does the transformational process summarily negate the characteristics of the individual or does it respect them as a potential resource?

Usually if institutions acknowledge difference they do so as a prelude to subordinating the other. Likewise, their acknowledgment of the other as equal serves as a prelude to the other's assimilation (Todorov 1984). I believe that contemporary educational and political institutions remain baffled about how to consider their obligations to others when those others demand consideration as both different *and* equal. Such institutional confusion is understandable; finding a way to treat the other as both equal and different strikes me as a painstakingly difficult project. This is because the project, barely five hundred years old, is so young that we have yet to develop a language for grasping its meaning. Nor have we built institutions for practicing its imperatives. Nevertheless, if we lack the experience of how to adequately treat others as different but equal, we have ample experience with the *difficulty* of trying to do so. Perhaps the first step toward reviving education and citizenship requires us to recognize this difficulty. I suspect that students leave anarchic learning formats with a stronger intuitive sense of this difficulty. I would *not* say that when students leave my course they naturally know how to become better citizens. Rather, I would say that sensing the difficulty of learning with and from others in a classroom begins to prepare us to engage the enormous challenge of creating a critical citizenry with different others.

## Notes

For their comments on an earlier draft, I thank Anna Aganthagalou, Keisha Audain, Jonathan Bach, Hannah Britton, Wayne Malcolm, Robin Riley, and the editors. My apologies to Hannah Britton and Robin Riley for not incorporating the depth of their criticism.

1. I take this to be especially true in the social sciences and humanities where the act of human study and learning influences and changes the object of study. See Giddens (1976, 153–54; 1979, 47, 244–45; 1984, xxxiv–xxxv, 27, 346–47, 353) for more on the central role of reflexivity in the social world.

2. The musical analogy is jazz or classical Indian music in which by design the interaction of the players, audience, and composition together determine the flow of sound and meaning.

3. See Harry Kariel's (1977) provocative essay.

4. I have lifted this sentence directly from Jonathan Bach's comments on a prior draft.

*11*

# Teaching Deliberation: Citizenship Education and Cross-Disciplinary Team Teaching

*Mark Rupert*

Deliberation suggests careful thought or reflection, consideration of alternatives, but may also imply public discussion, processes working toward collective judgments. For different reasons, liberals and their critics would agree that deliberation is central to citizenship. For liberals, deliberation in the public sphere is instrumental to the purposes and interests of free individuals, combining with other private citizens to articulate and pursue common interests. For those with a more communitarian perspective, public deliberation is part of the process through which citizens are socially constituted and democratic participation is thus intrinsically rather than instrumentally valuable. At Syracuse University's Maxwell School of Citizenship and Public Affairs, we have developed a team-taught, cross-disciplinary social science course that emphasizes public deliberation not only on policy issues, but on the meaning of citizenship itself. I write here about a collective project involving over the past few years several dozen people. Not all of them agree with all aspects of my interpretation of the course.

Our course entitled Critical Issues for the United States—along with its sister-course, The Global Community—originated with a year-long process of intensive discussion and planning among a group of faculty drawn from the various academic departments and programs of the Maxwell School.[1] The courses we developed were first offered during the 1993–94 academic year, and have undergone annual revisions—

189

some modest, some more substantial—ever since. The fundamental ideas underlying the courses have not changed, however: they remain focused upon citizenship, understood in terms of practices of public deliberation.

Our courses were designed as multidisciplinary survey courses that would, in the process of discussing issues important to the lives of our students, introduce them to some of the major concepts and modes of analysis employed in the various social science disciplines represented at the Maxwell School. There was from the outset, then, a sense of multiplicity of perspective built into the core concept of these courses. They would not present a single seamless vision of social life or seek to find the one right answer. Rather, they would present multiple interpretations of each issue we dealt with, some convergent, some in direct conflict. We would try to link these interpretations to fundamental assumptions about the nature of social life, and to show how these basic conceptual frameworks were related to different normative orientations and political positions—that is, to different practices of citizenship. We would invite students to ponder the implications of the various perspectives we discussed, to consider the consequences for their lives as citizens, but we would not push for closure or consensus. We would emphasize the *process* of deliberation, rather than any particular result.

We expose students to different ways of knowing social reality: the hypothesis-testing approach of orthodox social science, rudimentary rational choice theory, more interpretive understandings of social action, and critical theory models that seek organic links between knowing the world and recreating the world. We try to underscore the idea that different ways of knowing are associated with different modes of action and, ultimately, with alternative possible worlds. How knowledge is socially constructed is thus a crucial dimension of citizenship, and an important aspect of this course.

## Format

As part of our emphasis on processes of deliberation, we wanted to move away from the passive, lecture-based format typical of introductory survey courses at larger universities. In many such courses, if students are involved in smaller discussion sections at all, they are typically led by graduate teaching assistants and are at best an adjunct to the primary, lecture-driven substance of the course. In contrast, the

Maxwell courses were designed so that two-thirds of students' class time would be spent in discussion sections of no more than fifteen, led by members of a team representing a cross-section of the Maxwell School faculty. To underscore for students that these discussion sections were not merely the caboose on a lecture-driven train, but were rather the motor of this course, a substantial part of their final course grade (currently 25 percent) is directly linked to their level of participation in these discussions. Particular faculty members meet twice each week with the same discussion groups so that a sense of mutual familiarity and group identity could develop, fostering candor in discussion and a willingness to think out loud.

Once a week, rotating pairs of faculty share the responsibility of lecturing to a "plenary" in which all the discussion sections meet together. These lectures typically present alternative perspectives or ways of thinking about some general question or issue area. Faculty attempt to "model" intellectual activity for students, thinking through the strengths and weaknesses of various perspectives, underscoring their implications for politics and social life. Often, faculty will present perspectives with which they do not agree, and will state so at the outset. In this way, they may illustrate for students that there is an intelligible train of reasoning behind each position, and that our first task as critical thinkers and citizens is to try to understand that reasoning. Implicitly we pose the question: why would reasonable people hold such a view? In the first instance, then, our objective is to help students to feel the attraction that draws scholars and citizens to a particular perspective, its intellectual power, its political promise, its vitality. We then try to explore the tensions or limits of each perspective. Again, the emphasis is on deliberation rather than mastery of a given fund of "knowledge," but we do expect students to understand key concepts, arguments, and supporting evidence for each of the major positions we deal with, and ultimately to be able to incorporate these into their own critical judgments and deliberations.

To deemphasize rote learning, we abandoned conventional exams altogether. Instead, frequent writing assignments are integrated into the course as one more mode of deliberation and discussion. Students contribute regularly to a computerized "citizenship log" in which they are asked to exchange comments on a particular issue or idea in the course material. To encourage students to come to class prepared to actively discuss the material at hand, we may ask them to write a brief paragraph responding to each day's readings and perhaps to post this response on the electronic log for other members of the class to see. In addition to addressing regular prompts from the faculty, students may also engage each other on the electronic log, continuing or anticipating classroom discussions. Often, faculty will review students' e-log entries prior to class and use them to construct an agenda for more focused group discussion.

We also employ more traditional forms of writing. From time to time, we ask students to write very brief response papers (one or two pages) that focus their attention directly upon substantive points judged by the faculty team to be especially significant. Frequently these will be concepts or issues that will be important for future deliberative essays. This helps students early on to begin to come to grips with key claims or ideas, and enables the faculty to gauge their success in doing so. This may be a useful diagnostic tool: disappointing performance on response papers may then signal to us that particular students need additional help with key concepts, or they may reveal that the entire class needs to spend more time collectively working through some especially difficult points.

Finally, each major unit of the course culminates in a somewhat longer "deliberative essay" in which students are asked to critically assess various perspectives and formulate a position relative to the major theme or issue of that unit. These essays are kept short (typically around five pages) in order to encourage students to be as concise as possible, to make deliberate decisions about what material is most significant, to develop summarization skills, and to preclude the "kitchen sink" approach to paper writing. To aid students in the development of essay-writing skills, the faculty have prepared extensive writing guidelines that include such fundamentals as how to construct and support a reasoned argument, how such arguments differ from assertions of opinion, and how to use sources and avoid plagiarism. To reinforce our seriousness about the development of analytical writing skills, our grading criteria are keyed to these guidelines and we provide extensive written feedback on essays pointing out where there is significant room for improvement. We also make available to students annotated examples of especially strong essays so that students can see for themselves the kinds of work they are capable of producing and what faculty graders are looking for in student writing.

Altogether, students write five to eight papers of various lengths, and anywhere from a dozen to several dozen computer log entries. To aid faculty in designing these writing assignments, and to advise students on how to construct them, our faculty team includes an instructor from the university's writing program who has been involved in course planning from the outset, is familiar with the readings, attends all our lectures, and participates actively in faculty meetings. We have found the writing instructor to be especially valuable in helping us to design writing assignments that balance the open-endedness necessary for real deliberation with the concreteness required to hold student interest.

In keeping with this relatively open-ended format, we avoided adopting any standard textbooks, and instead assembled a custom reader that presents students with the challenge of interpreting multiple voices and engaging a variety of perspectives. In addition to our reader, we assign three books representing particular positions on each of the major issues under discussion. To maintain creative tension and space for deliberation, we are careful to include in our reader several counterpoints to each of the books we assign. Our goal is to provide students with enough material to construct both a critical and a supportive position with regard to each major reading.

We have also developed a home page on the World Wide Web in order to give students the opportunity to explore the vast array of resources available in cyberspace. For readers who would like to visit, our URL is:

http://www.maxwell.syr.edu/maxpages/classes/Max123/
Maxindex.htm

Our home page contains all the materials that would be found in a syllabus, together with guidelines for the different kinds of writing assignments students will encounter, annotated examples of strong student essays, information about members of the faculty team, links to computerized discussion forums for each class section, and links to a variety of resources external to the university. Newspapers and magazines, government agencies, political parties, advocacy groups, think tanks, databases, and archives are made accessible through our Web page. Our hope is that this array of electronic resources will not just facilitate learning through the classroom experience, but will also prompt students to consider the links between issues and perspectives discussed in class and those they encounter in the media and on the Web. To further encourage this, we directly incorporate Web materials into some of our class sessions: for example, we used material from the Web sites of industry, environmental, and citizens' groups to facilitate a role-playing exercise in which groups of students were asked to interpret the position of a particular group and to come to class prepared to assume their identity and negotiate with others based upon· what they had learned from the Web sites we assigned.


## Substantive Vehicle

The course Critical Issues for the United States began as a series of debates on issues that faculty planning teams thought to be important for students as citizens. Early versions of the course focused upon such issues as individual rights and the responsibilities of citizenship, the size and scope of federal government as well as the relative merits of governmental centralization and decentralization, unequal access to quality education, race and affirmative action, and the environment. However, over successive semesters, student evaluations suggested that these issues and the arguments relevant to them were being perceived as separate and disconnected. The course was not providing students with a way to connect these discussions to contested visions of civic life, to see that positions on different issues might be linked by similar understandings of citizenship, to understand that policy debates are also debates about the kind of society we wish to live in and the kinds of citizens we want to be.

To provide a substantive vehicle that would refocus the course on contested meanings of civic life and citizenship, and to help students see more clearly the linkages between these visions and particular political positions, we introduced a new integrative theme for the course as a whole: "The American Dream Reconsidered." We ask students to deliberate on questions such as the following: What has the American Dream meant historically? What meanings does it have for people today? How do visions of the American Dream help us to think about ourselves as citizens, and what difference does it make if we think about the Dream in one way or another? How have issues of race, class, and gender figured in various interpretations of the Dream? Are there nationalist or nativist undertones in some or all versions of the Dream? Can, or should, the prevailing interpretation of the American Dream survive into the twenty-first century?

To engage students on issues where they feel they have some stake and where they already know something, we approach these questions not in the abstract but as they have confronted us in three major areas of public controversy.

## Economy

We ask whether the American Dream has been associated with the rise of a large and prosperous "middle class," and if that version of the Dream is threatened by economic changes currently underway. What kinds of economic conditions are needed to support the Dream? Who can, or should, participate in such prosperity? What is the meaning of participation in an economy, and how is that participation related to different notions of citizenship and community?

This unit of the course introduces the basic market model, emphasizing individual choice and the role of prices as transmitters of both information and incentives. We present the case for the proposition that, in the absence of external intervention, individuals acting in pursuit of their own self-interest will realize through market institutions the most efficient allocation of resources. This implies a limited role for government and a tolerance for the economic and political inequalities that are intrinsic to a system of individualized incentives. We present the classic critique of governmental policies aimed at fostering greater equality: such policies are counterproductive insofar as they distort price signals and undermine incentives for the efficient allocation of resources, and are undesirable since they restrict individual liberty. On this view, then, the American Dream entails the protection of individual rights and liberties and a system of opportunity in which individuals are rewarded in proportion to their hard work and merit. America became a wealthy and powerful world leader through the pursuit of this vision of the Dream and, to the extent that we have in recent decades experienced diminished opportunity, prosperity, and power, it is because we have strayed from the original version of the Dream.

We also present in this unit a view of the American Dream of individual reward and prosperity as embedded in sets of social institutions that unequally allocate power, wealth, and knowledge, and that limit opportunities for meaningful self-government. These inequalities are woven through relations of class, race, and gender, and have intensified in recent years as the American economy has become more polarized in terms of power, income, and wealth. This view offers its own view of the American Dream, one that has markedly different political implications from the first view. The political horizon projected by this vision of the Dream constitutes a community of actively self-governing citizens. To the extent that economic institutions foster inequalities that preclude the realization of this Dream of participatory democracy for all citizens, institutional reforms aimed at equalization and democrati-

zation are warranted. We then explore some of the reforms proposed
by critics of the contemporary American political economy, as well as
the concerns that a more individualistic perspective would raise about
those proposed reforms.


## Education

We look at education as a pathway to a better life for individuals, or
as a prerequisite of an actively self-governing community. What kind
of educational system do we need in order to fulfill different versions
of the Dream? How are different visions of citizenship implicated in
contemporary debates about educational reform?

We explore problems of unequal access to quality education, both in
K–12 public schools and at the college level. We examine analyses that
argue that some Americans receive first-rate education at public expense, while there are entire classes of citizens who are not provided
with education adequate to enable effective participation in public deliberations, and thereby become disempowered, second-class citizens.
Accordingly, some prescribe a more centralized and uniform administration of public education in order to eliminate the grossest inequalities and ensure for all citizens the "equal protection of the laws"
promised by the Fourteenth Amendment. We also explore arguments
that locate the problems of public school systems in overcentralized
and bureaucratized administrations, and that prescribe institutional
reforms that move education closer to a competitive market model
based upon consumer sovereignty and choice. Finally, we grapple with
the dilemmas of affirmative action in college admissions, and ask how
a liberal individualist society can cope with persistent inequalities of
race in higher education.


## Environment

We look at the relationship between the natural environment and
the American Dream. Can the prevailing vision of the Dream coexist
with a healthy environment? Can we imagine more environmentally
friendly versions of the Dream? What would be the broader social and
political implications of enacting a more environmentally sustainable
vision of the American Dream?

We examine the anthropocentric view of nature as having value only
insofar as it serves human purposes, and which further suggests that
the market mechanism is the best way to determine to what extent

humans should exploit the natural environment. Establishing property rights over natural resources creates a direct incentive for their wise management. Further, the price signals and incentives of the market will call forth effective substitutes in response to resource shortages and new technologies that may minimize or eliminate our costliest environmental problems. This "free market environmentalism" is entirely consistent with the individualistic vision of the American Dream, promising consumers a world in which self-interested market behavior continues to generate high standards of living into the indefinite future. This view is encapsulated in Jay Leno's snack chip advertisement: "Eat all you want; we'll make more."

In contrast to this market-based view, we also examine the perspective of environmentalists who suggest that our relationship with nature is best viewed not in terms of the instrumental exploitation of an external object, but rather as a necessary aspect of any sustainable human community. On this view, then, our obligation as citizens of the community extends to future generations, and we must make environmental decisions based upon social norms of long-term sustainability. Such decisions cannot be made through the instrumental calculus of the market, but must instead be made through processes of public deliberation. This, in turn, requires institutions to support such processes of democratic deliberation and citizens competent to participate in them, and thus also suggests certain linkages to the other units of our course.

In addressing each of these critical issues we hope to lead students to ask: What does the American Dream promise? Does it mean individual liberty? Does it mean democracy? Does it mean equality? Does it mean opportunity for material success? A "middle-class" standard of living for most, if not all, citizens? The freedom to succeed or to fail? Freedom from oppression or poverty? Is it a promise of a better life for individuals? A better society in which all of us can live? Is mass consumption a necessary centerpiece of the Dream, or might it involve a more harmonious and balanced relationship with nature? What can, or should, we expect from the American Dream now and in the future? And what do those expectations mean for our own practices of citizenship?

In these ways, we try to encourage our students to see this course as being about themselves, their political community, and their future. In that sense, the course as a whole represents an invitation to enter into the public deliberations that are at the heart of various understandings of citizenship.

## Reflections

I came to these special courses with some modest experience of teaching discussion-oriented and writing-intensive courses. After an introduction to the teaching profession, which involved lecturing three times a week to faceless crowds of over two hundred students, I was fortunate to be able to teach international relations for several years in the Syracuse University Honors Program. These were some of the best students at Syracuse, accustomed to putting serious effort into their education and expecting a more intensive learning experience. It was exhilarating, a whole new kind of teaching for me: the students were eager to learn, and it seemed as though all I had to do was present them with some challenging material and prompt them with a few provocative questions and off they went, teaching each other and, in the process, teaching me about teaching. Eventually, though, I began to feel a nagging sense of guilt, inchoate at first, increasingly clear later on. I was doing my best teaching with those students who least needed my help. In that sense, I began to feel that I wasn't really doing my job. Then I was offered the opportunity to join the Maxwell courses.

Reflecting back now on five years of continuous teaching with these very special courses, the achievement from which I derive the greatest satisfaction is that we have been able to create for a cross-section of first- and second-year students a learning experience very much like that which was previously the privilege of Honors students. In that sense, our courses have been about the democratization of education, as well as the education of democratization.

## Notes

1. Maxwell School departments offering courses to undergraduates are Anthropology, Economics, Geography, History, Political Science, and Sociology, along with interdisciplinary programs in Public Affairs and International Relations.

*12*

# Using the Internet to Enhance Classroom and Citizenship Information

*William Ball*

The success of democratic politics depends on the basic political competencies of its citizens. As George Marcus and Russell Hanson write:

> If the public does not know what it wants, there is no popular will to reflect, and the whole idea of popular sovereignty is called into question. Similarly, if the public is incapable of expressing its views, political leaders can hardly be charged with making policies congruent with majority sentiment. How could they, given the absence of direction from the people? Thus, everything depends on public opinion, the greatest strength—and also the chief weakness—of democratic politics. (1993, 6)

Yet early research into the abilities of American citizens as political participants produced some very disconcerting results. For example, the well-known studies by Philip Converse (1964, 1970) challenged the fundamental rationality and coherence of the political views expressed by the public. While these particular results have been questioned, near universal concern remains about the ability of the average citizen to make informed political choices; for a presentation of all sides of the issue see the exchange between Donald Kinder and Don Herzog (1993) and James Farr (1993).

While political scientists continue to research the political competencies of the public, they also have the perfect opportunity to make a positive impact on these competencies through their teaching. In particular, introductory general education courses, such as Introduction to Political Science or American National Government, provide a chance to both inform and empower a broad selection of students with respect to their political system. As in any course, the key to success is to motivate students by making the subject matter meaningful to them, by engaging them directly with the "stuff" of politics and thus making it relevant to their lives. The personal relevance of the study of politics and its accessibility may be obvious to the instructor, yet the undergraduate has likely had little or no contact with the political system. Thus politics is likely to be seen by the student as a very abstract and distant subject. Until recently, the kind of experiential education discussed elsewhere in this volume was the only way to bring students into direct contact with political events and political actors, both politicians and other citizens.

While it is not a full substitute for more physical forms of contact with the political system, the Internet offers an opportunity to greatly enrich classroom-based citizenship education. Political views and events are communicated through the Internet. Indeed, politics is taking place on the Internet, from the informal discussion groups on a bewildering array of political topics, to the professionally crafted campaign materials of potential officeholders. Moreover, now that virtually all campuses have good connections to the Internet available for student use, and now that the technology has become vastly easier to use, the Internet provides a very cheap and convenient means of bringing politics directly into the student experience. Given the promise of the Internet to improve citizenship education, many political scientists have begun to employ the Internet in teaching politics. Gary Klass (1995) has compiled a database of more than forty-five examples; see also William Ball (1995) for an additional example, presented in considerably more detail.

This essay illustrates how the Internet can be used to develop citizenship among students—to encourage student participation in politics and to establish the relevance of political events to the personal lives of students—in addition to other educational objectives. I provide examples of four ways in which the Internet was incorporated into a course on American government and report student reactions to the experience. I also place the course in a context of types of Internet applications in education and briefly review the scant evaluative research on the use of the Internet as a teaching tool. Finally, I discuss the broader implications of the increasing ubiquity of the Internet for citizenship education.

# Examples of Incorporating the Internet into Teaching American Government

Courses employing the Internet can be classified along two dimensions: by the type of technique and by the intensity of integration of the Internet into the course. Internet techniques are generally of two types: those based on discussion lists or forums, and those using the Internet as a so-called virtual library. Discussion-type approaches emphasize person-to-person interactivity, while virtual library–type approaches take advantage of the Internet's ability to provide, on demand, a vast number of documents in different media. Klass (1996) has identified three increasingly intense levels of integration of the Internet into teaching: courses that use the Internet to parallel traditional forms (such as putting the course syllabus on-line as well as distributing it in print), courses that use the Internet in entirely new applications to supplement course-based learning (such as having students participate in Internet discussion groups), and courses that use the Internet to replace the classroom entirely. Klass finds that almost all of the "cyberclasses" in his database are at the first level of intensity.

I have used Internet resources with a variety of political science courses, from the history of political thought to research methods, as well as in informal settings outside the classroom. Most of my uses have employed the Internet as a virtual library. Yet even in this mode of application, the Internet provides a highly interactive and ultimately transforming experience for students and instructors alike. Students, and occasionally members of the community, approach me with questions about political events or processes with which I am often only vaguely familiar. By being able to access the text and explanatory material for a current California ballot initiative from my office in New Jersey, for example, I can not only help students find the material they are looking for but also show them how to find similar material themselves in the future and learn something new myself. I can greatly add to the impact of a discussion about the role of deliberation in ancient Athenian democracy by using Web sites to illustrate my topic. Once interested in a topic, students often continue class discussions via electronic mail, either privately with me or among themselves or more publicly in discussion groups.

Below, I provide more detailed examples drawn from a section of American National Government that I taught in the summer of 1996, a course specifically planned to try out and refine a variety of Internet-based assignments and multimedia presentations. Since the use of the

Internet in teaching politics is very recent, it is a practice that is still in the experimental stage. Instructors are trying out different types of assignments and different Internet technologies. The examples from my own teaching that follow are in this experimental spirit.

In some ways this course was identical to American government courses taught virtually everywhere in the United States. The course was a one-semester freshman-level survey of national institutions and processes. It was based on one of the major American government textbooks and employed both in-class exams and out-of-class writing assignments for the evaluation of students. In other ways, the course was uncharacteristic, but ideally suited for experimentation with Internet and multimedia resources. It was offered during the summer session, when my institution's only fully equipped multimedia classroom was available for use, and when the distractions of teaching multiple courses was absent. The course had an enrollment of seven students, which allowed me maximum flexibility in trying out assignments and allowed me to work individually with students whenever needed. The students represented three different home institutions and all four undergraduate classes—providing feedback from an unusually wide variety of perspectives for such a small group. None of the students was a political science major.

Of course, with seven students, systematic quantitative evaluation of data from the course was not possible. However, students were asked to comment frequently on the techniques and assignments employed, in both verbal and written form, including a daily journal. Moreover, to make the instructor experience more generalizable to large classes offered during a busy school year, I kept my additional preparation time down to an average of about thirty minutes per lecture.

The Internet was employed in four distinct ways during this course, three of which I regard as quite successful. The first, a discussion-type technique and least successful of the four, was to engage students in an on-line political discussion forum. The second was to have students compare the reporting on the same issue from on-line representatives of the media, government, and opinion polling. The third was to have students examine the way parties and campaigns portrayed themselves on-line. The fourth was to use multimedia resources on the Internet to liven up my own lecture presentations. Each of these last three represent virtual library-type techniques. The course operated at the first two levels of intensity of Internet integration. The syllabus and assignment instructions were provided to students in both print and on-line form. In contrast, the contents of the assignments themselves were located entirely on-line. However, the class met in traditional lecture/ discussion sessions.

As noted, the course was used to experiment with a variety of Internet multimedia applications. It is unlikely that an instructor would use all of these techniques in a single course on a regular basis. However, each individual assignment can be used effectively in American government and a wide array of other courses. The first three assignments do not require any special equipment in the classroom. An Internet-enabled lab is all that is necessary. In fact, many students now have adequate Internet access from dorm or home to do these assignments, and find them even more convenient than traditional library-based research.

## Assignment 1: Participation in Political Discussion

As their first assignment in the course, students were asked to participate in an on-line discussion. This type of assignment has been used by Klass (1995), Martha Bailey (1995), and many others (the next section notes the evaluation research on this type of assignment). The intent behind a discussion-type technique is primarily to engage the students in political discussion beyond the classroom and with people who are different from themselves. It is a form of direct, albeit informal, political participation.

For my course, students were asked to make a submission to existing usenet newsgroups. Existing newsgroups were used, rather than a special-purpose discussion forum created for the class, in order to reduce the time and resources necessary to prepare the assignment. Students were asked to write a personal position statement of a couple of paragraphs on one of the major controversies covered in the initial chapters of their textbook. These chapters were devoted to basic values in American government, the Constitution, civil rights, and civil liberties. Students were asked to make a reasoned argument for a particular viewpoint in this brief statement and then ask for responses. They submitted their statements to several of a limited selection of newsgroups including talk.politics.theory. This group seems to have the most appropriate level of discussion for the course. Responses were collected for about a week and then each student wrote a couple of pages based on the discussion their statements created.

My students submitted statements on a good selection of topics including the fairness of the jury system, the value of immigration restrictions, the use of quotas in affirmative action, and abortion laws as an issue of the separation of church and state. As others have observed (e.g., Klass 1995), knowing that their writing would be offered to a global audience motivated students to craft their statements with more care than is usual—if only they would write their exam essays with such care! Yet their statements generated only a moderate level of discussion, ranging from a single response up to six.

As is usually the case with Internet discussion groups, the quality of the responses varied greatly, from brief and incomprehensible notes to a four-page scholarly discourse. For example, one student noted that "responses tended not to be well thought out and some phrases I really couldn't understand." Another student, submitting a message on gun control, commented:

> *The respondents to these arguments did seem to be answer [sic] very passionately to these comments, the only problem was that they were not very argumentative. They only stated their case and made it clear that they agreed or disagreed and really did not say why. I felt that the answers did not explain the sides very well, so unfortunately I was forced to make some assumptions from the responses to this topic on the second amendment.*

These results were used in class to illustrate to students the same concerns about the reasoning abilities of the citizenry that opened this chapter. Yet student disappointment with the responses they received was clear.

As noted above, I regard this as the least successful Internet-based exercise in the course. Given the effort students put into familiarizing themselves with the software, writing their statements, and following the newsgroups, they were quite disappointed with the limited number of responses they received. Further, they had difficulty tracking responses to their particular submission through the wide-ranging discussions already taking place on their selected newsgroups. While existing discussion groups were employed in the assignment to save instructor time and effort, the exercise seems to have been rendered less successful as a result. Klass (1995) reports better results with discussion lists specially created for a course.

This type of assignment is riskier than those discussed below, because the instructor cannot predict the quantity and quality of responses that student submissions will generate. Further, the assignment appears to be a high-investment one for students, even when they are submitting only a paragraph or two, and thus requires considerable preparation by the instructor in order to be well received.

## Assignment 2: Comparing Political Information Sources

The second assignment for the course (as well as the third) made use of the Internet's role as a virtual library of unfiltered original data, rather than as a medium for discussion. In the second assignment students were asked to compare the coverage given to a single current issue in public policy—raising the minimum wage was recommended—by government, the media, and opinion polls. More specifically, they researched World Wide Web sites of the White House, Congress, several news magazines, and the Gallup polling organization. At these sites they encountered varying types of documents on their topic, including presidential speeches and congressional testimony, journalistic articles, and raw data. The assignment was modeled after one developed by Stephen Frantzich (1995), which was primarily intended to illustrate bias in media reporting of presidential press briefings. In the expanded version of the assignment that I employed, students were able to see not only media bias, but differences among branches of government in the way an issue is addressed, how well the rhetoric of public officials and journalists matches public opinion, and how informative each source is from a citizen's perspective. Students were required to write a three-page analysis of the Web sites they visited for this assignment.

While overall reaction to this assignment was quite positive, contained within student reaction was a mix of excitement and frustration. Students were excited about accessing the sources directly and conveniently (each site was linked from the class Web page). Their frustration—expected and very useful pedagogically—came from the relative incomparability of sources, even when addressing the same issue. Students discovered that the president and members of Congress are often talking past rather than to each other. This discovery provided good preparation for a presentation on the differing constituencies of the president and Congress, and on the differences between public speeches and private negotiation on legislation.

Moreover, students found it to be a very challenging task to piece together the "story" behind pending legislation by looking at the rhetoric of the actors directly involved or the brief coverage of news media. The assignment motivated students to create their own understanding of an issue by digging through original sources—and left them wanting more. This is illustrated by the following student comments: "I may feel this way because of the nature of this course, trying to think deeper about an issue that is being presented on the surface" and

"There is a lot of knowledge and general information out there—unfortunately I still don't feel like I really know how to find it and exploit it properly."

## Assignment 3: Comparing On-Line Campaigns

The 1996 presidential election provided a new opportunity for using the Internet in citizenship education. Although the Internet was used somewhat by campaigns during the 1992 election, the 1996 election was the first time that the full range of parties and candidates were represented. This meant that students had easy and direct access to a full array of campaign material, providing original data for class-related research on elections.

The third assignment took advantage of this opportunity, with emphasis on the interaction of political ideology and elections and citizen participation. Ideology was introduced in the first weeks of the course as a way of categorizing basic values in politics and explaining the conflicts over policy issues. For this assignment, ideology was explored as an important feature of elections—a way in which candidates try to distinguish themselves. The Web sites of major parties and candidates were also very useful in illustrating how these actors try to respond to voter apathy by encouraging any form of participation. Each of these Web sites included interactive elements such as games and some comic relief. These features allowed the class to consider issues surrounding citizen participation in the electoral process. In contrast to the major party and candidate sites, the minor party sites took a much drier tone, clearly preaching to the converted and the activists. Other features of elections explored in this assignment included the relative weight given to personality and issues, the strategies of parties versus individual candidates, and differences among major and minor parties. Students researched the Web sites of the Republican National Committee, Dole for President, Republicans for Bill Clinton, the Libertarian Party, and the National Party (a white supremacist group).

One of the most interesting elements of the highly positive student reaction to this assignment was created by the use of original sources. Students were very excited about being able to see how candidates and parties represented themselves directly, without the filtering effects of the media. Students expressed weariness at having every statement or act interpreted for them by the media. Further, they enjoyed being able to explore the election literature in greater depth on-line than is possible in a print article or broadcast sound bite. One student commented:

*I felt the sites were very informative. They do not even compare to the traditional campaign ads. The sites go into further detail and provide all sorts of perspectives on all the major topics. The sites are up to date and straight forward. They are biased, but the sites are open and encourage all readers. It was a pleasant experience searching through particular Web sites. I found them extremely informative.*

However, during extended class discussions over the assignment it slowly became clear to students that some interpretation and filtering of original sources is beneficial. We had a very fruitful discussion on issues of marketing and propaganda in campaigns, authoritativeness of sources, and investigative reporting. The students left the class with both an appreciation of the role of the media as a critical voice and a desire to get to the original sources to make judgments for themselves.

## Using the Internet as a Multimedia Resource

The final way in which the Internet was used in the course was as a virtual library for multimedia resources. The course had a strong multimedia component in addition to the Internet-based assignments. Some multimedia material was incorporated into my lectures from CD-ROMs and videotapes. However, the Internet also provided a range of multimedia material including illustrated documents, still photos, video, and audio. The classroom had a direct Internet link that allowed me to use Web pages to illustrate lecture points or spark class discussion. The advantage that this use of the Internet provides for citizenship education directly concerns student perception of relevance during lecture periods. American government textbooks try very hard to demonstrate why their content is relevant to the "real world" outside the classroom with generous illustrations and examples of semi-current events. However, heretofore, it has been very hard to do this in the classroom itself. The Internet allows the instructor to bring the real world into the classroom to share with students in a way not possible before.

The headline news services provided by several Internet directories were used to demonstrate the relevance of class material to breaking news. We also went beyond the headlines; the class visited and discussed Web sites covering issues such as homosexual rights, minimum wage legislation, censorship of the Internet, and the presidential election. Because of the vastly lower costs of publication compared with other media, the Web allows this kind of in-depth coverage of issues. Since Web browsers allow the user to control font sizes for most on-line documents, it was easy for me to have the Web browser used in the class format even lengthy Internet documents in font sizes large enough to be readable by everyone in the room when displayed through the projection equipment.

While documents relevant to the course are easy to find on the Internet, material in other media is currently more scarce, expensive, or prohibited from duplication. Yet the Internet can provide useful multimedia supplements for a course. Again, news services were used to provide still photos and short video clips on current events that, accessed directly off the services' Web sites from the classroom, eliminated worry about copyright issues. Other materials can be obtained from stock photo and government sources on the Internet. However, given the current costs of on-line stock photography, these resources were used very sparingly in the course. There are also pockets of relevant audio content on the Internet, most available for educational use without charge. I used several speeches of past presidents and the oral transcript of *Roe v. Wade* to enliven class presentations.

Not only can the Internet be used as a multimedia resource, but Internet software can be used to make and transport the presentation itself. Some class presentations were authored in the Web's format and presented in the Netscape Navigator Web browser. This worked best when the presentation was a simple outline with links to several Internet resources built into it. Other, more complex presentations were authored in PowerPoint. But even these were retrieved from my office PC and transported to the classroom via the Netscape Web browser. Moving presentations to the classroom via the Internet technology proved much more reliable and convenient than carrying around disk-based media.

Judging student reaction to many of the Internet multimedia resources was difficult because these were intermixed with multimedia material from CD-ROMs and videotapes. For example, students expressed high levels of appreciation for the video elements in the course but did not (and likely could not) distinguish the source of the video in their comments. The one area where the Internet resources made a clear difference was the use of on-line breaking news stories. Students reacted very positively to the class discussions based on these resources. One student characterized the multimedia elements obtained from news stories on the Internet as "very interesting and well organized which made it easier to follow class discussion." Given the long time to publication for most other media, breaking news is not feasible to share with students in class short of reading a newspaper to them, and it was much more of a pleasure to read *with*, rather than *to*, the students.

## The Internet as a Teaching Tool in Evaluative Context

In my judgment (and supported by student feedback), the course was quite successful aside from the unanticipated low response to the first assignment. It engaged the students more directly with the subject matter than is usually the case. It increased their interest in debating political issues. One student concluded: "I thought that use of the Internet for this class was a very good idea. It made the class more interesting and helped develop some discussions."

However, a subjective assessment of a single course is hardly adequate to evaluate the use of the Internet for classroom-based citizenship education. Unfortunately, the research literature on the impact of Internet technologies in learning is scant and narrowly focused on discussion-type techniques since they employ older and more familiar technologies. In this section I will try to set the stage for more systematic and comprehensive evaluation of all forms of Internet techniques by placing my course in the context of the broader range of experience with using the Internet in education.

At this point, the research literature on the impact of the Internet in education focuses narrowly on discussion-type techniques including applications at the first level of intensity (e.g., continuing in-class discussions via e-mail) and, to a lesser degree, at the second level of intensity (such as using Internet discussion groups to access a global audience). The literature on these techniques indicates that Internet applications not only produce positive learning results but also transform the nature of the learning experience by making it more collaborative and student-driven.

This general impression holds across disciplines and levels of education. Stephen Bruning (1995) reports that developing Internet skills in communications students, specifically the use of e-mail, leads students to communicate more frequently with the instructor and at a higher level of sophistication. Ron Barnette reports that the use of discussion lists in his philosophy courses enhances critical-thinking skills in collaborative work: "Members would respond to the discussion topic, defend their positions, raise critical objections, respond to challenges, reflect on implied new directions for analysis and further critical thought" (1995, 31). Robin Wagner and Bill Wilson (1995) note the beneficial impact of Internet techniques on active learning and group work in interdisciplinary courses. S. P. Fowell and P. Levy (1995) lay out the theoretical underpinnings of education via group collaboration employing Internet technologies and provide a framework for evaluating assignments in this area.

The positive response of students to Internet-based discussions can be seen in the quantitative results reported by Scott Althaus (1996). Ninety-four percent of 115 students participating in his on-line discussion section for an introductory sociology course believed it helped them learn the course material, and 75 percent of those with no prior experience reported an overall positive experience with the system. The breadth of participation among students in the class would be considered impressive compared to in-class discussions. Sixty percent of students took part in on-line discussions and 35 percent participated at least once per week. Althaus's statistical analysis of his data indicates no significant differences in participation between men and women, or across year in school. Frequent participants scored higher on the nonexam components of the course. Althaus concluded that the active participants were better writers and more motivated to attend class than the others.

The same kinds of results have been found in evaluating instructors rather than students. In a formal evaluation of a program to bring the Internet to math and science education in secondary schools, John Rogan (1995) describes some of the impacts for instructors. Teachers claimed that the Internet provided them with new resources, the sense of being part of a global community, and a renewed interest in trying different teaching techniques—especially in trying a more student-centered approach to learning. The instructors felt that students were becoming more motivated by the use of the Internet and that students were becoming "independent explorers and were taking more responsibility for their own learning" (Rogan 1995, 11). Further, students were engaged in more collaboration. The primary negatives reported were the lack of instructor time to prepare Internet-based assignments and the unreliability of network connections and resources. Similar results were found in a survey of users of the Texas Education Network (David 1993).

The transforming effects of Internet use have also been studied outside the classroom. Lewis Friedland (1996) ties different applications of the Internet as a communications tool in the nonacademic world to democratic theory. He notes that original expectations were for the Internet to expand *plebiscitary* democracy (offering new opportunities for citizens to register their opinion). However, Friedland reports on three models of how the Internet advances *deliberative* democracy (motivating citizens to improve their political knowledge and their level of political impact). The models include the use of the Internet by preexisting advocacy groups, the creation of new community groups through "free-nets," and the establishment of electronic public journalism. He concludes that access to network tools "allows for both the practical strengthening of grassroots democratic organizing and its growth and extension to new citizenship groups" (1996, 207).

The research noted above is quite preliminary. None of the studies cited employed controlled experiments, for example. Moreover, systematic evaluation needs to be done on the second type of technique, use of the Internet as a virtual library. While virtual library–type techniques are not as collaborative by nature as discussion-type techniques, they do place greater responsibility on the students to become independent and critical learners than do traditional exercises. As more instructors in political science are employing techniques of the virtual library type, and as they move beyond simply paralleling traditional forms to new applications at the second level of Internet integration, formal evaluations become appropriate. For example, the effectiveness of virtual library assignments needs to be measured against the effectiveness of the same assignments using traditional library resources. Furthermore, outcomes to be assessed include more than just the addition to a student's store of knowledge. To meet the objectives of citizenship education it is important to measure the impact of Internet assignments of the virtual library type on the student's ability to make informed political choices and on the level of the student's motivation to participate in political life.

## Conclusion

As political scientists continue to use and refine Internet applications to the teaching of politics, these more systematic evaluations need to occur. Ultimately, we need to be able to answer the general question: Does the Internet provide a means of improving the citizenship education of those exposed to it? Actually, I asked this of my students in their final exam. More specifically, I asked them, compared to traditional media and forms of participation and based on their experience, "Does the Internet make possible a better informed citizenry, or does it fail to make a difference?"

All the students astutely noted that the demographics of the Internet user are different from those of the typical citizen. At present, the Internet "surfer" is more likely to be affluent and educated. Moreover, other forms of disseminating political information are more passive. One has to work harder to find the "stuff" of politics on the Internet than passively viewing the reports on the evening news. Thus, students concluded that the Internet will have greater impact in the short run on those who are already more knowledgeable, better equipped, and more motivated than the average citizen.

Yet all the students argued that the Internet will have a positive impact on the political education of all those it reaches in the long run, because of the easy access to a wide array of viewpoints and the great depth of information available. Each member of the class responded similarly to the following student.

> *I do believe that the Internet will make possible a better informed citizenry, because you are providing an environment that is less restrictive in censorship. It is an area that will feature the positives of an issue and also the negatives. The lower level of control allows the reader to view the facts and opinions of many different types of people. It offers the opportunity for the reader to make a clear and objective opinion based on the information provided. I believe you will see a great deal more information because it is not catering to the masses. It is not competing for advertising dollars and the ratings needed in print and broadcasting . . . the nature of the information on the Internet can offer the opportunity for a citizen to become better informed.*

There are certainly limits to the use of the Internet to further citizenship education. It will never have the same level of activity and sense of immediacy that lies in direct participation in politics through traditional means. However, the Internet, whether used as a discussion forum or as a virtual library, can promote citizen participation in political life. Its primary potential for having that impact lies in the way it breaks down the walls between the classroom and what students usually refer to as "the real world." As clearly evidenced in my experiences, students are excited by the prospect of direct access to the opinions of other citizens and the messages of political actors without instructors, librarians, or even journalists as intermediaries. Moreover, students can discuss and debate what they see not only with fellow students and their instructor, but with people unlike themselves, who are part of their broader political community. It is perhaps ironic that the virtual reality of the Internet can reduce the unreality and isolation of the classroom, and can make a course an experience that is closer to what they find as citizens.

The degree to which this potential will be realized is as yet unknown. Not only does it depend on how effectively the Internet is used to teach, it also depends on how suitable the Internet remains as a teaching tool. The tremendous rise of interest in the Internet as a conduit for commerce has all but drowned out its initial objective of improving the flow of scholarly information and its later objective (mostly championed by the Clinton administration) of providing easier access by citizens to government and education. As political scientists and others become more effective in their use of the Internet as a way to motivate students to become more politically astute and active, they will simultaneously need to become advocates of maintaining the value of the Internet as a citizenship and education tool.

# The Internet as a Tool for Student Citizenship

*Kimberley P. Canfield*

This essay describes the optional Internet research project that I assign in my Introductory American Politics courses. It also explains the preparation I give for the assignment, assuming that each student has no experience with politics or computers. Some students arrive at an introductory course with an interest in politics, but many seem to come not only with a disinterest in politics that marks the current generation of college students, but also with an assumption that they cannot connect to the system in any meaningful way. In other words, they are unsure how to be effective citizens and unsure if citizenship would benefit them. In my experience this is due to a few different reasons. First, the political system is confusing and overwhelming to students. Next, they feel that the government is controlled by the elite. Finally, they believe that this elite is corrupt. Many of our college students do not feel that they should or can be effective citizens. These Internet projects are designed to respond to these conclusions in a timely and concrete manner. It is elementary for the political scientist to explain the theories of citizenship and the importance of political participation in an introductory course. The Internet can help students see that citizenship can and still does exist. More importantly, the Internet is a very individualized tool so that students can quickly discover meaningful links to the government for themselves. In this essay, I reflect on how these projects have succeeded in achieving the above goals and how the process might be improved.

In my reflection, I want not only to assess what students have learned but also to consider if the project enhances their individual citizenship. The evidence suggests that students learn some of the complexities of the U.S. system of politics but at the same time they are discouraged by what they find. They do, however, project an increased sense of empowerment in terms of their individual capacities to participate as effective citizens. University models of education strive both to educate students for growth and to train them for a competitive advantage. This project appears to enhance students' ability to critically analyze U.S. politics as well as give them advantages for effective citizenship.[1]

What do we do when we teach citizenship in an introductory political science course? We seek at a minimum to provide information that is useful for the activities of citizenship. But this information may not be useful without teaching other skills and even promoting certain values. In fact, the evidence suggests that as information has become more abundant, people no longer desire to use it. In order to enhance the citizenship skills of a student, a project on the Internet has to be more than simply information.

It is disputable which skills and values are most important for learning and teaching citizenship. In this essay I do not want to engage this debate, but instead I want to list some that seem to hold promise and describe how this project is relevant to those. In *Renewing Civic Capacity—Preparing College Students for Service and Citizenship*, Suzanne Morse (1989) describes what university systems have done in the past to promote citizenship and what they can do in the future. Morse believes that the citizens in our democracy "should be well educated and informed on the issues of the day, with the necessary skills to participate. Citizens must feel that they hold office in the country and have mastered a set of skills and competencies" (1989, iv). As our lives become more complex with technological advances, universities can no longer simply encourage this model of a citizen; we need to create citizens with ready-made skills for the democratic marketplace (Morse 1989, v).

It is interesting that Morse wants to be able to use the same strategy to enhance democracy that others blame in part for the crisis in democratic participation. This crisis is that as universities and society as a whole have enhanced preparation for increasingly compartmentalized lives in order to bolster productive success, we have become less able to communicate with each other in our own communities. But now we should add the ability to participate as citizens to the ready-made product that the university generates. This lack of communication and its relation to a successful democracy is evident to all and is nicely described in William Greider's desire for a "connective tissue" between citizens, Benjamin Barber's demand for "public talk," and Robert Bellah's discussion of "habits of the heart" where citizens search out and analyze new alternatives for society with their fellow citizens in a habit that could rival the way Americans channel surf on a daily basis (Greider 1992; Barber 1984; Bellah, et al. 1985).

Morse describes a need for the university to enhance the skills and values that lead to the ability of citizens to participate in "public talk." By this she means that students will be able to talk, listen, and act together with a group of other citizens. The students will also be able to think about and judge alternative plans for public action. This process requires that students think critically, use their imagination, and have the courage to take action when appropriate (Morse 1989, vi).

With this above-described need for public participation, let me list the benefits that students can gain from interaction with the Internet. I want to describe these attributes generally, and then later show specifically how the Internet helps the students progress toward them. First, in the idea of the ready-made citizen, is practical skills. These skills could range from filling out voter registration forms and reading and analyzing news stories to writing a letter to a politician or fellow citizen in order to begin a political dialogue. Second, students need to put the idea of citizenship in a historical context. This history should include the American development of the concept since the eighteenth century and also the current manifestations of what citizenship means to different groups and what the future could hold. Included in these discussions should be the broadening of the concept of political environment to mean much more than the voting booth. Third, we need to provide information about our governmental system. We also need to provide the pathways for the students to get more information when needed. Fourth, as we give the historical context and the information about government it is important that the student does not simply "take," but instead develops the ability to critically analyze what is encountered. Finally, we want to encourage what I will call the "social skills of the citizen." These include the art of conversation, the ability and propensity to be honest, and a sense of multicultural tolerance.

With all this to strive for, I am assuming that my students will not be ready-made citizens with these skills and values in tow. Besides the fact that many studies show the decrease in citizen participation, most students could tell you themselves that "no one cares" and "why should they?" I want to share what I have found from my entrance surveys about the prior assumptions and beliefs of the students I have encountered. This information is useful in that the Internet project seems to have a unique effect on these ideas as compared with information from texts or lectures.

Many students lack some of the most basic skills for citizenship. All but a few have never voted and many are not registered. Most often this was not a conscious decision, but instead they were unsure how to register and are not motivated to find out. As for party membership, most do not know how to go about contacting a political party or understand the purpose of political parties. The overwhelming majority have not written a political letter and many have not even written a business letter. In addition, only a small number have had experience with the Internet and a surprising minority have had no experience with computers.

In regard to the attitudes of my students, up to 99 percent in one class think that "all politicians are crooks." In the same proportions they do not trust the government. The attitudes of the students that I have encountered recently are similar to talk-radio hosts and listeners. They have a lot of vague criticism to levy against government and politicians in general. They have little specific to say about any political subject. Most telling of all, they spend virtually no time discussing any alternative versions of the situation.

That is the students' disposition, but what is involved in the Internet system they are to encounter? The booklet I have used to familiarize students with the Internet is the *Houghton Mifflin Guide to the Internet for Political Science* by Cecilia Manrique (1995). As with most written material concerning the Internet, the drawback is that it quickly becomes out of date. For instructors not familiar with the Internet the December 1995 issue of *PS* (companion to the *American Political Science Review*) has a nice collection of essays describing some previous uses in the classroom. In my class I give instruction specifically on five aspects of the Internet. There are other diversions on the Internet, even aspects that could relate to citizenship, but this is what I emphasize for my introductory course.

The first aspect is e-mail. Most students have some knowledge of e-mail systems on a local system, e.g., within the university or within a company. They understand the concept of machines being hooked together or sharing one large computer and being able to communicate through those connections. Many are surprised to learn about the numerous people they can communicate with across the world and in elite positions. Students will say, "I have e-mail but I'm not connected to the Internet." Learning about address books on the Internet and other searches is also very empowering to the students for enhancing the power of e-mail.

I describe the second aspect, the listservs, as e-mail community style. This is essentially a group e-mail system that has a single topic of focus. All the members of the group get each mailing sent from the other members. The ease of finding at least some lists that are of interest to each student, combined with the automatic format of the messages, serve, to socially connect the student to the Internet. Even if some lists are not directly political in nature, this experience is illuminating to make observations about the nature of all virtual communities. This communication process is also very basic in its structure.

The usenets are still structured as communities where information is shared, although they are less participatory and more basic in structure than the listservs. They are lists that are posted in a public space that users can visit. The main benefit these have over the listservs is that there does not have to be a commitment and you are less likely to become overwhelmed with the information you receive. You can browse the history of what is happening, you can decide you don't want to look at a few days, and you can easily ignore streams of topics altogether. You do not belong to a usenet but they exist like a public newspaper for users to come and see what has been published. Because of their lack of structure, both the listservs and the usenets are time-consuming if the student is trying to find information. One can search according to the subject line on each post, but one will usually have to wade through a good deal of nonsense before finding something useful.

The gopher menu system, almost entirely replaced by Web browsers, is still very useful from a teaching standpoint. It allows the student to start from somewhere, usually the home gopher server, and gives the student ideas for the next step. For instance, if a student wants to do a certain project and knows little about politics and less about the Internet, where does she go? The first page of a gopher is a good start. Students may look and see they want nonlocal connections, then see U.S. or government-related sources. They might then see a heading for state governments and pick that, not realizing that their state information could be accessed from this university in another state. Or they might see a listing for campaign-related materials and not realize that propaganda is included in the "information highway." One critique of the gopher system is that students tend to distrust set pathways and seem to prefer the fluidity of the World Wide Web.

The World Wide Web (WWW) is the main focus of most activity on the Internet. It includes all the text data available through the gopher menus as well as other data, including that in audio and graphic media. WWW access requires certain technological capabilities that many students' computers may not be equipped with, such as a high-speed modem. If the university supports a Web browser on its local network the instructor might do well to encourage students to come to campus until they are more familiar with the system, because even the most experienced user can be frustrated by the issues that are associated with remote log-in.

Unlike gopher, which gives the student structure, the WWW is very fluid because of its hypertext capability. It lets students wander through a political idea in a way that might help the student see connections that are normally obscured. When everything and anything can be footnoted there seem to be no stop signs. By no means is this everything that you can experience on the Internet, but these are the aspects that I have had success with in teaching citizenship.

Next I want to show how these aspects have all been used to create meaningful learning experiences concerning citizenship. I have summarized some of the attitudes that I have encountered from students in an introductory course. In this stereotype is not only a shortened attention span, but also a need for current information. Why read someone else's account of the campaign trail, like Bob Woodward's book *The Choice*, when you can get the minute-to-minute details of the campaign as well as the backlash from the book, with pictures, every half-hour on *Headline News* and still have time to tune into *The Real World* on MTV? The Internet is timely and outdated at the same time. It has good history and rash generalizations on the same topic. This is one of the challenges that we will discuss later.

The Internet can be very individualized, which also suits the stereotype from my student surveys. The Internet's individualized nature might add fire to the NIMBY attitude but it also makes it easier to become involved with an issue where the costs of participation off-line are very high to the student. Many students feel very strongly about vague issues, like support for education. The act of researching what types of activity occur around this issue is difficult enough without any actual activism on the student's part. But this issue is at least discussed on campus at some level. What if the student is concerned about subsidies for tobacco farmers? Imagine a student whose loved one died of lung cancer and would like to talk to others in this position who also oppose such subsidies. The Internet is an ideal tool for such an endeavor. This, of course, is a far cry from creating citizen-based visions for the future but it is also an improvement on what is presently occurring.

Furthermore, the Internet system is a real-life experience.[2] Many students have a natural dislike of texts and distrust of historical essays. The Internet allows the student to become a participant observer of a political environment. It does not replace internships or field trips, but it allows for student interaction with a wide variety of ideas and personalities. It has the added benefit of very low costs in terms of preparation, time, and money involved.

My assignment is one choice out of a project requirement. I ask the students to critique a small aspect of the Internet according to the promise it holds or doesn't hold for the enhancement of democratic ideals. According to what the students find interesting in their research, they usually pick about five different sites, listservs, or usenets. They examine the aspects for content, form, and presentation and then analyze the democratic potential. This potential is defined by each student's critique of democracy in general.

Some students have chosen to look at communication that occurs on the Internet. One student e-mailed representatives and sent them letters through the postal service and compared the responses. Another student e-mailed various types of representatives on different levels of government with the same basic letter and compared the responses.[3] Other students have joined several listservs that seemed to focus on political discussions. These students observed the electronic discussion and at times participated. Some would even participate for the purposes of experimentation. They would put forth certain ideas and wait to see what reactions would come of it. Many concluded by making comparisons between their observations of the electronic discussion groups and what occurs on talk radio. Most lists were interesting or amusing but like talk radio they did not seem to be moving toward public deliberation and public judgment. Most students found at least one group that they felt had some promise for useful deliberations.

Students have also investigated the different sources of government information. These investigations have led them to the sophisticated WWW servers that the federal government supports. Most were surprised to learn that they could access data such as information about legislation in progress and the details of the national budget. For many students, this was a direct contradiction of the secret corruption on which they imagine the government to be based.

Students have further examined the ways in which the Internet serves as a tool for the role of citizen watchdog. Project Vote Smart is a good start for this model as well as the home page of the Federal Election Commission. With these sources, students do not have to rely on campaign rhetoric to make informed decisions. They can see previous voting records, current platforms, and detailed campaign finance records for themselves.

The ICONS project (Vavrina 1995) is another good model of ways to circumvent the elite-based communication systems. In this project, students create direct communications to people in other countries to learn about the state of affairs in that country. This way students have an alternative source for evaluating foreign policy.

Some student projects have revolved around attempts to witness citizenship occurring on the Internet. This has been done by observing communication through listservs and usenets but some students have found sites created by individuals who want to start a "public talk." These have mostly been college students who through university resources can create their own page. These pages tend to be temporary. Some interesting pages are based on the creation of a third political party. Students have found these especially interesting to democratic ideals because of their lack of a comprehensive platform of issue stances. Parties such as the Reform Party are based on the idea of including citizen concerns even if they are transient in nature.

In these activities and others, students have tried to create meaningful democratic links. This strategy is based on their assumption that money keeps citizenship difficult to engage in so that citizens will not communicate and will remain divided. When divided, citizens create little competition with elite interests. The students ask, can the Internet put citizens back on a more level playing field with monied interests? I also encourage them to think about the question of who gains from the growth and expansion of the Internet. Those with computer skills? Computer access? Are these easier to obtain than wealth? Even if access were universal, the Internet will still work to the advantage of those with superior language and communication skills. These issues are complex but they are worth noting.

One student who wanted to create a communication between herself and government tried to use the information she found on federal Web servers and write e-mail with concerns to appropriate officials. She found that the responses she received were still as vague as when she had little information, and she also felt that her impact on the issue was the same as before. She did feel, however, that she could communicate and mobilize other citizens more effectively and thought that

that communication could be enhanced through the Internet, although she did not have the time to investigate that further. Many students felt that in the future they would use the Internet, given access, to help them understand specific issues in government.

Projects on listservs aside, only one student investigated ways in which citizens' special interests could be mobilized through the Internet. He compared sites run by elites and corporations, sites created under an on-line service, and sites run by individuals. He felt that in the first two instances the activity mimicked what occurred in other forms of media with the exception of a larger audience for the intellectual elite. In the last instance he felt that the pages were not sophisticated but since the issues were so narrow they had some influence.

No student has taken on the general issue of how the Internet helps citizens communicate about general issues or find important issues. This is the topic of a lecture I give the day the projects are due. I ask if we can communicate and then create publicly supported ideas from this communication. The conclusion is that the Internet is not widely enough accessible yet, and even if it becomes so, the topic of citizenship needs to become trendy. It has its start in movements like the Reform Party. But what will happen when we want to make a comprehensive plan for the future that includes all issues, not just campaign finance reform? When party members discuss what national health care should look like or if it should exist at all, will they be able to stay unified? Or will the Internet actually encourage the party's downfall because of the possibility of including a limitless number of views?

It would be interesting to use the Internet to examine and promote democratic ideals, but this is an introductory course in political science and not computer science. Let me explain what is involved in preparing students for this activity. It is ideal if the instructor can take the students into an iconified environment and take them through a couple of icon choices that will get them to the browser. In my case the browser is Netscape. From this I show them the search and bookmark features that are important to a student who has not developed a list of relevant sources. The news reader is a part of the browser system.

I also show the students how to log-in and send an e-mail since this is the basis of Listservs as well. Students do not need a lesson on the history of the Internet, hardware, and the like. They need to be told the exact steps to take and what they need to do. This process does not create apt computer users at the moment, but if they are comfortable using the computer for these specific tasks, other skills can easily be added gradually.

The instructor should show them how to get to gopher menus from the mainframe prompt as well as an icon if the system supports turbo-gopher. In the past, even the most computer-illiterate student mastered these focused tasks within a half-hour. I spend the remainder of the hour session helping each student get to a site on the Web that may be of interest to them. I ask each of them if they want information, connection with government, special interests, or citizens generally, or assistance with their own creations. This allows me to get them started in a productive direction.

There are two main obstacles to the training. First, students must be convinced that it is worthwhile and painless. This can be avoided if the workshop is mandatory. Second, all students must have a computer account and know it and their password. This can be avoided by obtaining class accounts for training purposes. I would discourage this since it leaves the task of students getting their own accounts until after the training session.[4]

Class listservs are a good way not only to monitor the interaction the students are having with the Internet but also to create a political environment for the students to participate in. To do this you create a listserv (with help from the computer support service at the university) where the members of the list are the students in the class. They can discuss any issue relating to class.[5] These lists serve as a basis for a variety of discussions about citizenship. Students can observe who takes leadership roles and why. They can note who fails to participate and examine their concerns. The instructor can participate in the group and spur discussion by submitting questions for the class to discuss: How do the participants feel about those who do not participate? How do the nonparticipants feel about those who dominate the discussions? Electronic discussions are unique in that as opposed to discussions in class, students have time to think out what they want to say and no one will interrupt them. There is also time for everyone to take a turn. Even if one student overly dominates the discussion, other students can ignore those posts. This is an added advantage over town meeting–type models of discussions as well.

So that the instructor does not require an artificial response to every topic just for credit from each student, he or she might assign a minimum number of posts throughout the semester. My assignment was one choice out of a journal requirement. I think the interaction would have been enhanced if there was some minimal level required from each student.

I have received only positive feedback from students about the project and their training on the Internet. About half the students found some real potential in the Internet and all found some useful information and entertainment value in what they found.

Below are some useful hints and citations that will not only note some interesting political activity but also give the reader a more concrete idea of what the students were interacting with.

## Listservs

Subscribe to each of these by writing to the administration of the list owner (usually listserv or listproc at each address with a message that reads: "subscribe list-name your-real-name"). But how to know what lists to subscribe to and out of what address they are based? One way is word of mouth; another is that once one subscribes to some lists, the members will share addresses of new lists that may be of interest. One cite on the WWW that will be a good place for students to begin is the Political Science List of Lists:

http://osiris.colorado.edu/POLSCI/RES/lists.html

This gives a list of political science–related listservs and their addresses. Another good site on the WWW for addresses that allows a search for the e-mail addresses of individuals is:

http://www.qucis.queensu.ca/FAQs/email/finding.html

## Usenets

Usenets are organized by thread, which is the topic heading that the posts should follow. Below are some citations for several threads that my students have found interesting.[6]

alt.politics
soc.politics
talk.politics.misc
talk.politics.theory

## World Wide Web

The Netscape browser will have a line prompt that begins with LOCA-
TION: Type these addresses into that line to go to that site. These are
some interesting and important political sites.

　http://www.vote-smart.org/

This is one of the students' favorite sites. It lists federally elected officials and candidates for federal office. For each person there is a list of
information such as voting records, performance scores from special
interest groups, and campaign finance information. There is some
state-level information as well.

　http://www.democrats.org

This site is sponsored by the Democratic Party and has a lot of textual
data.

　http://www.rnc.org

This site is sponsored by the Republican Party and has some good
video clips.

　http://www.reformparty.org

This site is sponsored by the National Reform Party.

　http://www.whitehouse.gov

This site is sponsored by the White House and has some nice graphical
features including tours of famous Washington buildings.

　http://www.fec.gov

This site is sponsored by the Federal Election Commission and is a
nice start for election material. It has all the official campaign finance
material on candidates and even compiles summaries about the trends
of finances for all candidates.

　http://www.house.gov
　http://www.senate.gov

These are counterparts to the White House site. They give information about Congress, committee work, and the data listed in the *Congressional Record*.

http://www.civnet.org

This site is entitled CIVNET. It is an "international resource for civic education."

http://voter.cq.com

This site gives information on voting sponsored by *Congressional Quarterly*.

http://www.familyInternet.com/fitimes

This is an on-line citizen-oriented magazine. It is attempting to use the Internet to promote citizenship.

There are many good pages to start from to do political searches. They try to compile links to interesting Web sites in one location. This is especially good if students are using computers in a common cluster where they do not have their own bookmarks and have not kept good records of previous sites visited. The following are some the students tend to use.

http://www.mebbs.com/tenny/politics.html

This is called Tenny's Political Page. It is a good start for election information and magazine-formatted political material.

http://www.yahoo.com/Government/Politics

Like the rest of the search engines, Yahoo is good but it tends to be difficult to use during peak hours.

http://www.apsanet.org

The APSA page starts here with other political science links.

http://www.ditell.com/Government/GovernmentIndex.html

This site has government-related links.

http://www.law.vill.edu/Fed-Agency/

This is the Federal Web Locator. It lists all the Web servers in the federal government.

http://www.trincoll.edu/~pols/guide-home.html

This page, by Peter Adams, is entitled the Political Scientists Guide to the Internet. It serves as a link to interesting sites.

http://www.access.gpo.gov/su_docs/

This is the Web page for the Government Printing Office. There are a variety of documents that one can read, download, and print.

General pages like these tend to be a bit redundant in their listing of links to other Web pages. Therefore, a list of interesting sites should be available so that students do not have to spend too much time searching pages whose paths lead to the same place.

These addresses are not meant to be a complete list of what is on the Internet or of what my students encountered. It is instead a list of what I use to help lead my students to interesting areas and of what my students have enjoyed.

## Conclusions

My conclusions about the effectiveness of the Internet as a tool for education for citizenship are positive but mixed. The Internet does allow students to create a public space with little cost and effort. Representatives are the only ones in our society who have a public space arranged for them by the governmental structure. The rest of us are on our own, even though citizenship is supposed to be the basis of our democracy. This creates a skewed agenda in governmental affairs, because of the advantages money affords when participating in politics. The Internet levels that playing field to some extent for an expanded set of citizens. This set is still skewed but with one difference. Any group of students, even the poorest, should be able to come together and get some access to the Internet, mostly because of the widespread use of the system on university campuses. Citizen advocates should be able to raise enough money from a citizen group to subscribe to an Internet provider and become politically active without a major time commitment.

In my observations, the Internet seems to do the best at helping students play the game rather than create the "connective tissue" that William Greider describes. This, however, is not as bleak as it sounds. The simple fact that different types of people are playing the game will necessarily have an effect on the structure of political activity. This outlook is difficult to relate to the cynical student. And for students to become effective citizens they need to have the hope that there can be change.

The students' observations were marked by their feelings of competence. Students would remark that they could easily express their views to elected officials through e-mail, that they could easily find the text of legislation in each stage of the process, and that they could easily find a space to communicate with other citizens who have like-minded and opposing views. Students were split in regard to their enthusiasm. Some felt that their efforts would be fruitful and others felt that the Internet created a space for citizen activity, but they were hesitant to believe that this activity would have meaningful effects on the decisions of government. In all, the students predicted that their interactions would continue.[7]

In the future, I would change at least the training session to be a required element of the course instead of optional. Even students who have attended the training halfheartedly have had great success in their projects. This might be a good project for a democratic theory class and a nice break from the traditional texts. In this type of class, the students would also be able to explore their analysis of democratic theory more completely.

I might also experiment with increasing the time spent on the subjects of democracy and citizenship. Possibly an in-class assignment could be added where students explore what are the essential and the ideal qualities of a citizen. Do they vote, discuss, act, serve, and protest? Where should they do these activities: in work, at local, state, federal, or international levels? What are the rights of a citizen? What are the responsibilities? What if a citizen does not live up to these expectations? What is the role of government in ensuring that each person is able to live up to these expectations? This might serve as a nice background to their Internet searches.

There is also a set of questions that seem to have been glaringly absent from my students' research that I might want to encourage some thought about in the future: How are gender, ethnicity, and economic status are affected by the Internet in terms of the role they play in political relationships? I might also want students at the end of their projects to reflect on whether their feelings about power and leadership have been altered in any way. This has been underlying much of the work I have seen, but it would be interesting to ask the question specifically.

Finally, I hope that no one would want the Internet to replace face-to-face contact with other citizens even if access became universal. Aside from the variety of problems associated with fraudulent representation, physical experiences are significant because the most powerful means of expression is still human expression. We want to enhance our communication possibilities but not replace the power of physical community and family. I suggest that the Internet can enhance our students' development as citizens by enlarging their access to information, teaching them new skills that will empower them for the inevitable changes in society, and giving them a concrete experience that can serve as a basis for future political interaction.

## Notes

1. See Doris Graber's 1996 essay that comments on the differences in the potential of the Internet for the rich and poor. She notes that the Internet is still a tool for the educationally and economically privileged.

2. I will discuss later what it lacks compared to face-to-face experiences.

3. See Carleton, et al. (1996) for another experience of students communicating with political representatives. The authors note the limits of e-mail in their classroom experience.

4. I would recommend a hands-on out-of-class training. This seems to be time efficient. See Carleton, et al. (1996) for an example of the drawbacks of in-class training.

5. A good example of this is discussed in the Gary Klass article.

6. Also see Martha Bailey's 1995 *PS* article for a discussion of a project based solely on interaction with usenets.

7. These results are similar to the conclusions found in the classroom study described by Carleton, et al. (1996).

# Bibliography


Achebe, Chinua. 1987. *Anthills of the Savannah*. New York: Anchor Books.

Alexander, James R. 1982. "Institutional Design of Public Service Internships: Conceptual, Academic, and Structural Problems." *Teaching Political Science* 9 (Spring): 127–33.

Althaus, Scott. 1996. "Computer-Mediated Communication in the University Classroom: An Experiment with On-Line Discussions." Paper presented at the Annual Meeting of the American Political Science Association, San Francisco.

Anderson, Charles W. 1990 *Pragmatic Liberalism*. Chicago and London: University of Chicago Press.

Aristotle. 1966. *The Ethics of Aristotle: The Nicomachean Ethics*. Baltimore: Penguin Books.

Astin, Alexander W. 1994. *Higher Education and the Future of Democracy*. Inaugural lecture, Allan M. Carter Symposium, University of California, Los Angeles, October 26.

Bahmueller, Charles, ed. 1991. *Civitas, A Framework for Civic Education*. Center for Civic Education.

Bailey, Martha. 1995. "USENET Discussion Groups in Political Science Courses." *PS: Political Science and Politics* 28, 4: 721–22.

Ball, William J. 1995. "Using the Internet as a Teaching Tool: Why Wait Any Longer?" *PS: Political Science and Politics* 28, 4: 718–20.

Balutis, Alan P. 1977. "Participation Through Politics: An Evaluation of the New York State Assembly Intern Program." *Teaching Political Science* 3 (April): 319–28.

Barber, Benjamin R. 1984. *Strong Democracy*. Berkeley: University of California Press.

———. 1989. "Public Talk and Civic Action: Education for Participation in a Strong Democracy." *Social Education* 53: 355–70.

———. 1992. *An Aristocracy of Everyone: The Politics of Education and the Future of America*. New York: Ballantine.

Barber, Benjamin R., and Richard M. Battistoni. 1993. "A Season of Service: Introducing Service Learning into the Liberal Arts Curriculum." *PS: Political Science and Politics* 26, 2: 235–40.

Barnette, Ron. 1995. "Reflections on Electronic Frontiers in Education." Paper presented at the Annual Meeting of the Association of Small Computer Users in Education, Myrtle Beach, S.C.

Barr, Robert B., and John Tagg. 1995. "From Teaching to Learning—A New Paradigm for Undergraduate Education." *Change* (November/December): 13–25.

Battistoni, Richard M. 1995. "Service Learning, Diversity, and the Liberal Arts Curriculum." *Liberal Education* 81: 30–35.

———. 1996. "Service-Learning in a Democratic Society: Essential Practices for K–12 Programs." *Community Service-Learning: A Guide to Including Service in the Public School Curriculum*. Albany: SUNY Press.

Battistoni, Rick, and Keith Morton. 1995. "Service and Citizenship: Are They Connected?" *Wingspread Journal* 17, 3: 17–19.

Bellah, Robert N., Richard Madsen, William M. Sullivan, Ann Swidler, and Steven M. Tipton. 1985. *Habits of the Heart: Individualism and Commitment in American Life*. New York: Harper and Row.

———. 1991. *The Good Society*. New York: Knopf.

Benson, Norman. 1987. "Citizenship and Student Power: Some Strategies for the Classroom." *The Social Studies* 78: 136–39.

Bikson, T. K., and S. A. Law. 1994. "Global Preparedness and Human Resources." Santa Monica, Calif.: Rand Corporation.

Blaney, David, and Naeem Inayatullah. 1994. "Prelude to a Conversation of Cultures? Todorov and Nandy on the Possibility of Dialogue." *Alternatives* 19, 1 (Spring): 23–51.

Bloom, Allan. 1979. "Introduction," in Jean-Jacques Rousseau, *Emile*, trans. Allan Bloom. New York: Basic Books.

Boyer, Ernest. 1994. "Creating the New American College." *Chronicle of Higher Education*, March 9.

Boyte, Harry. 1991. "Community Service and Civic Education." *Phi Beta Kappan* (June): 765–67.

———. 1993. "Practical Politics," In *Education for Democracy*. Dubuque, Iowa: Kendall-Hunt.

Boyte, Harry C., and Rebecca Breuer. 1992. "Service, Citizenship and Politics: A Perspective from Project Public Life." *Compact News* (Winter): 1–5.

Boyte, Harry C., and Nancy N. Kari. 1996. *Building America: The Democratic Promise of Public Work*. Philadelphia: Temple University Press.

Boyte, Harry C., and Frank Reissman. 1986. *The New Populism: The Politics of Empowerment*. Philadelphia: Temple University Press.

Brandhorst, Alan. 1990. "Teaching Twenty-First Century Citizenship: Social Psychological Foundations." *Theory and Research in Social Education* 18, 2: 157–68.

Brown, David W., ed. 1996. *Higher Education Exchange*. Dayton, Ohio: Kettering Foundation.

Bruner, Jerome. 1963. *The Process of Education*. New York: Vintage Books.

Bruning, Stephen. 1995. "Classroom Exercise That Incorporates Internet Discussion Groups as an Integral Element in a Communication Course." Paper presented at the Annual Meeting of the Central States Communication Association, Indianapolis.

Burnham, Walter Dean. 1987. "The Turnout Problem," in *Elections American Style*, ed. James Reichley. Washington, D.C.: Brookings Institution Press.

Canfield, Kimberley, and Grant Reeher. 1996. "Encouraging the Better Angels: On Designing the Introductory Course in American Politics." Paper presented at the Annual Meeting of the American Political Science Association, San Francisco.

Carleton, Francis, Scott R. Furlong, and Denise Scheberle. 1996. "Educating Towards the 21st Century: Active Learning in American Government and Politics." Paper presented at the Annual Meeting of the American Political Science Association, San Francisco.

Cell, Edward. 1993. "Personal Development in Organizational Contexts." *NSEE Quarterly* 19 (Fall): 1 + .

Chesler, M., and R. Fox. 1966. *Role-Playing Methods in the Classroom*. Chicago: Science Research Associates.

Chesney, James, and Otto Feinstein. 1996. *The Urban Agenda Project*. Englewood Cliffs, N.J.: Prentice-Hall.

Converse, Philip. 1964. "The Nature of Belief Systems in Mass Publics," in *Ideology and Discontent*, ed. David Apter. New York: Free Press.

———. 1970. "Attitudes and Non-attitudes: Continuation of a Dialogue," in *The Quantitative Analysis of Social Problems*, ed. Edward Tufte. Reading, Mass.: Addison-Wesley.

Conway, Margaret. 1988. *Political Participation in the United States*. Washington, D.C.: CQ Press.

Coplin, W. D., and M. K. O'Leary. 1992. *Public Policy Skills*, 2nd ed. Croton-on-Hudson, N.Y.: Policy Studies Associates.

Couto, Richard A., and Theodore L. Becker, eds. 1996. *Teaching Democracy by Being Democratic*. Westport, Conn.: Praeger.

Cox, Archibald. 1981. *Freedom of Expression*. Cambridge: Harvard University Press.

Cromwell, Lucy. 1994. "An Internship Seminar: Integrating the Academic and Professional Worlds." *NSEE Quarterly* 20 (Winter): 8 + .

Cross, Patricia. 1994. "The Coming Age of Experiential Education." *NSEE Quarterly* 9 (Spring): 1 + .

David, Jane. 1993. "TENET After One Year." Naples, Fla.: WEB Associates.

Dewey, John. 1899. *The School and Society*, rev. ed. Chicago: University of Chicago Press.

———. 1916. *Democracy and Education*. New York: Macmillan.

———. 1938. *Experience and Education*. New York: Macmillan.

Edmondson, Mark. 1994. "Bennington Means Business." *New York Times Magazine*, October 23.

"Educating for Citizenship." 1984. *PS: Political Science and Politics* 17, 2: 193–219.

Ehrenhalt, Alan. 1995. *The Lost City: Discovering the Forgotten Virtues of Community in the Chicago of the 1950's*. New York: Basic Books.

Eissey, Edward M. 1996. *Did You Know?* Palm Beach Community College, September.

Emerson, Thomas. 1970. *The System of Freedom of Expression*. New York: Random House.

Endersby, James, and David Webber. 1995. "Iron Triangle Simulation: Role-Playing Game for Undergraduates in Congress, Interest Groups, and Public Policy Classes." *PS: Political Science and Politics* 28, 3 (September): 520–23.

Etzioni, Amitai. 1993. *The Spirit of Community: Rights, Responsibilities, and the Communitarian Agenda*. New York: Crown.

Eyler, Janet, and Beth Halteman. 1981. "The Impact of a Legislative Internship on Students' Political Skill and Sophistication." *Teaching Political Science* 9 (Fall): 27–34.

Farr, James. 1993. "Framing Democratic Discussion," in *Reconsidering the Democratic Public*, ed. George Marcus and Russell Hanson. University Park, Pa.: Pennsylvania State University Press.

Ferguson, LeRoy C., and David W. Winder. 1981. "Evaluation of Political Science Fieldwork." *Teaching Political Science* 8 (January): 191–200.

Fowell, S. P., and P. Levy. 1995. "Computer-Mediated Communication in the Information Curriculum: An Initiative in Computer Supported Collaborative Learning." *Education for Information* 13: 193–210.

Fox, Janet. 1995. *Amtrak Express*, July/August: 11.

Frantzich, Stephen. 1995. "Press Briefing Exercise," in "Using the Internet in the Political Science Classroom." *PS: Political Science and Politics* 28, 4 (December): 728–30.

Freire, Paulo. 1970. *Pedagogy of the Oppressed*. New York: Continuum.

Friedland, Lewis. 1996. "Electronic Democracy and the New Citizenship." *Media, Culture, and Society* 18: 185–212.

Galston, William A. 1995. "Liberal Virtues and the Formation of Civic Character," in *Seedbeds of Virtue*, ed. Mary Ann Glendon and David Blankenhorn. Lanham, Md.: Madison Books.

Gant, Michael, and Norman Luttbeg. 1993. *American Electoral Behavior*. Itasca, Ill.: Peacock.

Gardner, Howard. 1982. *Frames of Mind: The Theory of Multiple Intelligences*. New York: Basic Books.

Gastil, John. 1993. *Democracy in Small Groups: Participation, Decision Making and Communication*. Philadelphia: New Society.

———. 1994. *Democratic Citizenship and the National Issues Forums*. Doctoral dissertation, University of Wisconsin–Madison.

Giddens, Anthony. 1976. *New Rules of Sociological Method*. New York: Basic Books.

———. 1979. *Central Problems in Social Theory*. Berkeley: University of California Press.

———. 1984. *The Constitution of Society*. Berkeley: University of California Press.

Glendon, Mary Ann. 1991. *Rights Talk: The Impoverishment of Political Discourse*. Cambridge: Harvard University Press.

Gorham, Eric B. 1992. *National Service, Citizenship, and Political Education*. Albany: SUNY Press.

Graber, Doris A. 1996. "Disparity in Information Resources: The Widening Gap Between the Rich and Poor." Paper presented at the Annual Meeting of the American Political Science Association, San Francisco.

Greider, William. 1992. *Who Will Tell the People: The Betrayal of American Democracy*. New York: Simon and Schuster.

Guarasci, Richard, and Craig A. Rimmerman. 1996. "Public Service and Civic Education," in *Teaching Democracy by Being Democratic*, ed. Ted Becker and Richard Couto. New York: Praeger.

Haiman, Franklyn. 1981. *Speech and Law in a Free Society*. Chicago: University of Chicago Press.

Halva-Neubauer, Glen A. 1991. "Teaching Public Policy and Government in an Internship Setting: The First Year of Furman University's Local Government Program." Presented at the Annual Meeting of the National Society for Internships and Experiential Education, Sarasota, Fla.

———. 1995. "Journaling: How It Can Be a More Effective Experiential Learning Technique." Paper presented at the Annual Meeting of the American Political Science Association, Chicago.

Harwood, Richard C. 1991. "Citizens and Politics: A View from Main Street America." Dayton, Ohio: Kettering Foundation.

Harwood Group. 1993. *College Students Talk Politics*. Dayton, Ohio: Kettering Foundation.

Heinemann, Harry N., and Anthony A. De Falco. 1990. "Dewey's Pragmatism: A Philosophical Foundation for Cooperative Education." *Journal of Cooperative Education* 27 (Fall): 38–44.

Hepburn, Mary A. 1993. "Concepts of Pluralism and the Implications for Citizenship Education." *Social Studies* 84: 20–26.

Hibbing, John, and Elizabeth Theiss-Morse. 1995. *Congress as Public Enemy: Public Attitudes Toward American Political Institutions*. New York: Cambridge University Press.

Higher Education Research Institute. 1995. "The American Freshman: National Norms for Fall 1994." 1–4.

———. 1996. "The American Freshman: National Norms for Fall 1995."

Hutchings, Pat, and Allen Wutzdorff. 1988. "Experiential Learning Across the Curriculum: Assumptions and Principles," in *Knowing and Doing: Learning*

*Through Experience*, ed. Pat Hutchings and Allen Wutzdorff. San Francisco: Jossey-Bass.

Inayatullah, Naeem. 1994. "Diversity as Degeneration: Temporal and Spatial Representations of the 'Other' in Early Modern European Social Theory," manuscript. Ithaca, N.Y.: Ithaca College.

"Internship Program." 1996. Polisci Connection, Department of Political Science Alumni Newsletter, University of Minnesota (Fall): 10.

Johnson, Roberta Ann. 1993. "Applying Theory to Practice in Public Administration Internships." Paper presented at the Annual Meeting of the American Political Science Association, Washington, D.C.

Kariel, Henry. 1977. "Becoming Political," in *Teaching Political Science*, ed. V. Van Dyke. Atlantic Highlands, N.J.: Humanities Press.

Kinder, Donald, and Don Herzog. 1993. "Democratic Discussion," in *Reconsidering the Democratic Public*, ed. George Marcus and Russell Hanson. University Park, Pa.: Pennsylvania State University Press.

Klass, Gary. 1995. "Bringing the World into the Classroom: POLS302-L—The Race and Ethnicity Seminar Discussion List." In "Using the Internet in the Political Science Classroom." *PS: Political Science and Politics* 28, 4 (December): 723–25.

———. 1996. "A Survey of Political Science Cyberclasses." Paper presented at the Annual Meeting of the American Political Science Association, San Francisco.

Knowles, Malcolm. 1986. *Using Learning Contracts*. San Francisco: Jossey-Bass.

Kolb, David. 1984. *Experiential Learning: Experience as the Source of Learning and Development*. Englewood Cliffs, N.J.: Prentice-Hall.

Kozol, Jonathan. 1995. *Amazing Grace: The Lives of Children and the Conscience of a Nation*. New York: Crown.

Lappe, Frances Moore, and Paul Martin DuBois. 1994. *The Quickening of America: Rebuilding Our Nation, Remaking Our Lives*. San Francisco: Jossey-Bass.

Lasch, Christopher. 1995. *The Revolt of the Elites*. New York: Norton.

Lawrence, David G. 1995. "Shall We Dance? Applying the Theory of Multiple Intelligences to American Government Courses." Paper presented at the Annual Meeting of the American Political Science Association, Chicago.

Lipset, Seymour Martin, and William Schneider. 1987. *The Confidence Gap: Business, Labor and Government in the Public Mind*, 2nd ed. New York: Free Press.

Loeb, Paul Rogat. 1994. *Generations at the Crossroads: Apathy and Action on the American Campus*. New Brunswick, N.J.: Rutgers University Press.

Luger, Stan, and William Scheuerman. 1993. "Teaching American Government." *PS: Political Science and Politics* 26, 4: 749–53.

MacKinnon, Catharine. 1993. *Only Words*. Cambridge: Harvard University Press.

Manrique, Cecilia G. 1995. *The Houghton Mifflin Guide to the Internet for Political Science*. Boston: Houghton Mifflin.

Marcus, George, and Russell Hanson, eds. 1993. *Reconsidering the Democratic Public*. University Park, Pa.: Pennsylvania State University Press.

Markus, Gregory, Jeffrey Howard, and David King. 1993. "Integrating Community Service and Classroom Instruction Enhances Learning: Results from an Experiment." *Educational Evaluation and Policy Analysis* 15: 4.

Marriott, Michel. 1996. "Taking Education Beyond the Classroom." *The New York Times*, August 4.

Mathews, David. 1994a. "... afterthoughts." *Kettering Review* 68.

———. 1994b. *Politics for People: Finding a Responsible Public Voice*. Urbana and Chicago: University of Illinois Press.

McClosky, Herbert, and Alida Brill. 1983. *Dimensions of Tolerance: What Americans Believe about Civil Liberties*. New York: Russell Sage Foundation.

McKenzie, Robert H. 1994. *Public Politics*. Dubuque, Iowa: Kendall-Hunt.

———. 1996. "Experiential Education and Civic Learning." *NSEE Quarterly* 22 (Winter): 1+.

McKenzie, Robert H., and Daniel W. O'Connell. 1995. "Teaching the Art of Public Deliberation—National Issues Forums in the Classroom." *PS: Political Science and Politics* 28, 4: 230–32.

Michaelis, John U. 1963. *Social Studies for Children in a Democracy*. Englewood Cliffs, N.J.: Prentice-Hall.

Morin, Richard. 1996. "So Much for the 'Bowling Alone' Thesis." *Washington Post Weekly Edition*, June 17–23.

Morrill, Richard L. 1982. "Educating for Democratic Values." *Liberal Education* 68: 365–76.

———. 1989. *Renewing Civic Capacity—Preparing College Students for Service and Citizenship*. ASHE-ERIC Higher Education Report No. 8. Washington, D.C.: School of Education and Human Development, George Washington University.

———, ed. 1992. *Politics for the Twenty-First Century: What Should Be Done on Campus?* Dubuque, Iowa: Kendall/Hunt.

Morse, Suzanne W. 1993. "The Practice of Citizenship: Learn By Doing." *Social Studies* 84: 164–67.

Mosher, Ralph, Robert A. Kenny, Jr., and Andrew Garrod. 1994. *Preparing for Citizenship*. Westport, Conn.: Praeger.

Murray, Charles. 1984. *Losing Ground: American Social Policy, 1950–1980*. New York: Basic Books.

Nandy, Ashis. 1984. *The Intimate Enemy: Loss and Recovery of Self Under Colonialism*. Oxford: Oxford University Press.

Newmann, Fred M. 1990. "Reflective Citizen Participation," in *Combining Service and Learning: A Resource Book for Community and Public Service*, vol. I, ed. Jane C. Kendall and Associates. Raleigh, N.C.: National Society for Internships and Experiential Education.

"Next Steps Team Training Manual." n.d. Bethel, Me.: National Training Laboratories.

Ostrom, Elinor. 1996. "Civic Education for the Next Century: A Task Force to Initiate Professional Activity." *PS: Political Science and Politics* 29, 4: 755–58.

Pauly, Edward. 1991. *The Classroom Crucible: What Really Works, What Doesn't, and Why.* New York: Basic Books.

Pederson, William D., and Norman W. Provizer. 1995. "A Comparison of Washington Semesters at Public Colleges and Universities: Who Gets What, When, and How." *PS: Political Science and Politics* 28, 2 (June 1995): 232–35.

Penny, Timothy, and Major Garrett. 1995. *Common Cents: A Retiring Six-Term Congressman Reveals How Congress Really Works and What We Must Do to Fix It.* New York: Avon Books.

People for the American Way. 1989. *Democracy's Next Generation: American Youth Attitudes on Citizenship, Government, and Politics.* Washington, D.C.

Pettman, Ralph. 1992. "Teaching World Politics (as Well as Teaching for It)," in *Teaching World Politics: Contending Pedagogies for a New World Order,* ed. Lev Gonick and Edward Weisband. Boulder, Colo.: Westview.

Pierce, Roy, and Converse, Philip. 1990. "Attitudinal Sources of Protest Behavior in France: Differences Between Before and After Measurement." *Public Opinion Quarterly* 54: 295–316.

Profughi, Victor, and Edward Warren. 1978. "Role Relationships in Internship Program Management." *Teaching Political Science* 5 (January): 199–207.

Putnam, Robert. 1995. "Bowling Alone: America's Declining Social Capital." *Journal of Democracy* 6, 1: 65–78.

———. 1996. "The Strange Disappearance of Civic America." *American Prospect* 24 (Winter): 34–48.

Reeher, Grant. 1995. "Citizens and Professionals in the Political Science Polity." *Perspectives on Political Science* 24: 197–201.

Rimmerman, Craig A. 1991. "Democracy and Critical Education for Citizenship." *PS: Political Science and Politics* 24, 3: 492–95.

———. 1997. *The New Citizenship: Unconventional Politics, Service, and Activism.* Boulder, Colo.: Westview.

Rogan, John. 1993. *Presidency by Plebiscite.* Boulder, Colo.: Westview.

———. 1995. "The Use of the Internet by Math and Science Teachers." Paper presented at the Annual Meeting of the American Educational Research Association, San Francisco.

Shah, Idries. 1969. *Tales of the Dervishes: Teaching Stories of the Sufi Masters over the Past Thousand Years.* New York: Dutton.

Shaver, James P. 1985. "Commitment to Values and the Study of Social Problems in Citizenship Education." *Social Education* 49: 194–97.

Shor, Ira, and Paulo Freire. 1987. *A Pedagogy for Liberation: Dialogues on Transforming Education.* New York: Bergin and Garvey.

Smythe, Ormond. 1990. "Practical Experience and the Liberal Arts: A Philosophical Perspective," in *Combining Service and Learning: A Resource Book for Community and Public Service,* vol. I, ed. Jane C. Kendall and Associates. Raleigh, N.C.: National Society for Internships and Experiential Education.

Stanley, Mary. 1988. "Six Types of Citizenship." *Civic Arts Review* 1: 12–15.

Stanton, Timothy, and Kamil Ali. 1994. *The Experienced Hand: A Student Manual for Making the Most of an Internship.* 2nd rev. ed. New York: Sulzburger and Graham.

Stern, Carol Simpson. 1994. "Academic Freedom and Artistic Expression," in *Academic Freedom: An Everyday Concern*, ed. Ernst Benjamin and Donald R. Wagner. San Francisco: Jossey-Bass.

Stoll, Clifford. 1996. "Invest in Humanware." *The New York Times*, May 19.

Stouffer, Samuel. 1955. *Communism, Conformity, and Civil Liberties.* New York: Doubleday.

Sullivan, John L., James E. Piereson, and George E. Markus. 1982. *Political Tolerance and American Democracy.* Chicago: University of Chicago Press.

Svinicki, Marilla D., and Nancy M. Dixon. 1987. "The Kolb Model Modified for Classroom Activities." *College Teaching* 35 (Fall): 141–46.

"Symposium Report of the Bennington College Board of Trustees." June 1994.

Taylor, John, and Rex Walford. 1972. *Simulation in the Classroom.* New York: Penguin Books.

Tarrow, Sidney. 1989. *Democracy and Disorder: Protest and Politics in Italy, 1965–1975.* New York: Oxford University Press.

Teixera, Ruy. 1987. *Why Americans Don't Vote: Turnout Decline in the United States, 1960–1984.* Westport, Conn.: Greenwood Press.

Times-Mirror Center for the People and the Press. 1990. Press release, June 28.

Tocqueville, Alexis de. 1945. *Democracy in America.* New York: Modern Library.

Todorov, Tzvetan. 1984. *The Conquest of America: The Question of the Other.* New York: Harper.

Tompkins, Jane. 1991. "Pedagogy of the Distressed." *College English* 52, 6.

Towne, Douglas, Ton deJong, and Hans Spada. 1993. *Simulations and Learning.* New York: Verdung-Lang.

van Ments, Morry. 1989. *The Effective Use of Role-Play.* New York: Nichols.

Vavrina, Vernon J. 1995. "Poughkeepsie to Persian Gulf Revisited: ICONS, the Internet, and Teaching International Politics." *PS: Political Science and Politics* 28, 4: 725–27.

Verba, Sidney, Kay Lehman Schlozman, and Henry E. Brady. 1995. *Voice and Equality: Civic Voluntarism in American Politics.* Cambridge: Harvard University Press.

Wagner, Robin, and Bill Wilson. 1995. "Mosaic as a Vehicle for Collaborative Learning." Paper presented at the Annual Meeting of the Association of Small Computer Users in Education, Mytle Beach, S.C.

Waldman, Steven. 1995. *The Bill.* New York: Viking.

Walt Whitman Center. 1996. *Measuring Citizenship: Assessing the Impact of Service Learning on America's Youth.* New Brunswick, N.J.: Walt Whitman Center, Rutgers University.

Williams, Thomas J. 1976. "The Faculty Advisor's Role in Intern Supervision." *Teaching Political Science* 4 (October): 101–10.

Wineman, Sheila A., and Rosalind Hammond. 1987. "Citizenship Education Through the Webbing Approach." *Social Studies* 78: 169–72.

Wingspread Group on Higher Education. 1993. *An American Imperative: Higher Expectations for Higher Education.* Racine, Wisc.: The Johnson Foundation.

Wolfinger, Raymond, and Steven Rosenstone. 1980. *Who Votes?* New Haven: Yale University Press.

Wright, Ian. 1993a. "Citizenship Education and Decision Making." *International Journal of Social Studies* 3: 55–62.

———. 1993b. "Civic Education Is Values Education." *Social Studies* 84: 149–52.

Wuthnow, Robert. 1995. *Learning to Care: Elementary Kindness in an Age of Indifference.* New York: Oxford University Press.

Yankelovich, Daniel. 1991. *Coming to Public Judgment: Making Democracy Work in a Complex World.* Syracuse, N.Y.: Syracuse University Press.

# Index


active learning, 3–4, 10–13, 83
Adams, John, x
Adams, Peter, 228
affective development, 92–94
Alexander, James, 81
alienation, political, 1–2, 20–21, 27, 32, 52–53, 94, 97, 101–2, 106, 116–18, 215
Althaus, Scott, 210
Alverno College Curriculum, 87
Anderson, Charles, 136–39
Aristotle, 136
Astin, Alexander, 32
Athenian Oath, 79–80

Bailey, Martha, 203
Balutis, Alan, 97
Barber, Benjamin, 3, 129, 217
Barnette, Ron, 209
Bellah, Robert, 217
Boyte, Harry, 22, 26, 28, 32
Becker, Theodore, 96–97
Breuer, Rececca, 28
Brill, Alida, 126–27
Bruner, Jerome, 105
Bruning, Stephen, 209

Cell, Edward, 93
citizenship, xi, 17–18, 33–44, 51, 57–62, 103, 163, 186, 199–200

civic literacy, 51
civic responsibility. *See* citizenship
*Cohen v. California*, 131–32n3
Common School movement, xi
communitarianism, 2, 21, 123, 128, 189
community service. *See* public service
Couto, Richard, 96–97
critical thinking, 7, 44, 88, 191, 217

democracy, ix–xiv
Dewey, John, 32, 34, 64, 85–87, 162
diversity, xii, 8, 13, 26, 35–38, 40–42, 61, 158, 166, 187–88, 212, 217; and assimilationism, 187
Dolch, Norman, 150
Douglas, William O., 132n8

education: democracy in, xiii, 3, 8, 12, 19, 42–43, 76, 106, 153–57, 163–65, 173–75; interdisciplinary, 189–98; political economy of, 5; professionalism in, 4–5
equality, social and civic, xiv
*Erznoznick v. Jacksonville*, 132n4
Etzioni, Amitai, 123
experiential learning. *See* internship; public service; simulations
Eyler, Janet, 97

Faneuil, Douglas, 133n12
Farr, James, 199
Federal Election Commission, 222
Finocche, Emmett, 133n13
Fowell, S. P., 210
Frantzich, Stephen, 205
free speech, 11, 119–33; and Supreme
　　Court, 122, 125
freedom, ix
Freire, Paolo, 43, 159
Friedland, Lewis, 210

Garrod, Andrew, 154
Gastil, John, 149
gender, 180
Gorham, Eric, 23
Graber, Doris, 230n1
Greider, William, 3, 217, 229

Halteman, Beth, 97
Harwood Group, 32
Herzog, Don, 199
Hibbing, John, 102
Hutchings, Pat, 86

Individual Learning Contract (ILC),
　　13, 153–70
individualism, 5, 7, 11, 14, 24, 64, 139
Internet, 6, 14–15, 72–73, 146, 193,
　　200–213, 215–31; gophers, 219; list-
　　servs, 219, 225; and socioeconomic
　　inequality, 212; usenets, 219, 225;
　　as virtual library, 201, 211; World
　　Wide Web, 193, 220, 226
internships, 9–10, 83–99; critiqued,
　　96–97
introduction to American politics
　　(course), 24, 53, 202

Jackson, Robert, 125
James, William, xiii
Jefferson, Thomas, x
journals, 95, 191
justice, 22

Kennedy, Robert, 154
Kettering, Charles, 141
Kettering Foundation, 19, 141, 142,
　　144
Kinder, Donald, 199
Klass, Gary, 200–201, 203–4
Kolb, David, 87–88, 94
Kozol, Jonathan, 27

Levy, P., 210
Lewin, Kurt, 87
learning cycle theory, 88–89
liberal arts, xii, 9, 63
liberty. *See* freedom
Loeb, Paul, 139

MacKinnon, Catharine, 123
Madison, James, x, 132n9
Manrique, Cecilia, 218
Markus, Gregory, 32
Mathews, David, 136–37, 141
McClosky, Herbert, 126–27
McKenzie, Robert, 88–89, 143
Michaelis, John, 154
Mill, John Stuart, 131
Morse, Suzanne, 216–17
Mosher, Ralph, 154
multiculturalism. *See* diversity

National Issues Forums (NIF) on
　　Campus, 12, 19, 135–51
National Issues Convention, 149
National Issues Forums Institute
　　(NIFI), 141
Newmann, Fred, 97

Pederson, William, 81
Piaget, Jean, 87
Plato, 3, 51, 53, 58, 62
political participation. *See* citizenship
populism, 2
Project Public Life, 28
Project Vote Smart, 222
Provizer, Norman, 81
Public Agenda Foundation, 141

public deliberation, 135–151, 189, 211
public service, xii–xiii, 6–10, 16n3, 16n5, 17–29, 31–50, 66–67, 70, 136; critiqued, 22–28, 32; and moral judgment, 47; student enthusiasm for, 27–28, 33; teams in, 47; training sessions for, 25–26

racial issues in learning. *See* diversity
representation, 171–72, 183
Ritchie, Daniel, 5
Rogan, John, 210
role-playing. *See* simulations
Rousseau, Jean-Jacques, ix, 5
*Rowan v. U.S. Post Office*, 131n2

service learning. *See* public service
simulations, political, 10–11, 26, 70–71, 101–18, 193; critiqued, 108; structuring of, 110
Smythe, Ormond, 86

Stern, Carol Simpson, 122

Taylor, John, 105
team teaching, 189–98
technology, change in, 3, 14
*Terminiello v. Chicago*, 125, 132n8
Texas Education Network, 210
Theiss-Morse, Elizabeth, 102
*Tinker v. Des Moines School District*, 132n7
Tocqueville, Alexis de, x, xii, 3, 44

Wagner, Robin, 209
Walford, Rex, 105
Walt Whitman Center, 32, 48
Wilson, Bill, 209
Wingspread Group, 31
Wuthnow, Robert, 25
Wutzdorff, Allen, 86

Yankelovich, Daniel, 144

# About the Contributors

**William Ball** is assistant professor of political science at the College of New Jersey (formerly Trenton State College), where he teaches courses in political philosophy and research methods. He is the founder of three important Internet resources for political scientists: PSRT-L, Political Science Manuscripts, and the American Political Science Association gopher. In 1997 he served on the APSA Publications Committee and as president of the APSA Computers and Multimedia Section.

**Richard M. Battistoni** is professor of political science and director of the Feinstein Institute for Public Service at Providence College. He also taught political science and served as director of the Citizenship and Service Education Program at Rutgers University and of the Civic Education and Community Service Program at Baylor University. He is the coeditor, with Benjamin Barber, of *Education for Democracy*, and has written extensively in the areas of democratic theory and community service learning.

**Joseph Cammarano** is assistant professor of political science at Syracuse University's Maxwell School of Citizenship and Public Affairs. Prior to coming to Syracuse he taught at Drew University and Mansfield University of Pennsylvania. His research focuses on how politicians and citizens behave in a post-institutional era, and on the connection between social well-being and politics. In 1997 he was recognized by Syracuse University as the undergraduate academic advisor of the year.

**Kimberley P. Canfield** is a Ph.D. candidate in political science at Syracuse University's Maxwell School of Citizenship and Public Affairs.

Her research concerns theories of political participation and employs narrative accounts of uninvolved citizens to enhance these theories.

**James D. Chesney** is senior staff investigator with the Henry Ford Health System in Detroit and has been on the faculties of the University of Illinois, University of Michigan, and Wayne State University. His focus is on civic literacy and health care policies and politics, and he is currently working on the evaluation of Medicare and Medicaid managed care policies. Chesney and Otto Feinstein developed the Civic Literacy and Urban Agenda Project and expanded the project to other postsecondary institutions, high schools, and middle schools.

**William D. Coplin** is director of the Public Affairs Program at Syracuse University's Maxwell School of Citizenship and Public Affairs. The program serves only undergraduates and has as its mission the development of educated and thoughtful citizens. He has published extensively in the fields of international relations, public policy analysis, teaching social sciences, and political risk analysis.

**Otto Feinstein** is professor of political science at Wayne State University in Detroit. His areas of interest include civic literacy, the education of adults, ethnicity, and innovation in higher education. He initiated the Civic Literacy and Urban Agenda Project as part of a basic American government course in 1986.

**Linda L. Fowler** is director of the Rockefeller Center for the Social Sciences and Frank O. Reagan Chair of Policy Studies at Dartmouth College. She is the author of *Political Ambition: Who Decides to Run for Congress* (1989) and *Candidates, Congress, and the American Democracy* (1993). While on the faculty at Syracuse University she received two awards for excellence in undergraduate teaching.

**John F. Freie** is associate professor and chair of the political science department at LeMoyne College. He is head of the Teaching and Learning Section of the New York State Political Science Association and has published numerous articles on political participation and civic education. In his forthcoming book, *Counterfeit Community*, he extends his argument about democratizing the classroom to the societal level.

**Glen A. Halva-Neubauer** is Dana Associate Professor of Political Science and the director of the Christian A. Johnson Center for Engaged

Learning at Furman University. He directs the university's urban studies program and the political science department's state and local public affairs internship program. His previous published work has been in the area of state legislative abortion politics.

**Naeem Inayatullah** is assistant professor of politics at Ithaca College. His interests include exploring the role of non-Europeans in the construction of Western social theory and the relationship among space, time, and participatory processes.

**Marc Lendler** has taught American politics at a number of schools, most recently Yale University. He is the author of *Just the Working Life* (1990) and *Crisis and Political Beliefs* (1997).

**Daniel W. O'Connell** is associate professor of political science/law and Eissey Endowed Chair for Community Building at Palm Beach Community College. He is also political science and law coordinator for the National Issues Forums on Campus network and member of the board of the National Issues Forums Institute, and senior associate in the Choices for the Twenty-First Century Education Project at the Watson Institute for International Studies, Brown University.

**Grant Reeher** is assistant professor of political science at Syracuse University's Maxwell School of Citizenship and Public Affairs. He is author of *Narratives of Justice: Legislators' Beliefs about Distributive Fairness* (1996) and *Health Care, Reform, and Distributive Justice* (forthcoming). In 1993 he was awarded the American Political Science Association's William Anderson Prize and during 1995–97 he was a Robert Wood Johnson Foundation Scholar in Health Policy Research at the University of Michigan.

**Craig A. Rimmerman** is professor of political science at Hobart and William Smith Colleges, author of *Presidency by Plebiscite: The Reagan-Bush Era in Institutional Perspective* (1993) and *The New Citizenship: Unconventional Politics, Activism, and Service* (1997), and editor of *Gay Rights, Military Wrongs: Political Perspectives on Lesbians and Gays in the Military* (1996). He teaches courses on democratic theory, American politics, environmental policy, urban policy, lesbian and gay politics, and the presidency. During 1992–93 he was the American Political Science Association's William Steiger Congressional Fellow.

**Mark Rupert** is associate professor of political science at Syracuse University's Maxwell School of Citizenship and Public Affairs and teaches in the areas of international relations and political economy. He is the author of *Producing Hegemony: The Politics of Mass Production and American Global Power* (1995). His current research focuses on ideologies of globalization in popular common sense.